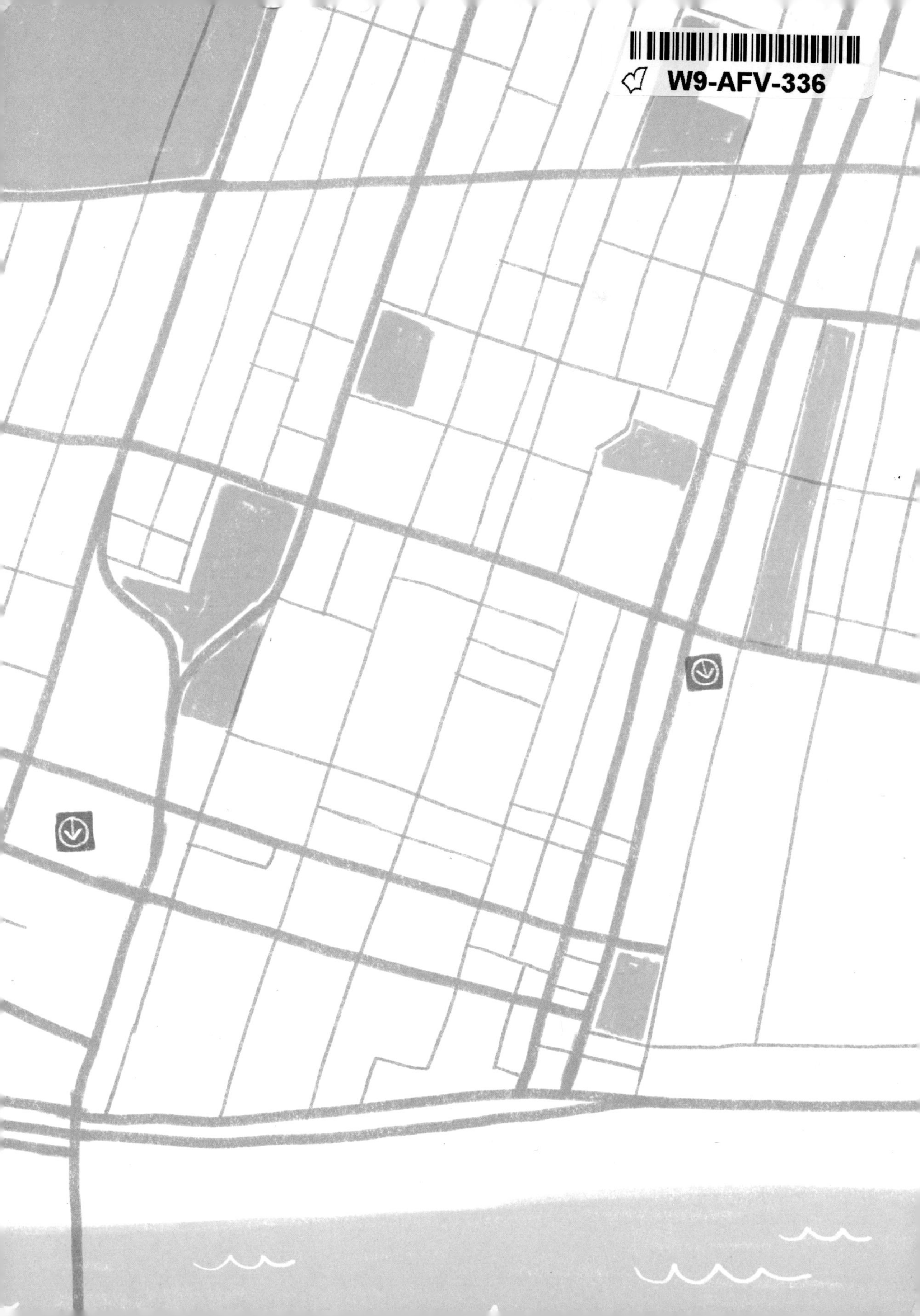

VALÉRIE PLANTE
DELPHIE CÔTÉ-LACROIX

okay, universe

CHRONICLES OF A WOMAN IN POLITICS

DRAWN & QUARTERLY

DRAWNANDQUARTERLY.COM

ISBN 978-1-77046-411-7
FIRST EDITION: OCTOBER 2020
PRINTED IN CANADA
10 9 8 7 6 5 4 3 2 1

CATALOGUING DATA AVAILABLE FROM LIBRARY AND ARCHIVES CANADA.

PUBLISHED IN THE USA BY DRAWN & QUARTERLY, A CLIENT PUBLISHER OF FARRAR,
STRAUS AND GIROUX. PUBLISHED IN CANADA BY DRAWN & QUARTERLY, A CLIENT
PUBLISHER OF RAINCOAST BOOKS. PUBLISHED IN THE UNITED KINGDOM BY DRAWN
& QUARTERLY, A CLIENT PUBLISHER OF PUBLISHERS GROUP UK.

DRAWN & QUARTERLY ACKNOWLEDGES THE SUPPORT OF THE GOVERNMENT OF CANADA
AND THE CANADA COUNCIL FOR THE ARTS FOR OUR PUBLISHING PROGRAM, AND THE NA-
TIONAL TRANSLATION PROGRAM FOR BOOK PUBLISHING, AN INITIATIVE OF THE ROADMAP
Canada FOR CANADA'S OFFICIAL LANGUAGES 2013-2020: EDUCATION, IM-
MIGRATION, COMMUNITIES, FOR OUR TRANSLATION ACTIVITIES.

DRAWN & QUARTERLY RECONNAÎT L'AIDE FINANCIÈRE DU GOUVERNEMENT DU QUÉBEC
PAR L'ENTREMISE DE LA SOCIÉTÉ DE DÉVELOPPEMENT DES ENTREPRISES CULTURELLES
(SODEC) POUR NOS ACTIVITÉS D'ÉDITION. GOUVERNEMENT DU QUÉBEC—PROGRAMME
DE CRÉDIT D'IMPÔT POUR L'ÉDITION DE LIVRES—GESTION SODEC.

TO PIERRE-ANTOINE, ÉMILE, AND GAËL.

THANK YOU, ISABELLE. THANK YOU, MAUDE.
THANK YOU, PAUL AND RICHARD. AND THANK
YOU, TRISTAN, FOR YOUR SENSITIVE AND
PERCEPTIVE SUPPORT ALONG THE WAY.

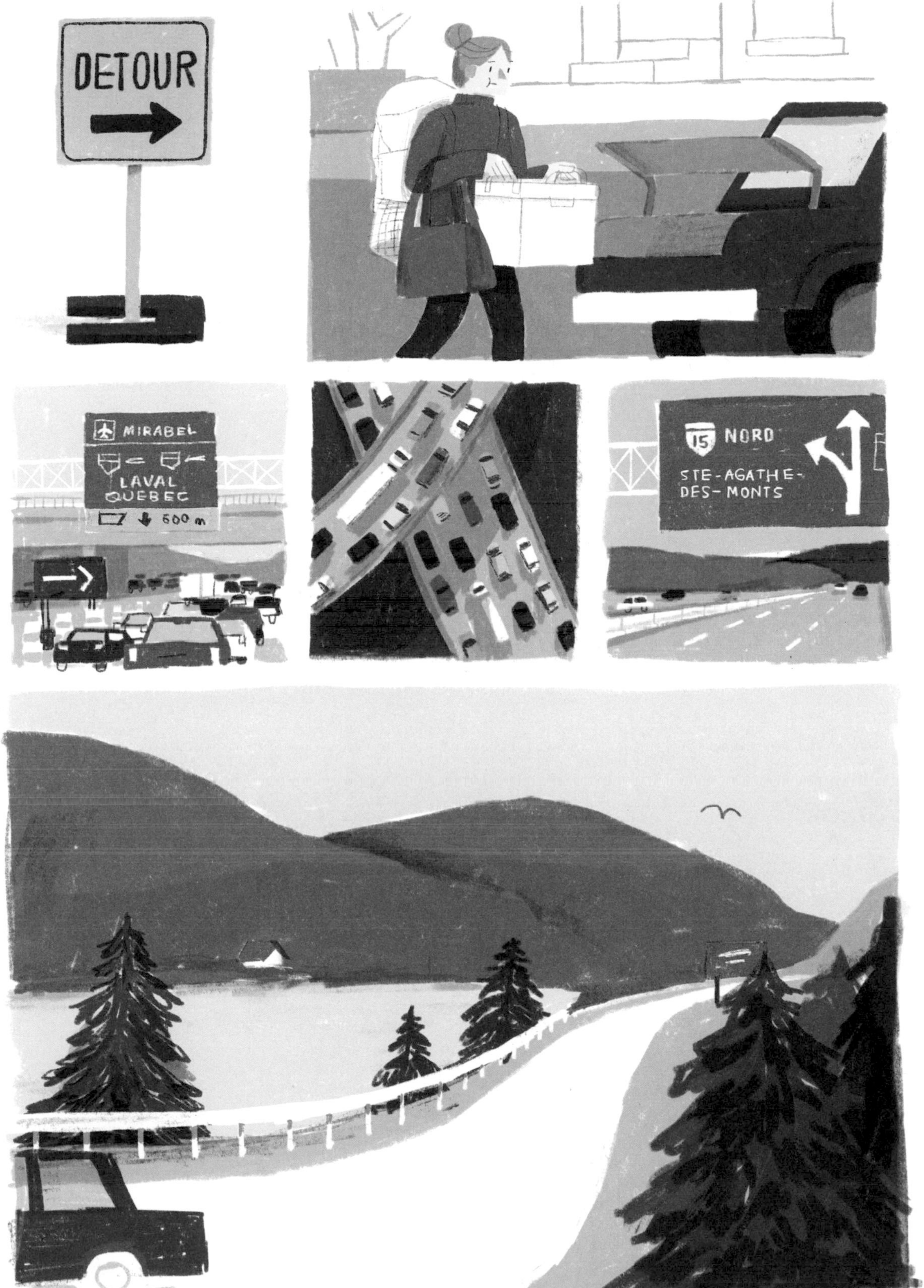
DETOUR
MIRABEL
LAVAL
QUEBEC
600 m
15 NORD
STE-AGATHE-
DES-MONTS

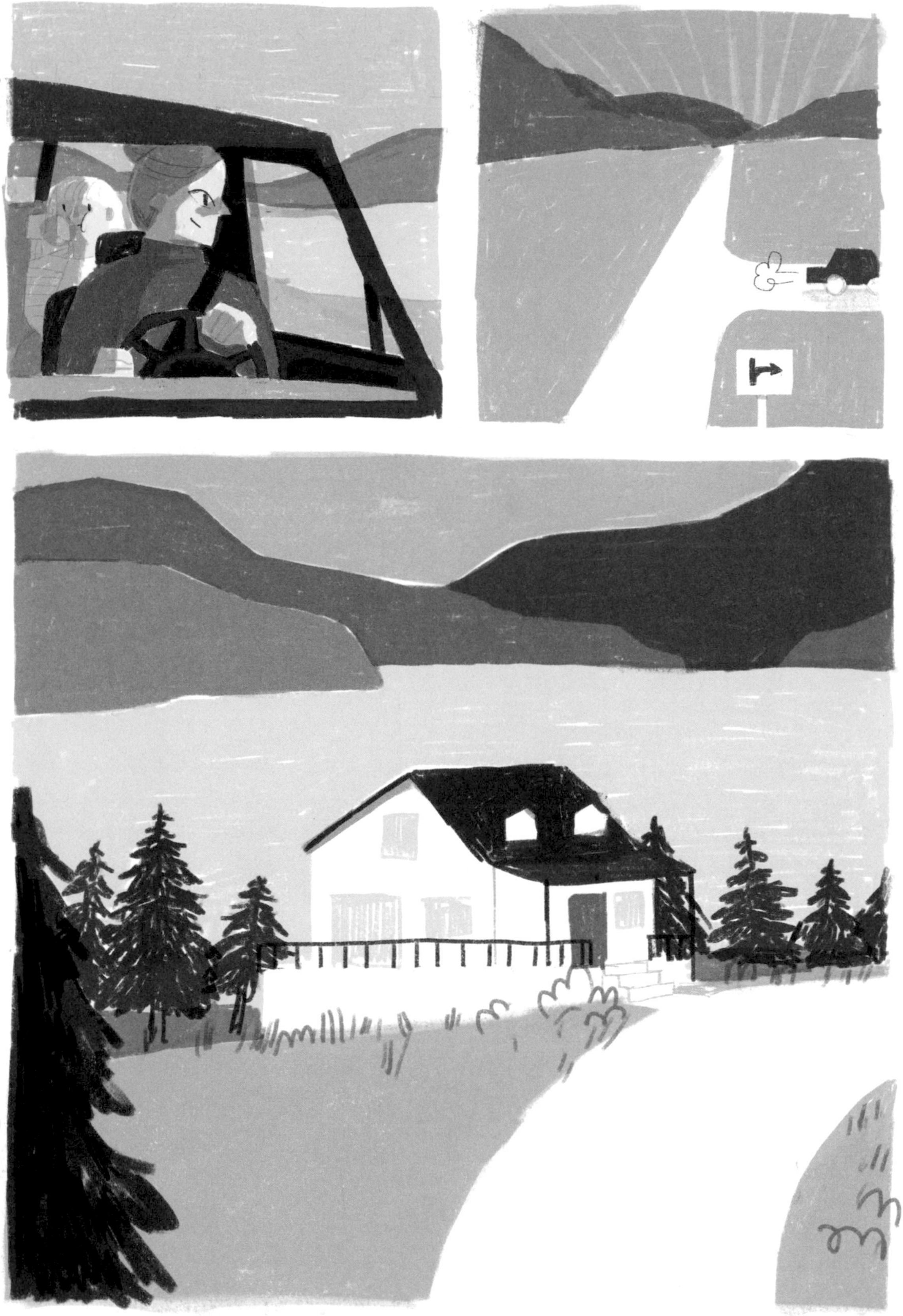

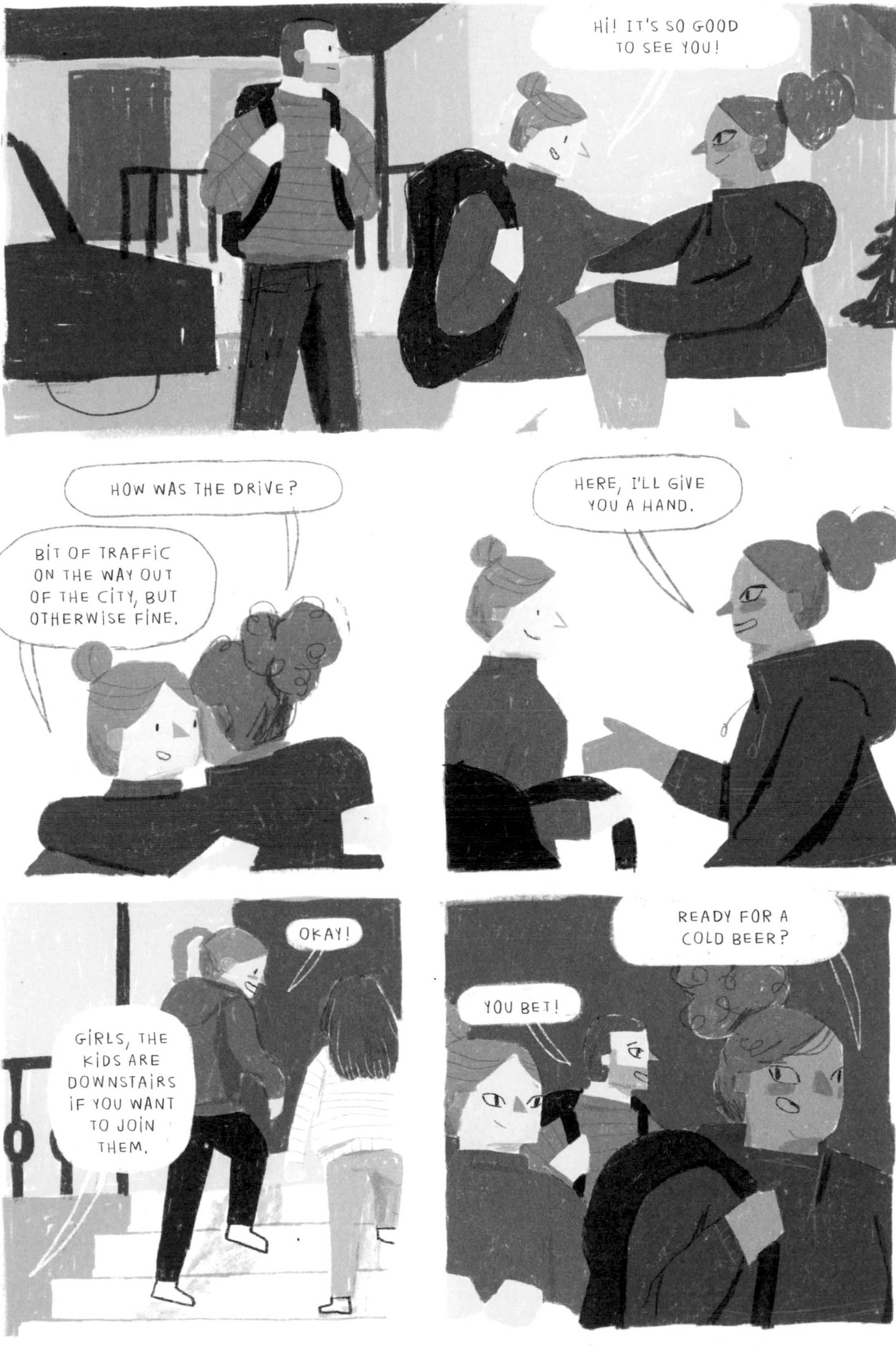
HI! IT'S SO GOOD TO SEE YOU!
HOW WAS THE DRIVE?
BIT OF TRAFFIC ON THE WAY OUT OF THE CITY, BUT OTHERWISE FINE.
HERE, I'LL GIVE YOU A HAND.
OKAY!
GIRLS, THE KIDS ARE DOWNSTAIRS IF YOU WANT TO JOIN THEM.
READY FOR A COLD BEER?
YOU BET!

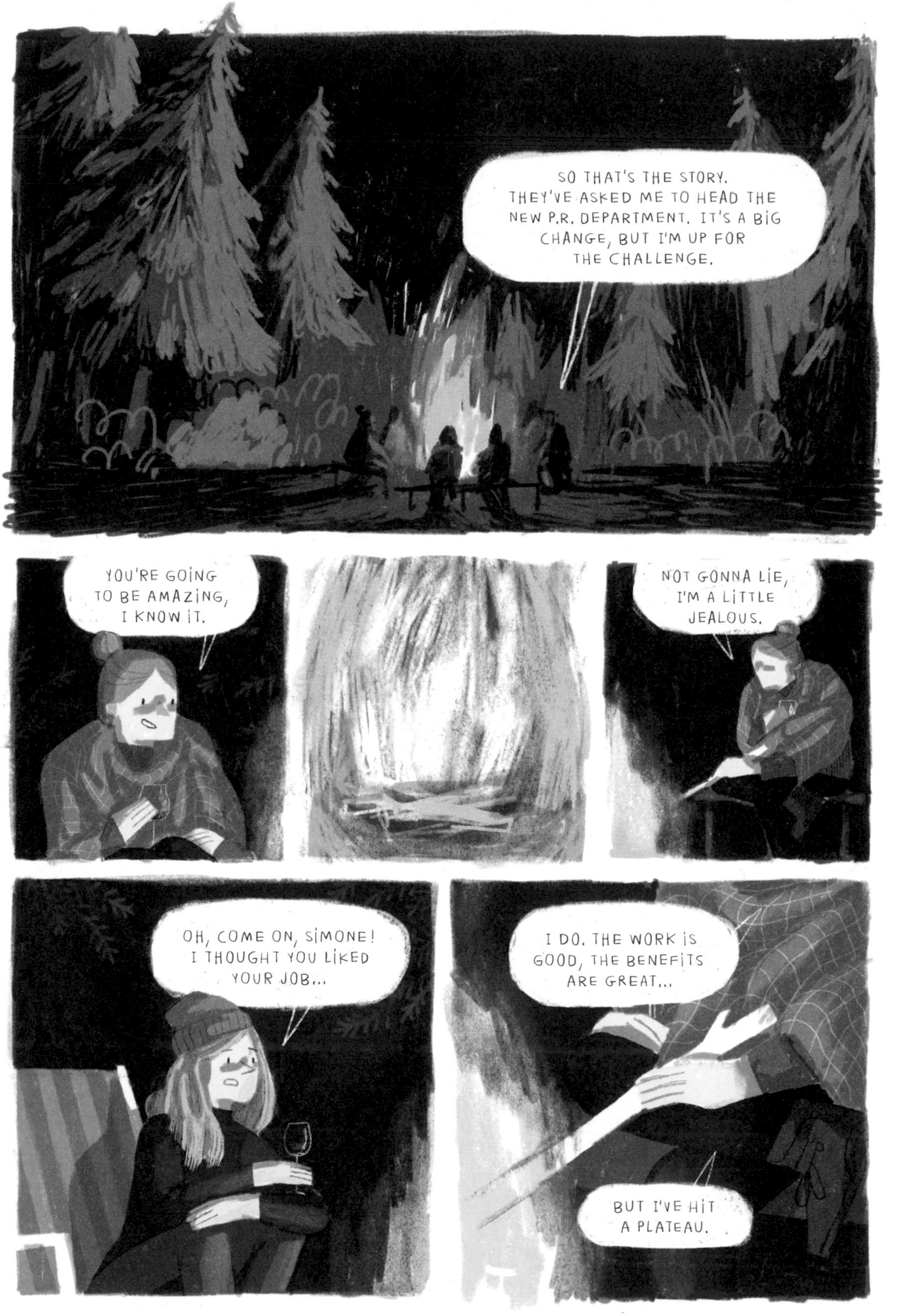
SO THAT'S THE STORY. THEY'VE ASKED ME TO HEAD THE NEW P.R. DEPARTMENT. IT'S A BIG CHANGE, BUT I'M UP FOR THE CHALLENGE.
YOU'RE GOING TO BE AMAZING, I KNOW IT.
NOT GONNA LIE, I'M A LITTLE JEALOUS.
OH, COME ON, SIMONE! I THOUGHT YOU LIKED YOUR JOB...
I DO. THE WORK IS GOOD, THE BENEFITS ARE GREAT...
BUT I'VE HIT A PLATEAU.

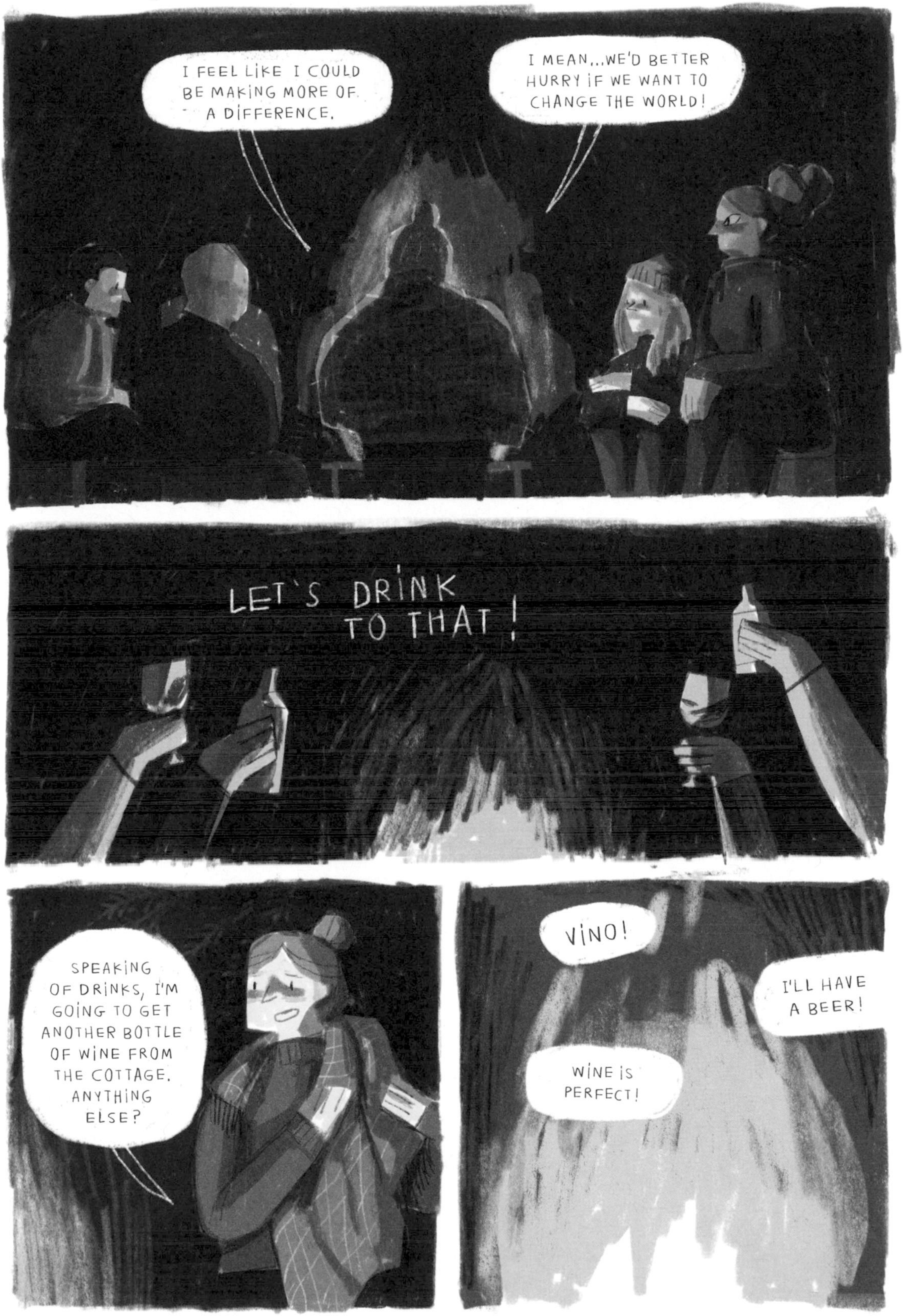
I FEEL LIKE I COULD BE MAKING MORE OF A DIFFERENCE.
I MEAN...WE'D BETTER HURRY IF WE WANT TO CHANGE THE WORLD!
LET'S DRINK TO THAT!
SPEAKING OF DRINKS, I'M GOING TO GET ANOTHER BOTTLE OF WINE FROM THE COTTAGE. ANYTHING ELSE?
VINO!
I'LL HAVE A BEER!
WINE IS PERFECT!

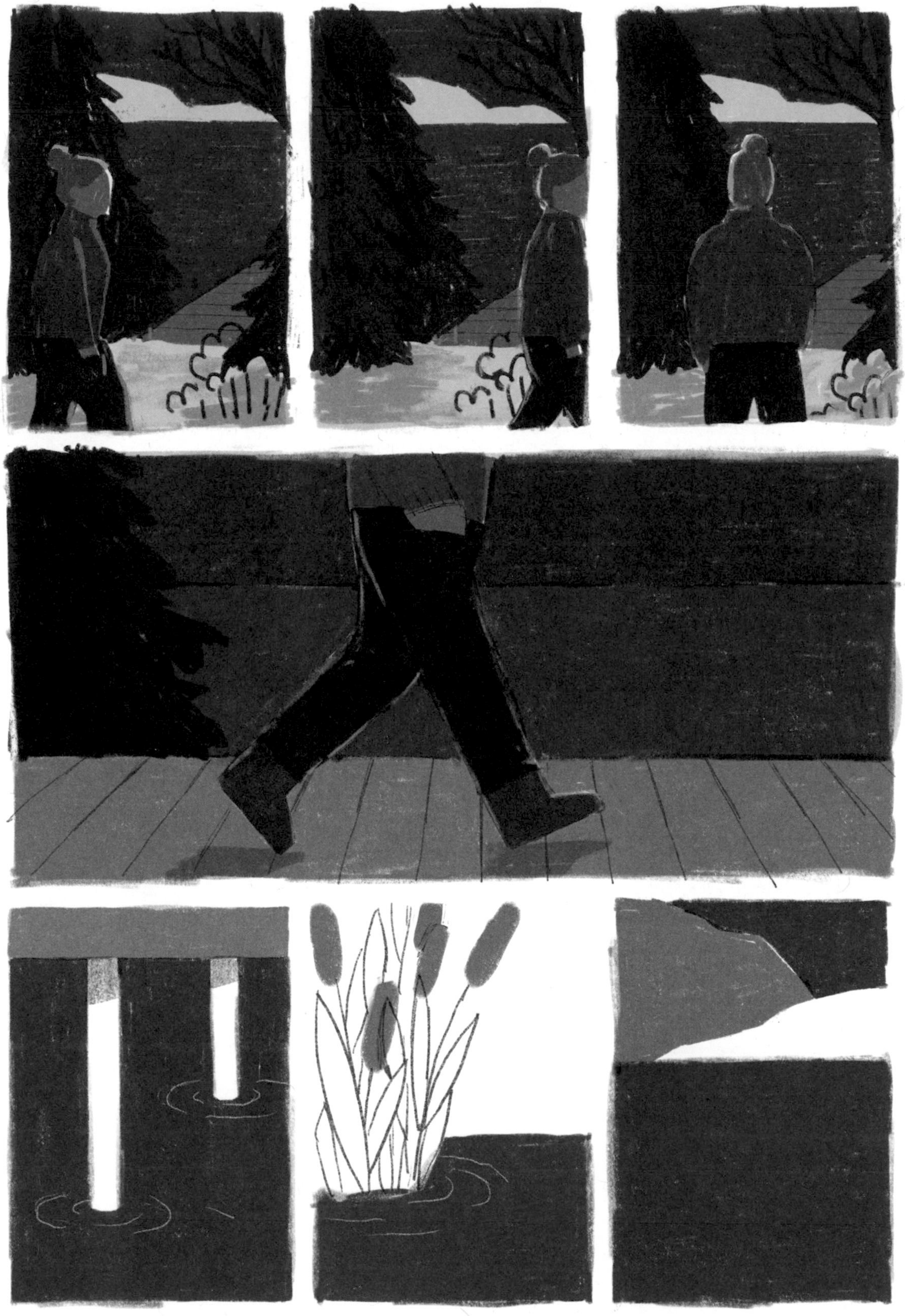

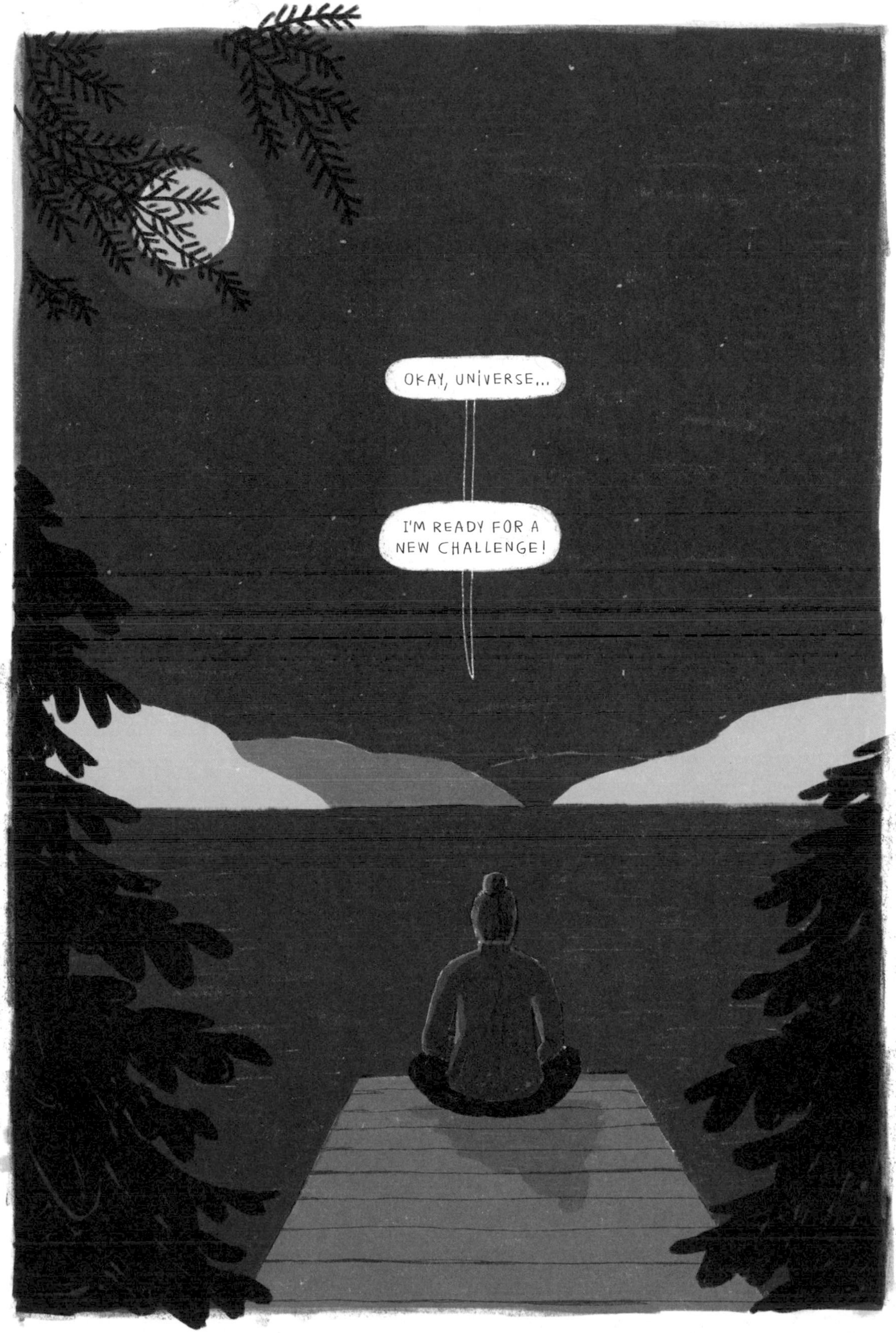
OKAY, UNIVERSE...
I'M READY FOR A NEW CHALLENGE!

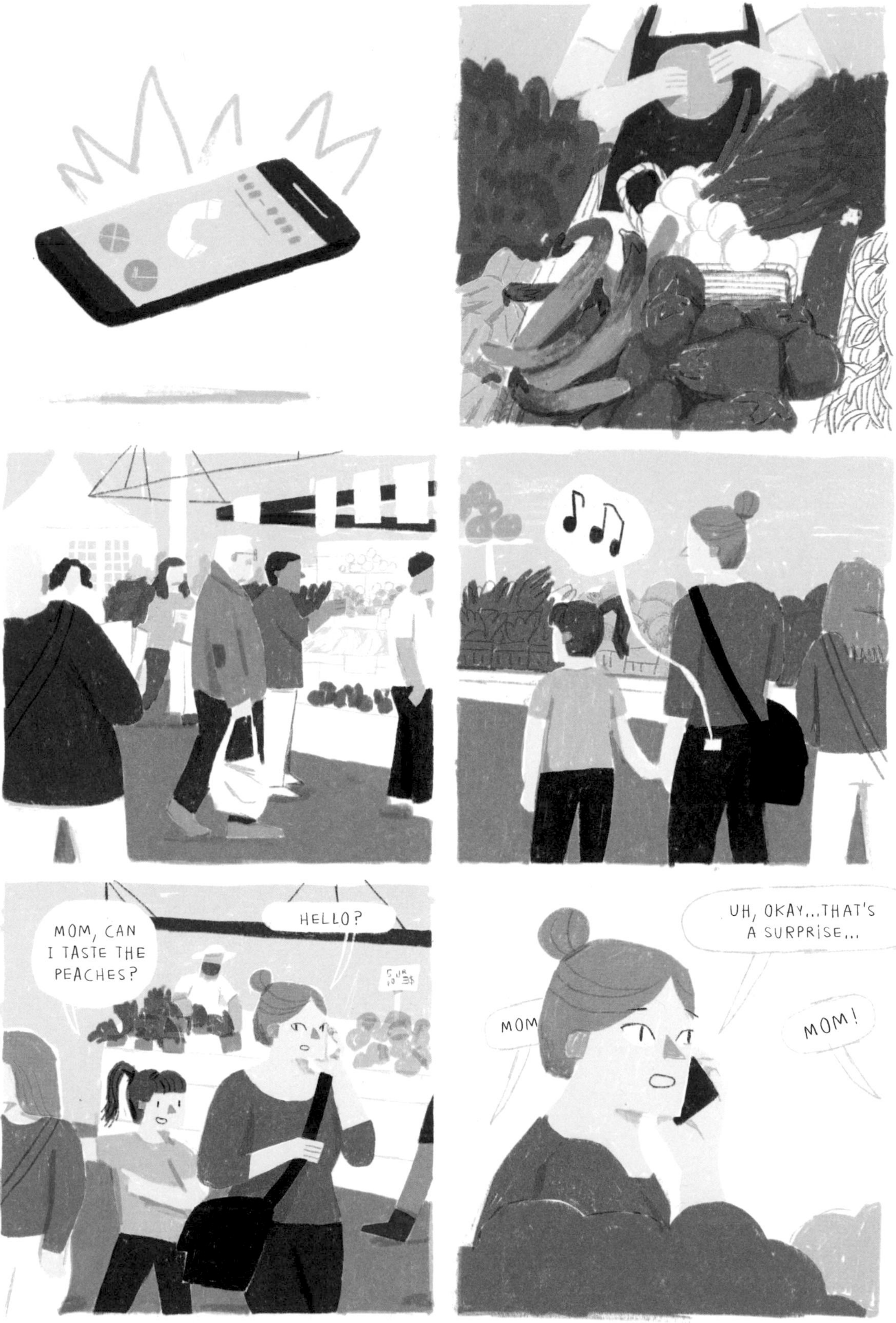
MOM, CAN I TASTE THE PEACHES?
HELLO?
UH, OKAY...THAT'S A SURPRISE...
MOM
MOM!

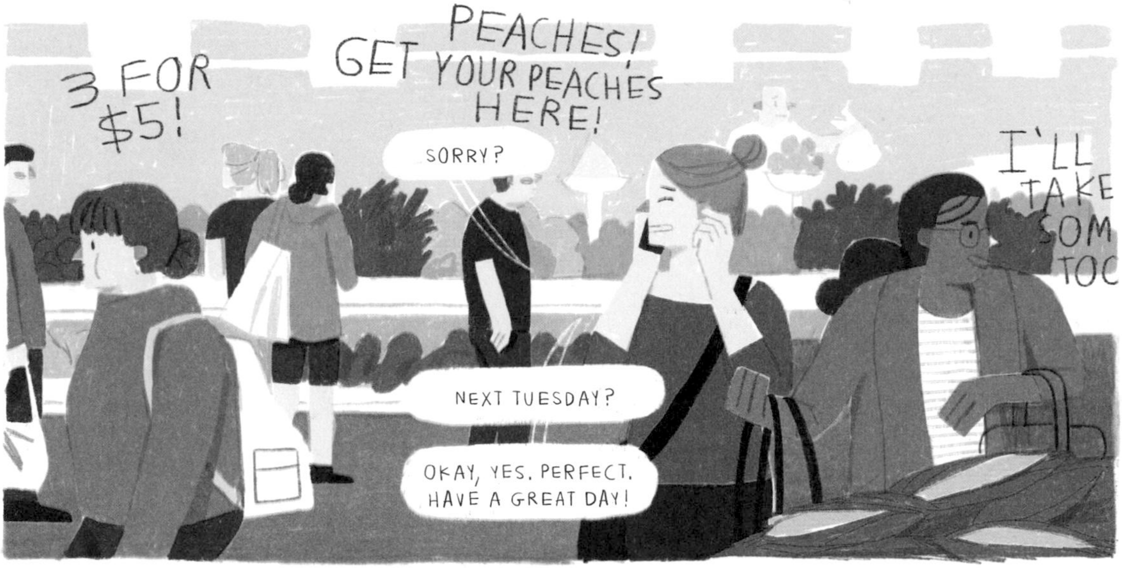
3 FOR $5!
PEACHES! GET YOUR PEACHES HERE!
SORRY?
NEXT TUESDAY?
OKAY, YES. PERFECT. HAVE A GREAT DAY!
I'LL TAKE SOM TOO

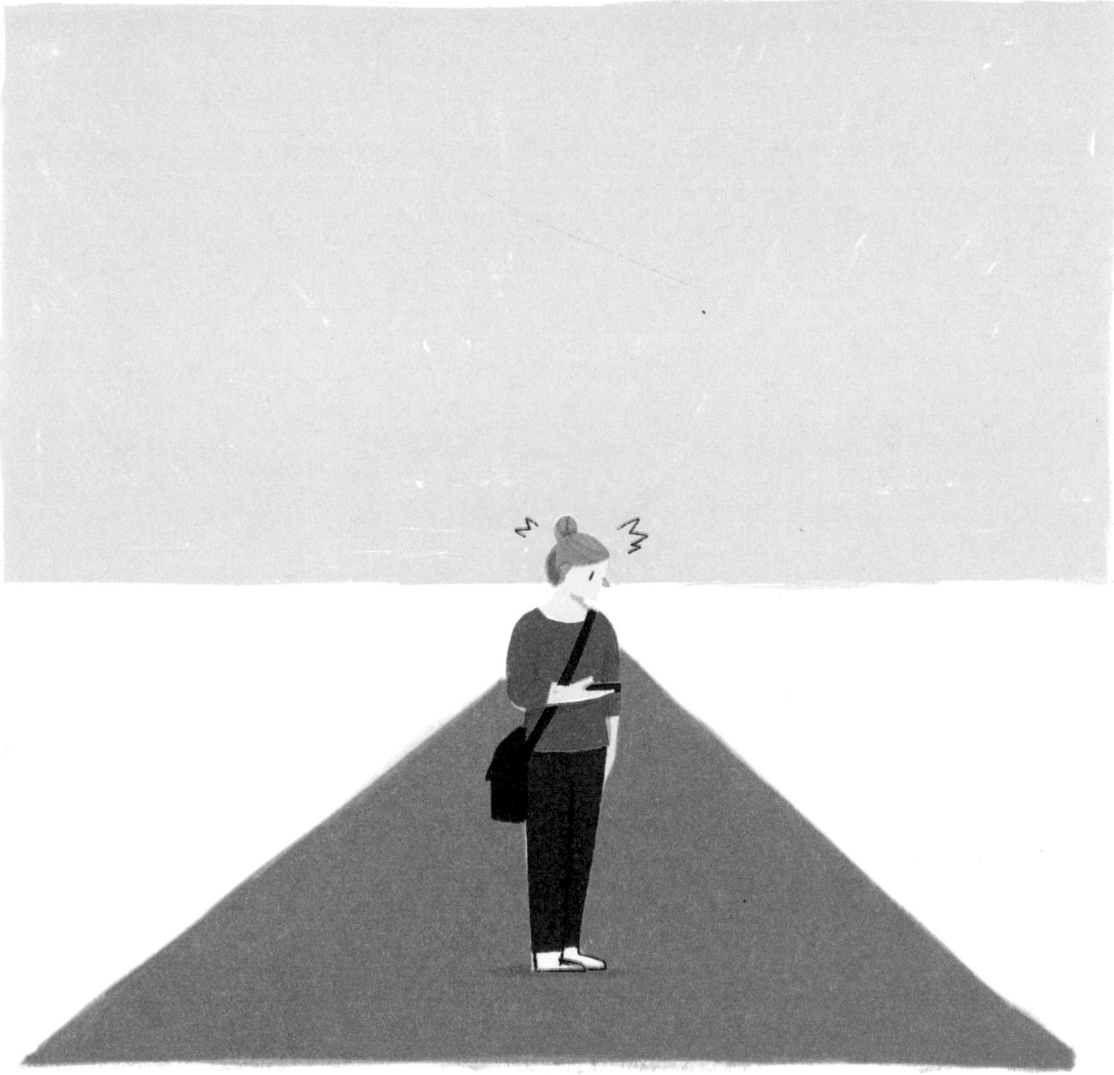

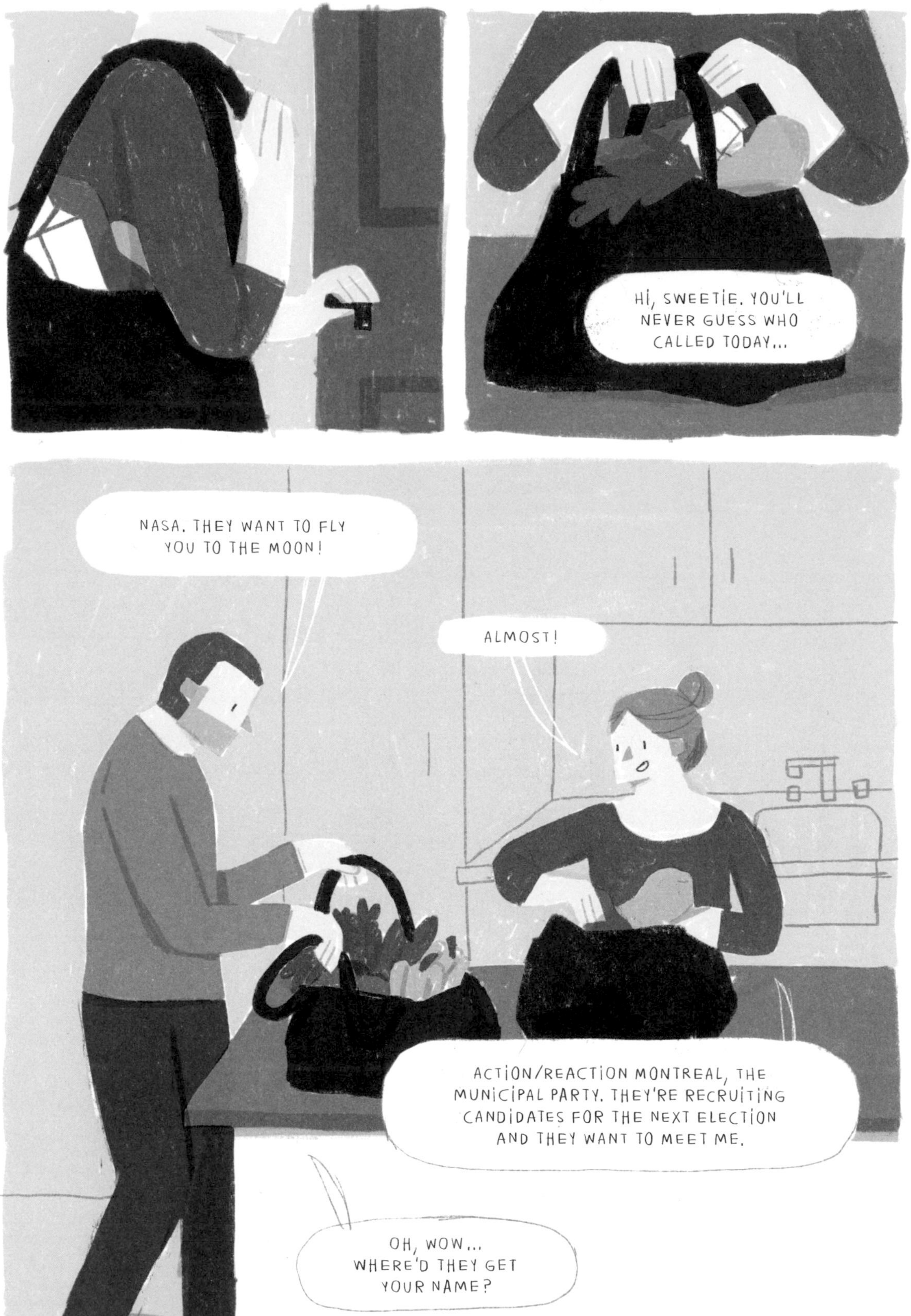
HI, SWEETIE. YOU'LL NEVER GUESS WHO CALLED TODAY...
NASA. THEY WANT TO FLY YOU TO THE MOON!
ALMOST!
ACTION/REACTION MONTREAL, THE MUNICIPAL PARTY. THEY'RE RECRUITING CANDIDATES FOR THE NEXT ELECTION AND THEY WANT TO MEET ME.
OH, WOW... WHERE'D THEY GET YOUR NAME?

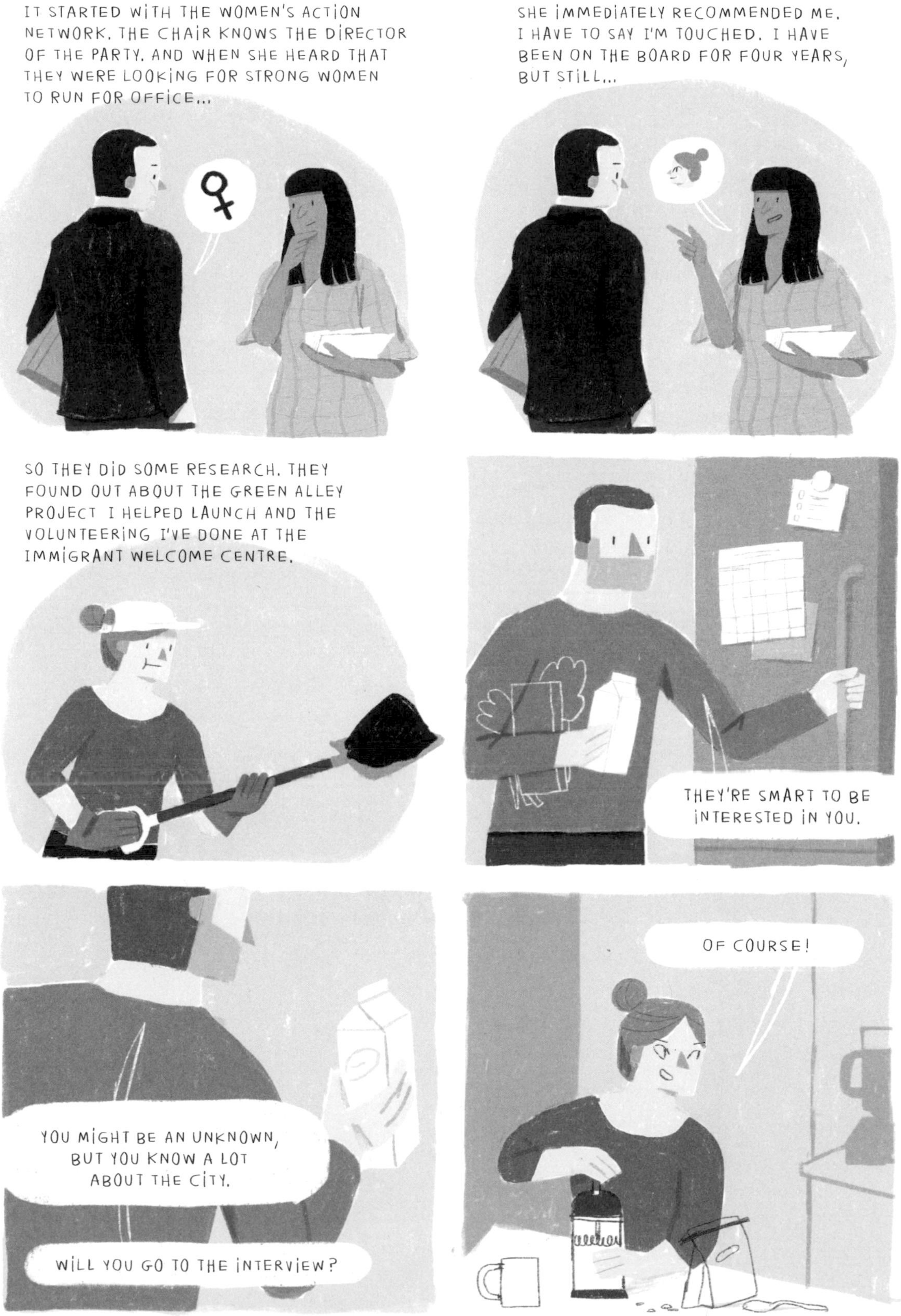
IT STARTED WITH THE WOMEN'S ACTION NETWORK. THE CHAIR KNOWS THE DIRECTOR OF THE PARTY. AND WHEN SHE HEARD THAT THEY WERE LOOKING FOR STRONG WOMEN TO RUN FOR OFFICE...
SHE IMMEDIATELY RECOMMENDED ME. I HAVE TO SAY I'M TOUCHED. I HAVE BEEN ON THE BOARD FOR FOUR YEARS, BUT STILL...
SO THEY DID SOME RESEARCH. THEY FOUND OUT ABOUT THE GREEN ALLEY PROJECT I HELPED LAUNCH AND THE VOLUNTEERING I'VE DONE AT THE IMMIGRANT WELCOME CENTRE.
THEY'RE SMART TO BE INTERESTED IN YOU.
YOU MIGHT BE AN UNKNOWN, BUT YOU KNOW A LOT ABOUT THE CITY.
WILL YOU GO TO THE INTERVIEW?
OF COURSE!

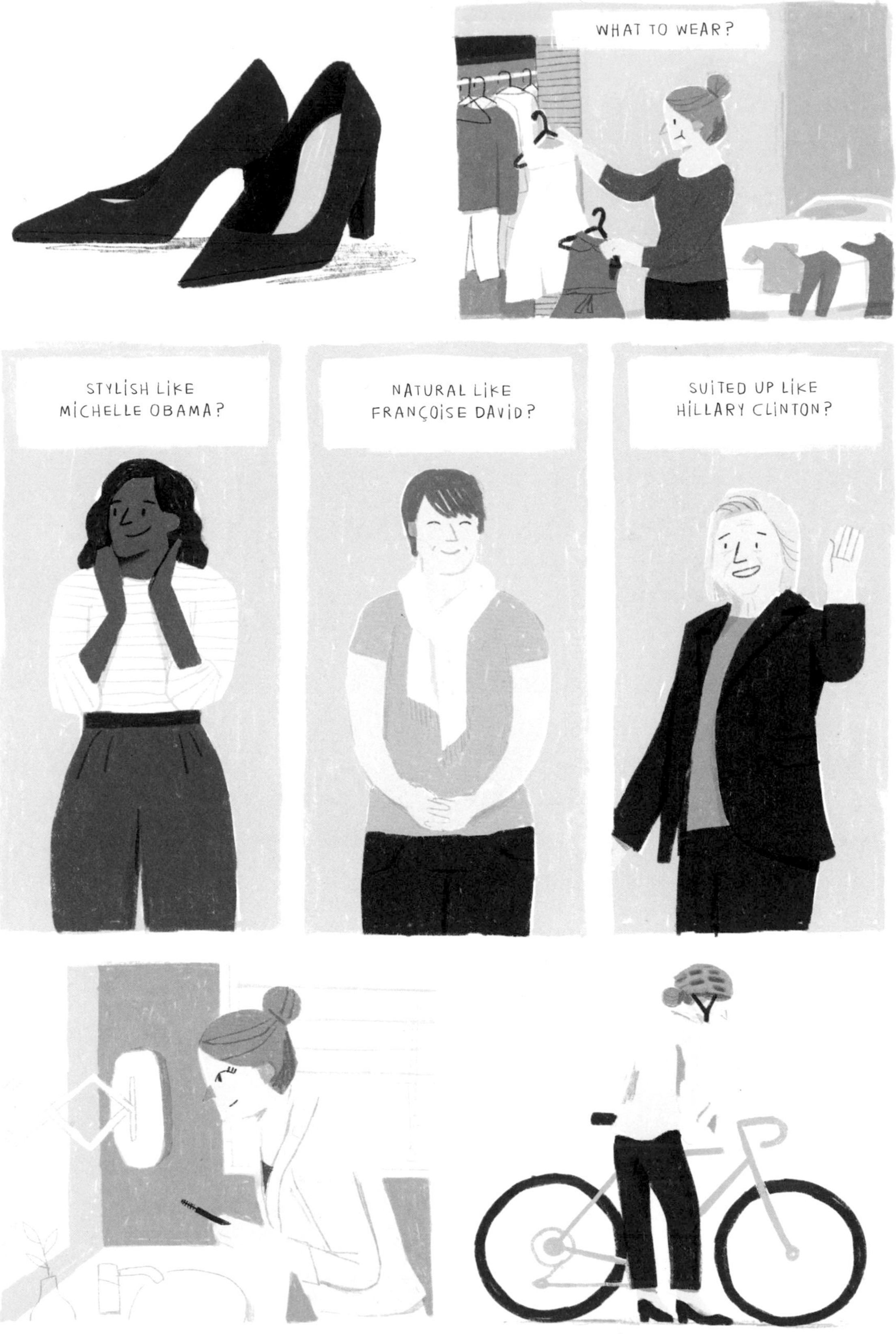
WHAT TO WEAR?
STYLISH LIKE MICHELLE OBAMA?
NATURAL LIKE FRANÇOISE DAVID?
SUITED UP LIKE HILLARY CLINTON?

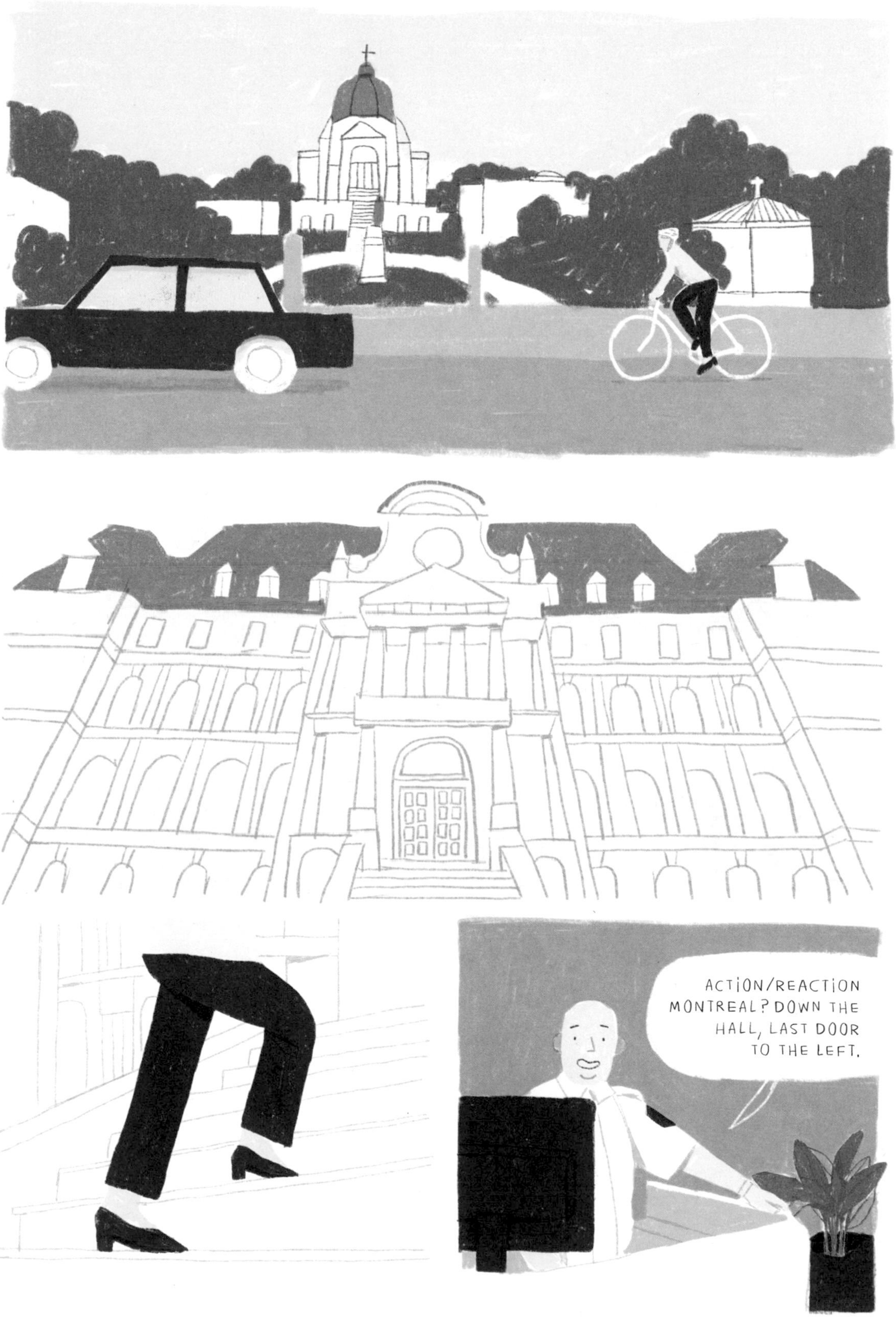
ACTION/REACTION MONTREAL? DOWN THE HALL, LAST DOOR TO THE LEFT.

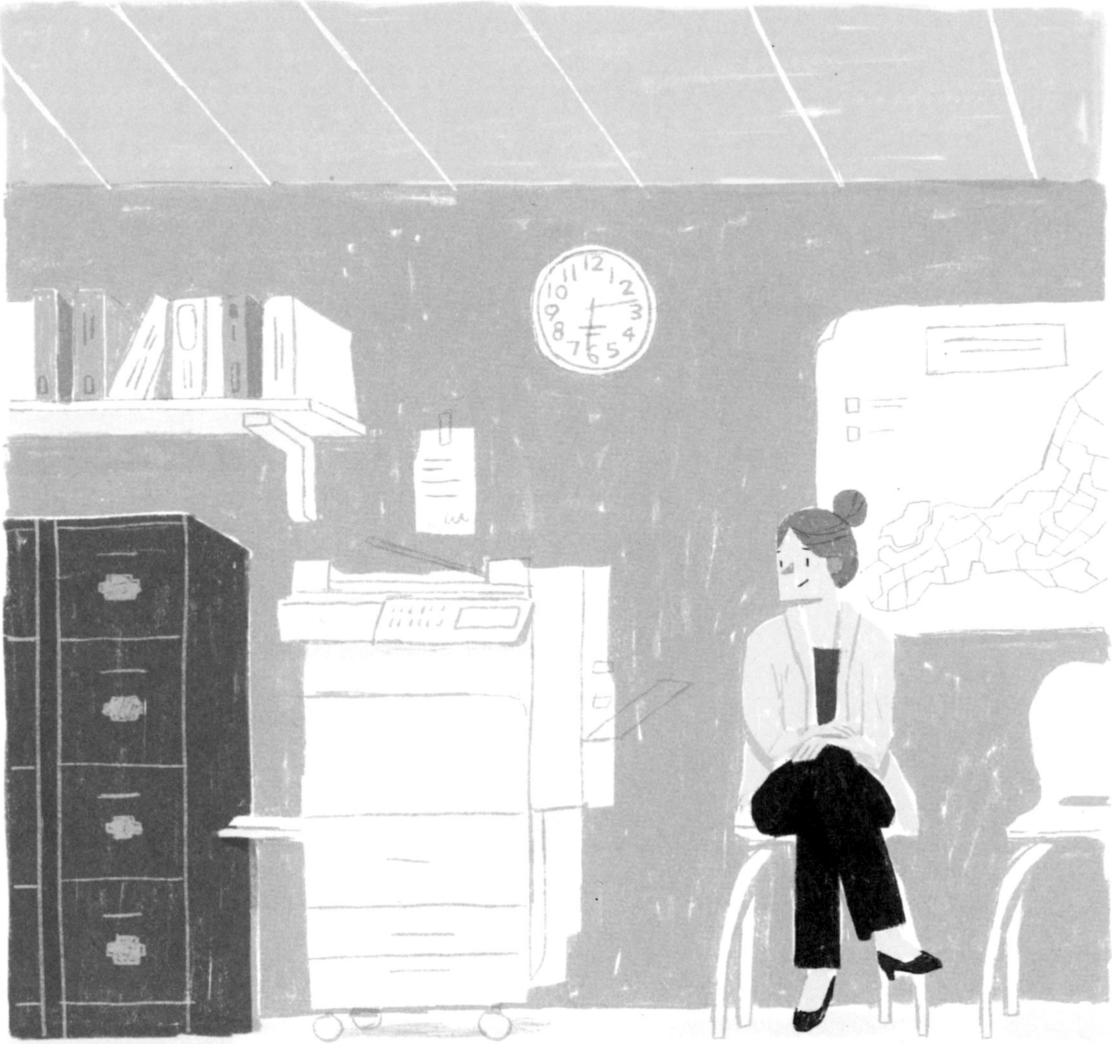

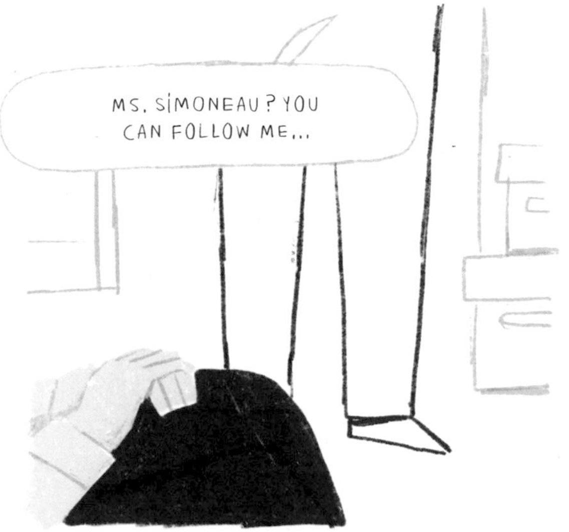
MS. SIMONEAU? YOU CAN FOLLOW ME...

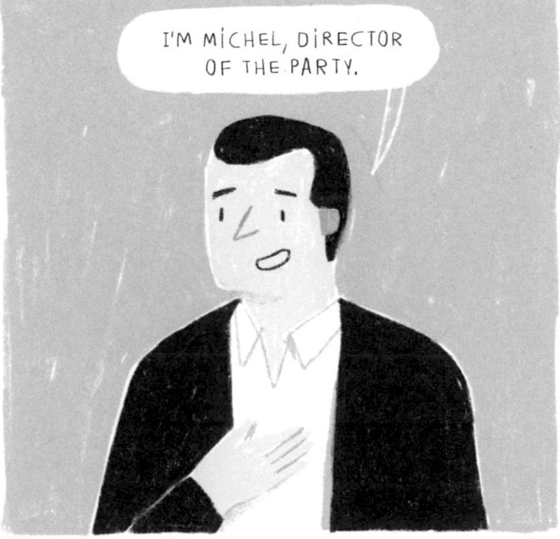
I'M MICHEL, DIRECTOR OF THE PARTY.

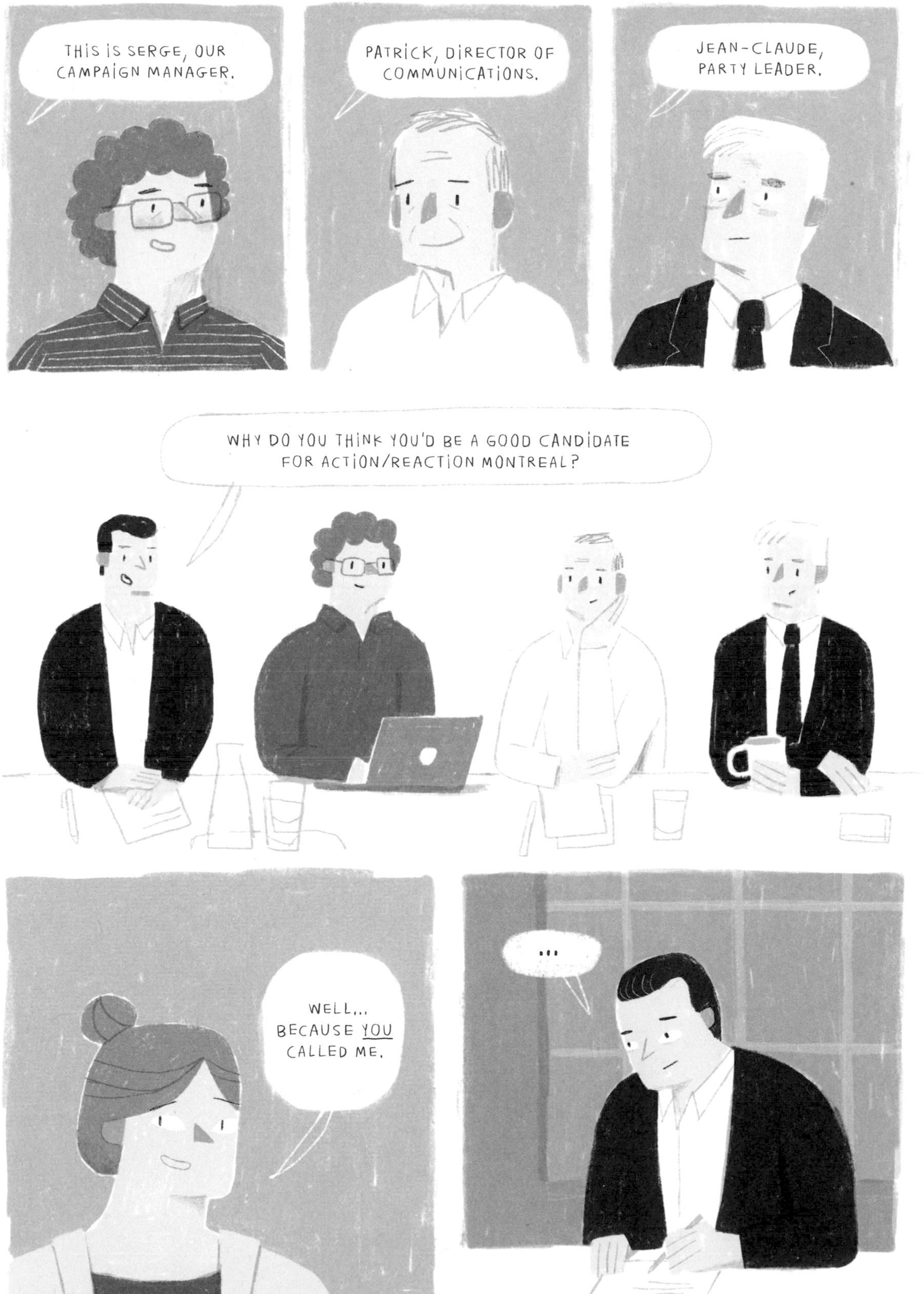
THIS IS SERGE, OUR CAMPAIGN MANAGER.
PATRICK, DIRECTOR OF COMMUNICATIONS.
JEAN-CLAUDE, PARTY LEADER.
WHY DO YOU THINK YOU'D BE A GOOD CANDIDATE FOR ACTION/REACTION MONTREAL?
WELL... BECAUSE YOU CALLED ME.
...

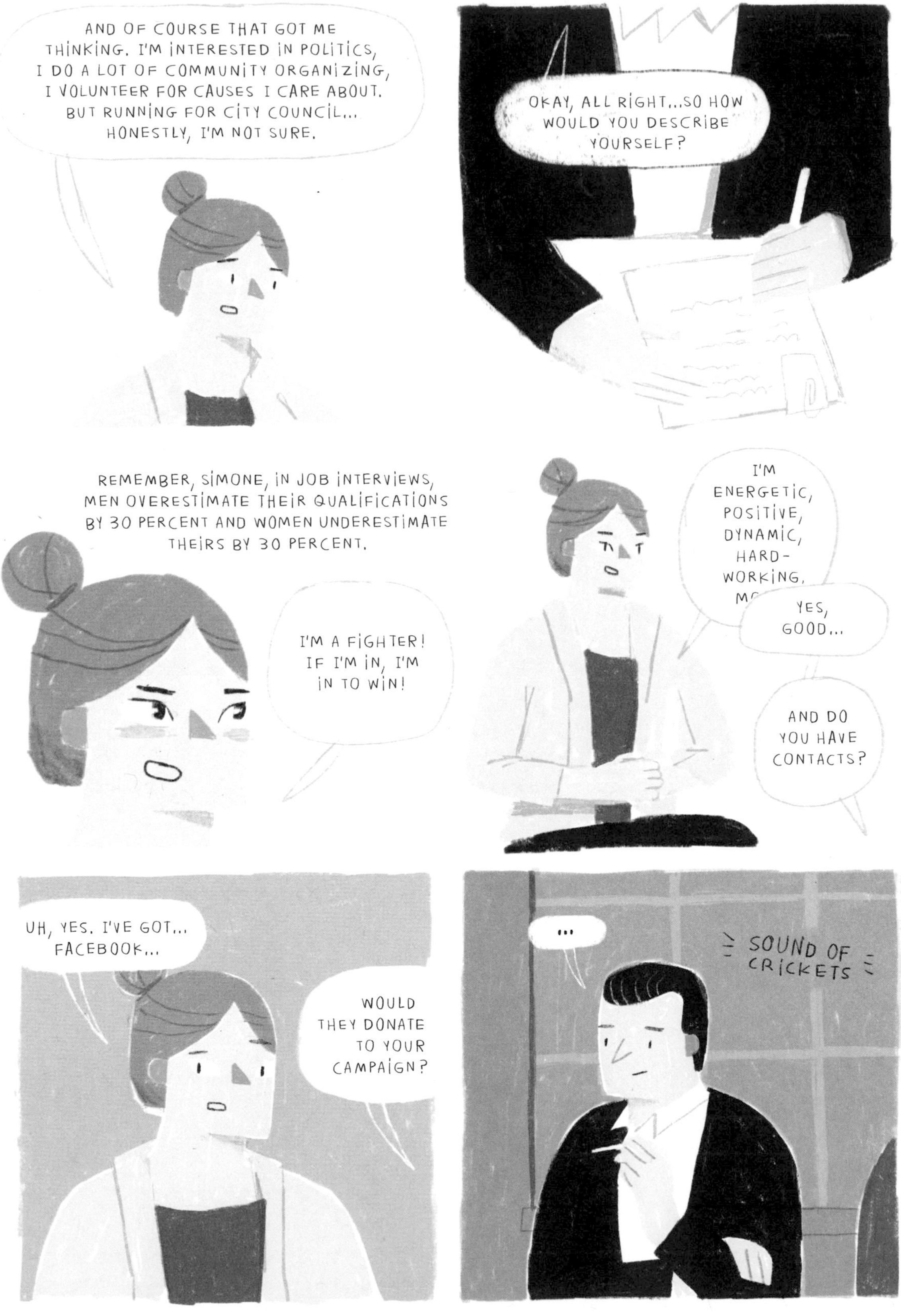
AND OF COURSE THAT GOT ME THINKING. I'M INTERESTED IN POLITICS, I DO A LOT OF COMMUNITY ORGANIZING, I VOLUNTEER FOR CAUSES I CARE ABOUT. BUT RUNNING FOR CITY COUNCIL... HONESTLY, I'M NOT SURE.
OKAY, ALL RIGHT...SO HOW WOULD YOU DESCRIBE YOURSELF?
REMEMBER, SIMONE, IN JOB INTERVIEWS, MEN OVERESTIMATE THEIR QUALIFICATIONS BY 30 PERCENT AND WOMEN UNDERESTIMATE THEIRS BY 30 PERCENT.
I'M A FIGHTER! IF I'M IN, I'M IN TO WIN!
I'M ENERGETIC, POSITIVE, DYNAMIC, HARD-WORKING,
YES, GOOD...
AND DO YOU HAVE CONTACTS?
UH, YES. I'VE GOT... FACEBOOK...
WOULD THEY DONATE TO YOUR CAMPAIGN?
...
SOUND OF CRICKETS

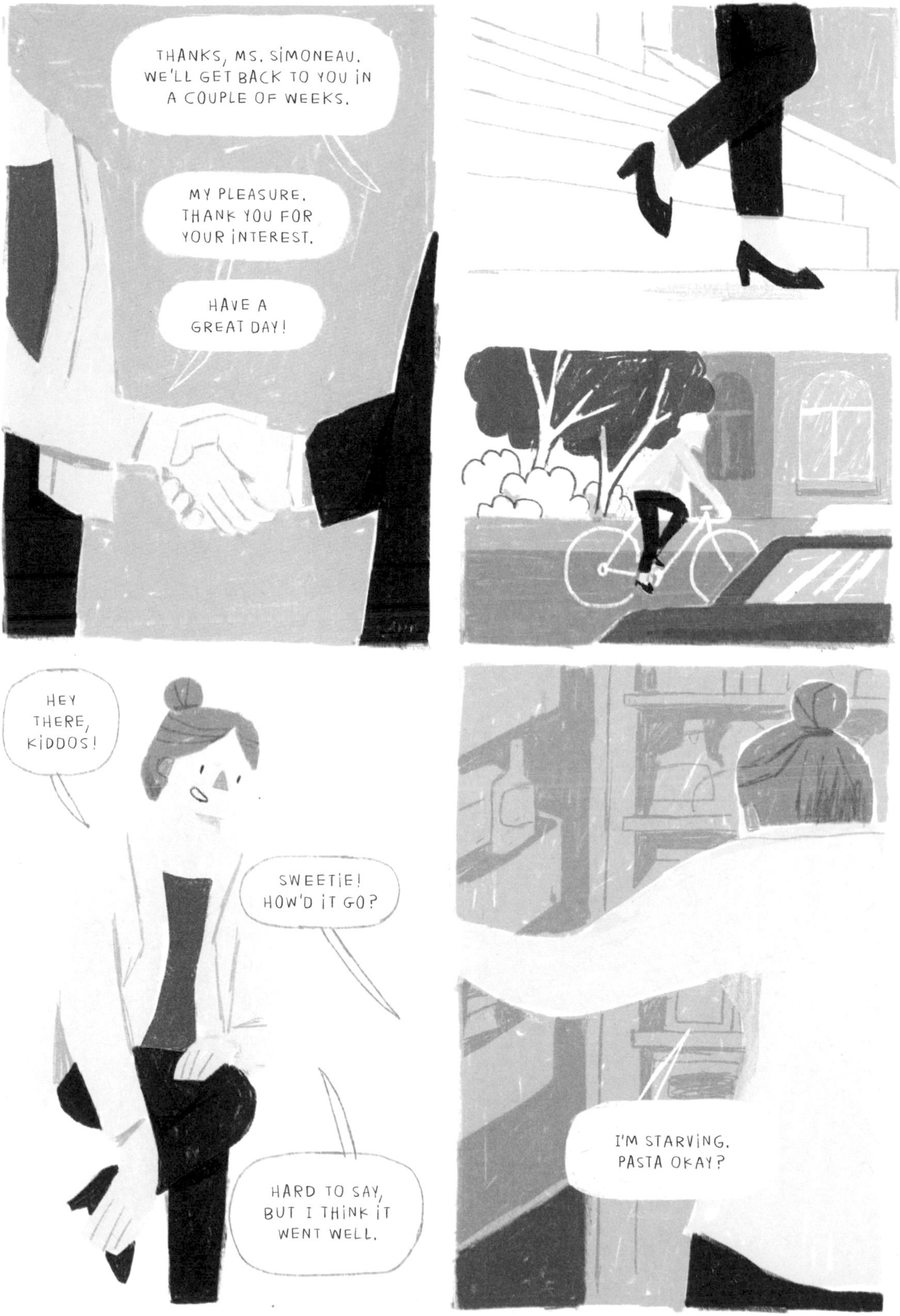
THANKS, MS. SIMONEAU. WE'LL GET BACK TO YOU IN A COUPLE OF WEEKS.
MY PLEASURE. THANK YOU FOR YOUR INTEREST.
HAVE A GREAT DAY!
HEY THERE, KIDDOS!
SWEETIE! HOW'D IT GO?
HARD TO SAY, BUT I THINK IT WENT WELL.
I'M STARVING. PASTA OKAY?

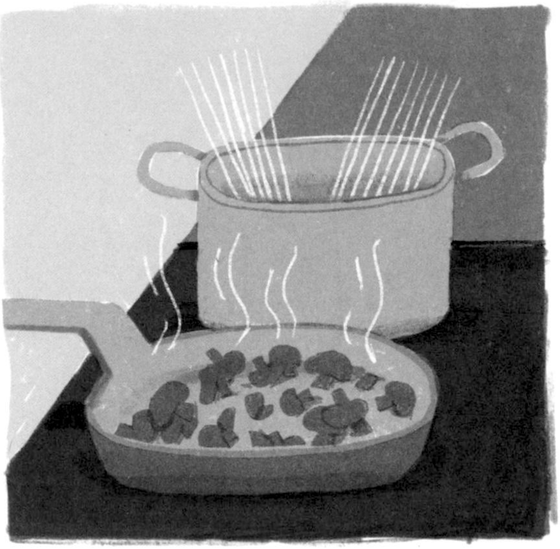

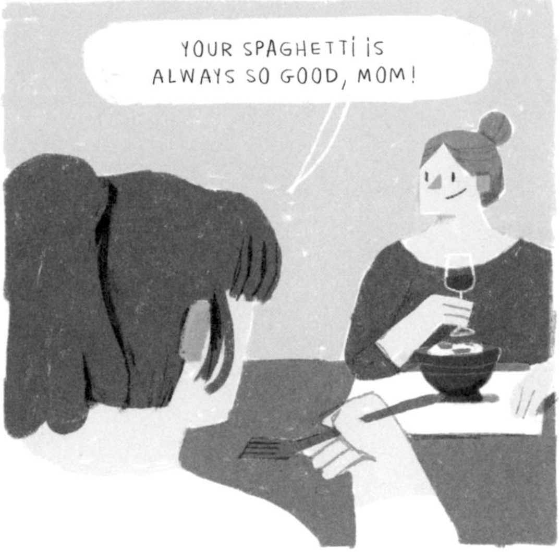
YOUR SPAGHETTI IS ALWAYS SO GOOD, MOM!

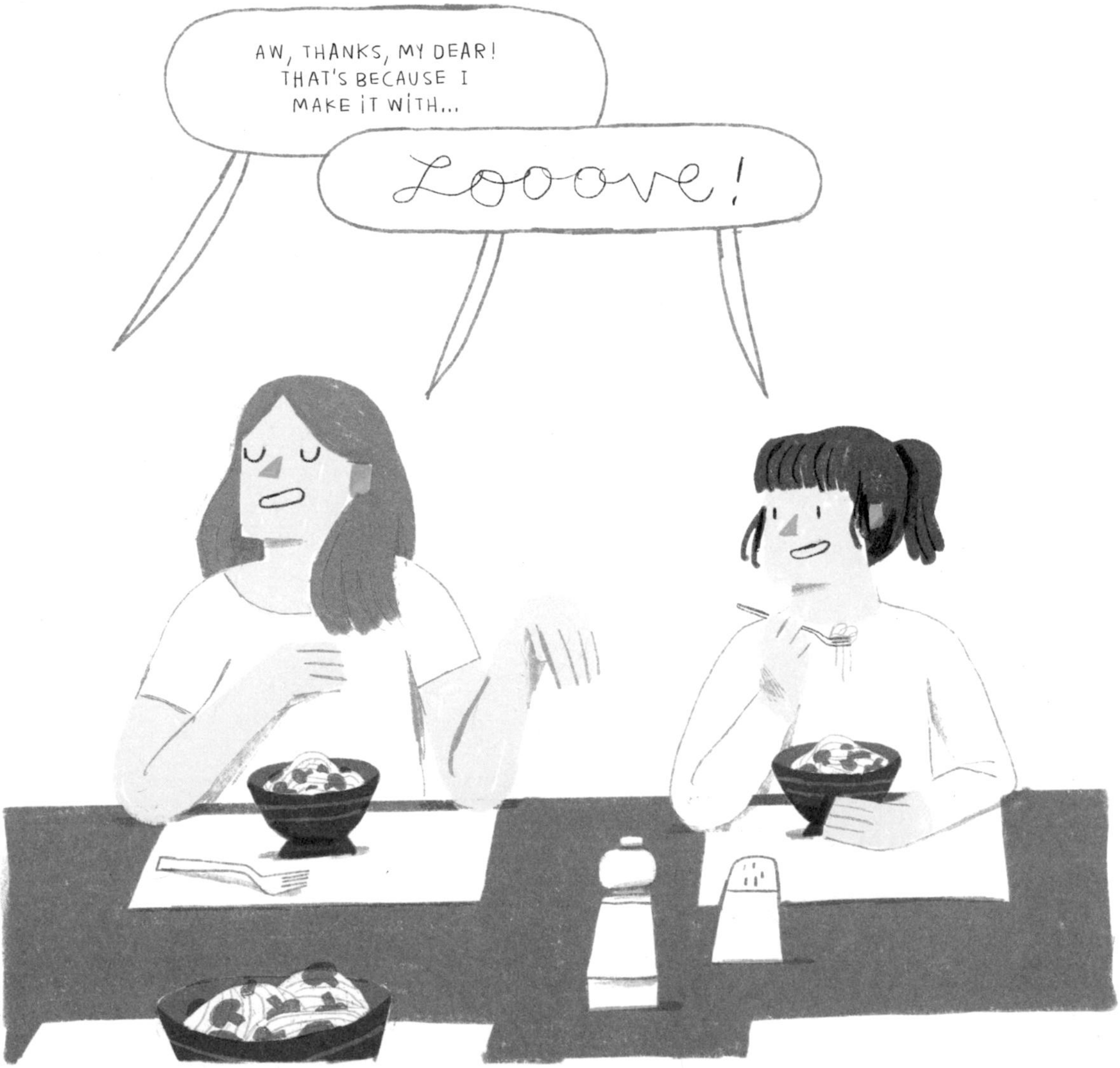
AW, THANKS, MY DEAR! THAT'S BECAUSE I MAKE IT WITH...
Looove!

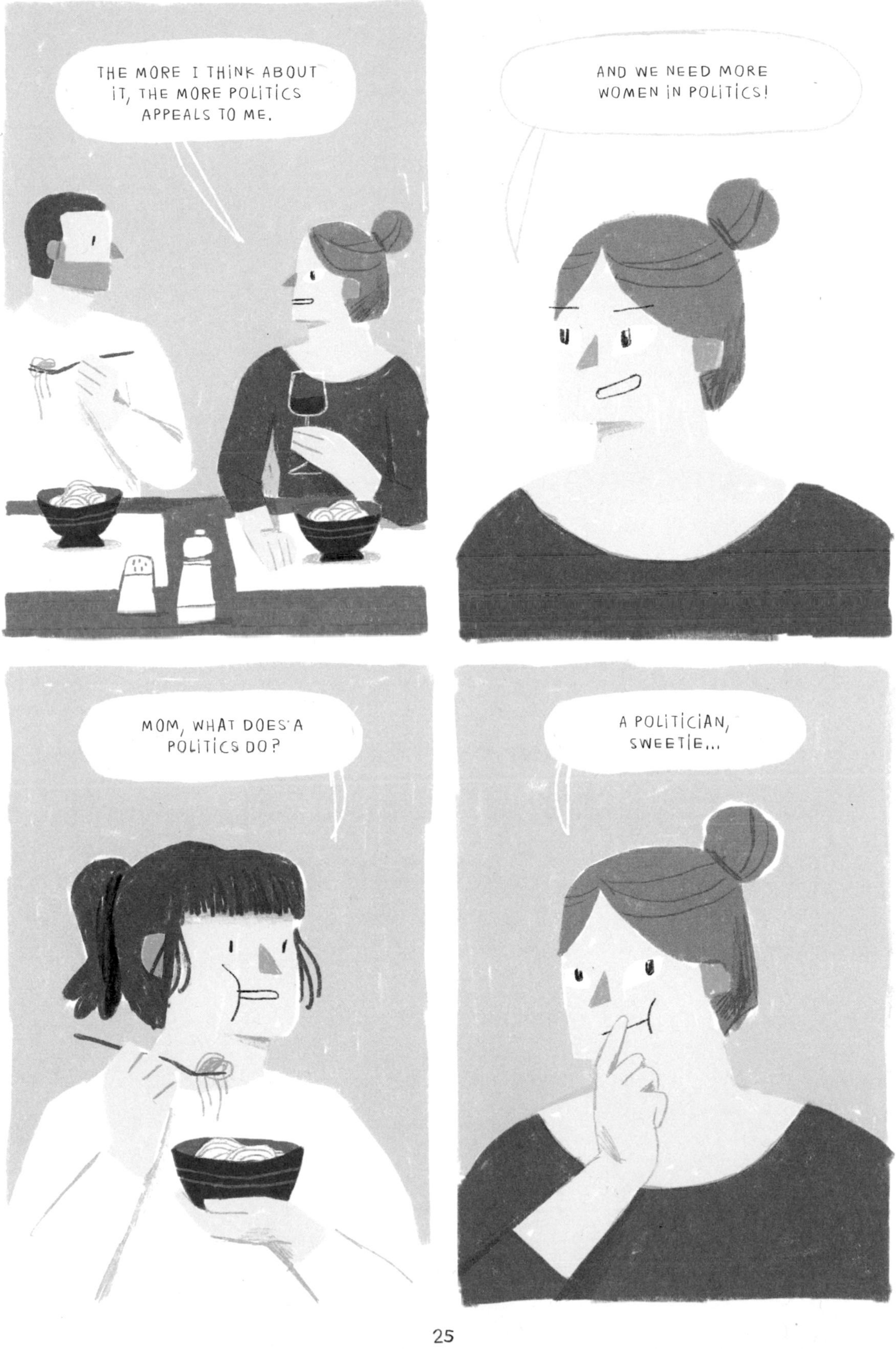
THE MORE I THINK ABOUT IT, THE MORE POLITICS APPEALS TO ME.
AND WE NEED MORE WOMEN IN POLITICS!
MOM, WHAT DOES A POLITICS DO?
A POLITICIAN, SWEETIE...

WELL, POLITICIANS LISTEN.
THEY LISTEN TO EVERYBODY.

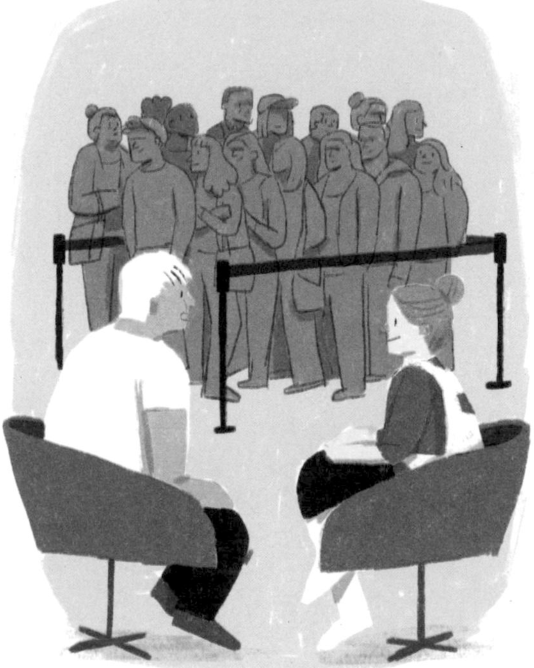

THEY HELP PEOPLE GET THEIR
PROBLEMS SORTED OUT.

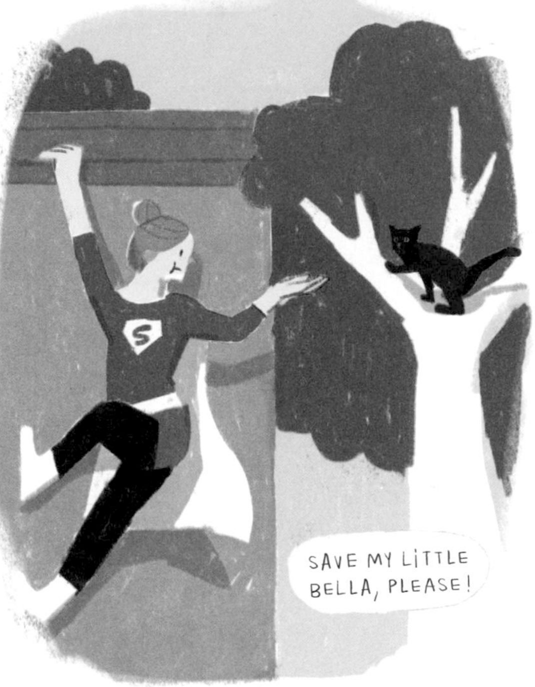
SAVE MY LITTLE BELLA, PLEASE!

THEY HOLD MEETINGS
IN THE COMMUNITY.

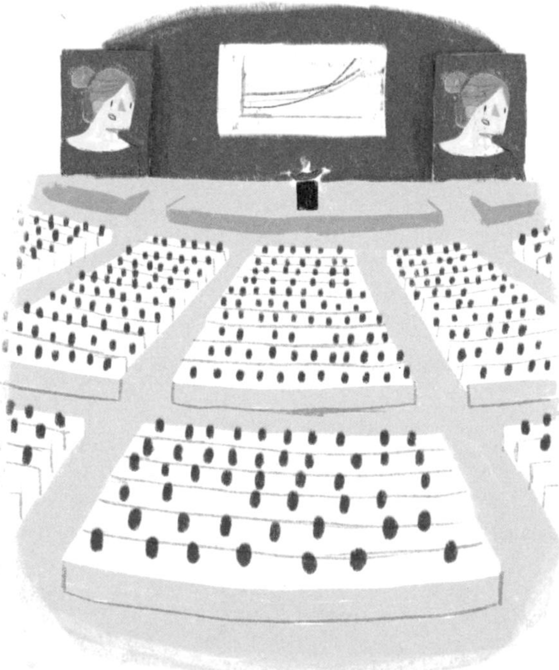

AND WHEN SOMETHING'S
BROKEN, THEY FIX IT.

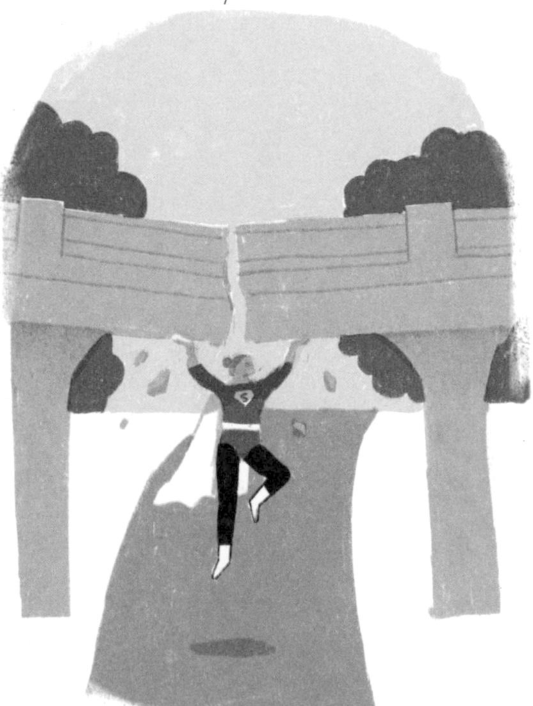

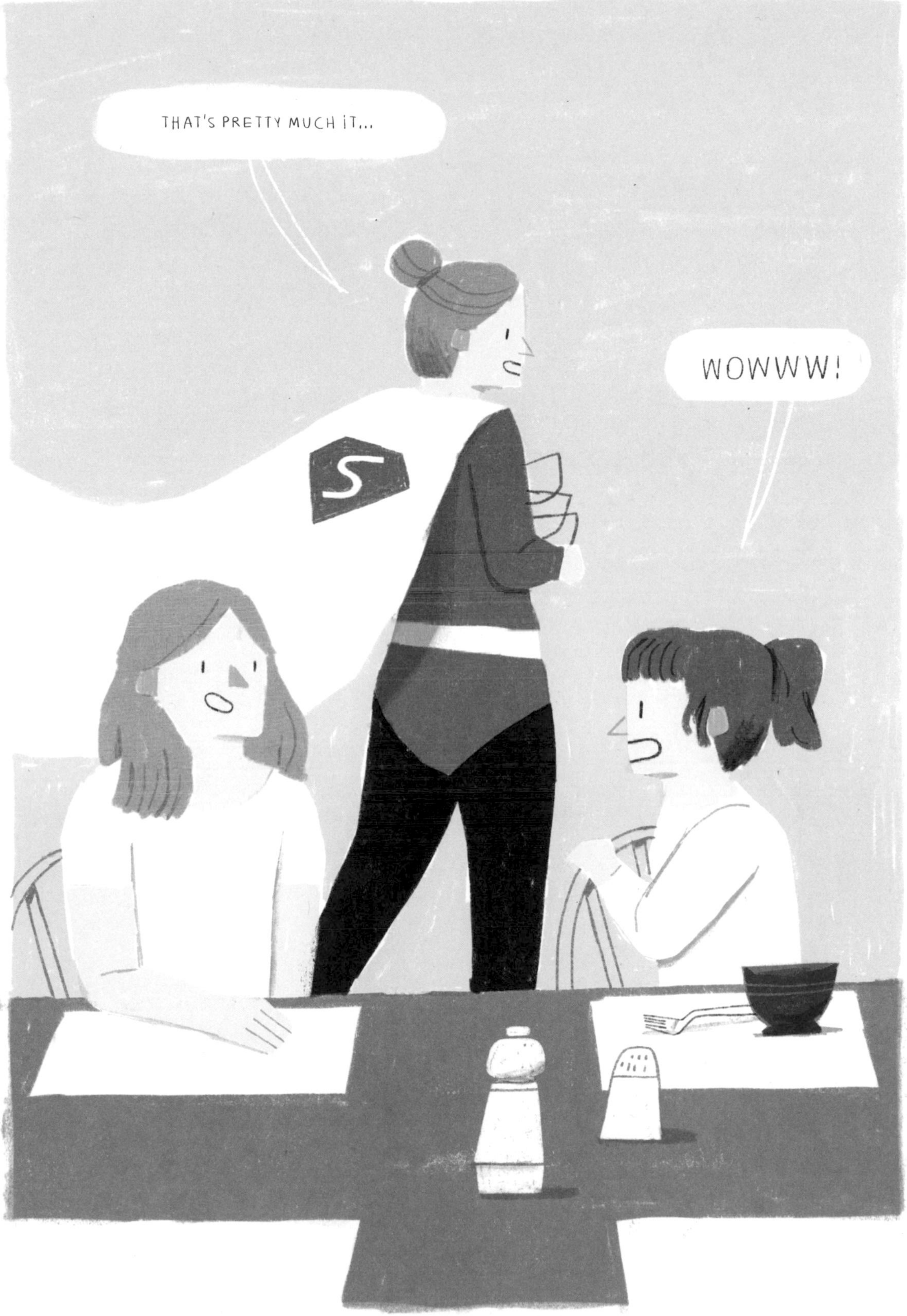
THAT'S PRETTY MUCH IT...
WOWWW!

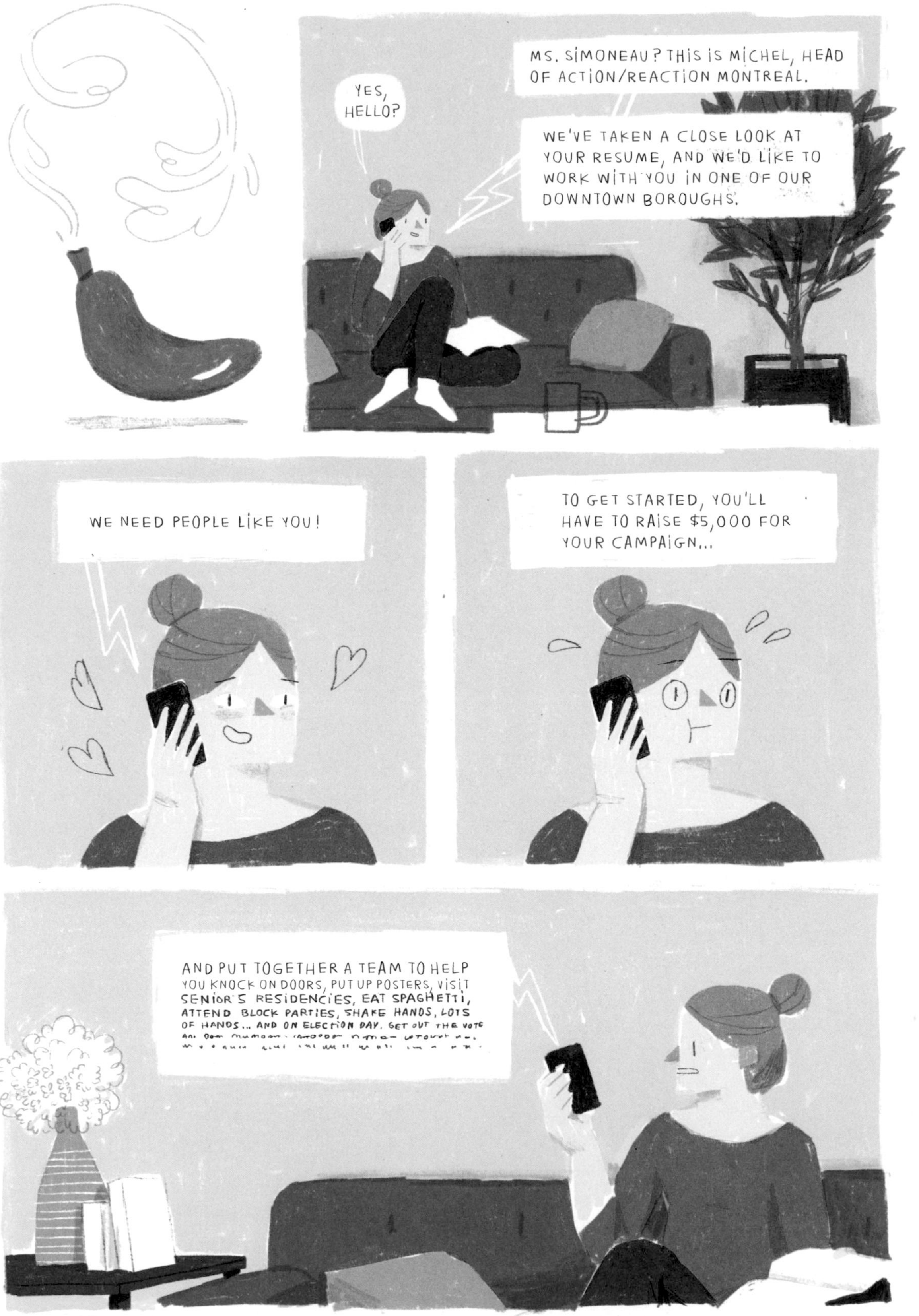

YES, HELLO?
MS. SIMONEAU? THIS IS MICHEL, HEAD OF ACTION/REACTION MONTREAL.
WE'VE TAKEN A CLOSE LOOK AT YOUR RESUME, AND WE'D LIKE TO WORK WITH YOU IN ONE OF OUR DOWNTOWN BOROUGHS.
WE NEED PEOPLE LIKE YOU!
TO GET STARTED, YOU'LL HAVE TO RAISE $5,000 FOR YOUR CAMPAIGN...
AND PUT TOGETHER A TEAM TO HELP YOU KNOCK ON DOORS, PUT UP POSTERS, VISIT SENIOR'S RESIDENCIES, EAT SPAGHETTI, ATTEND BLOCK PARTIES, SHAKE HANDS, LOTS OF HANDS... AND ON ELECTION DAY, GET OUT THE VOTE

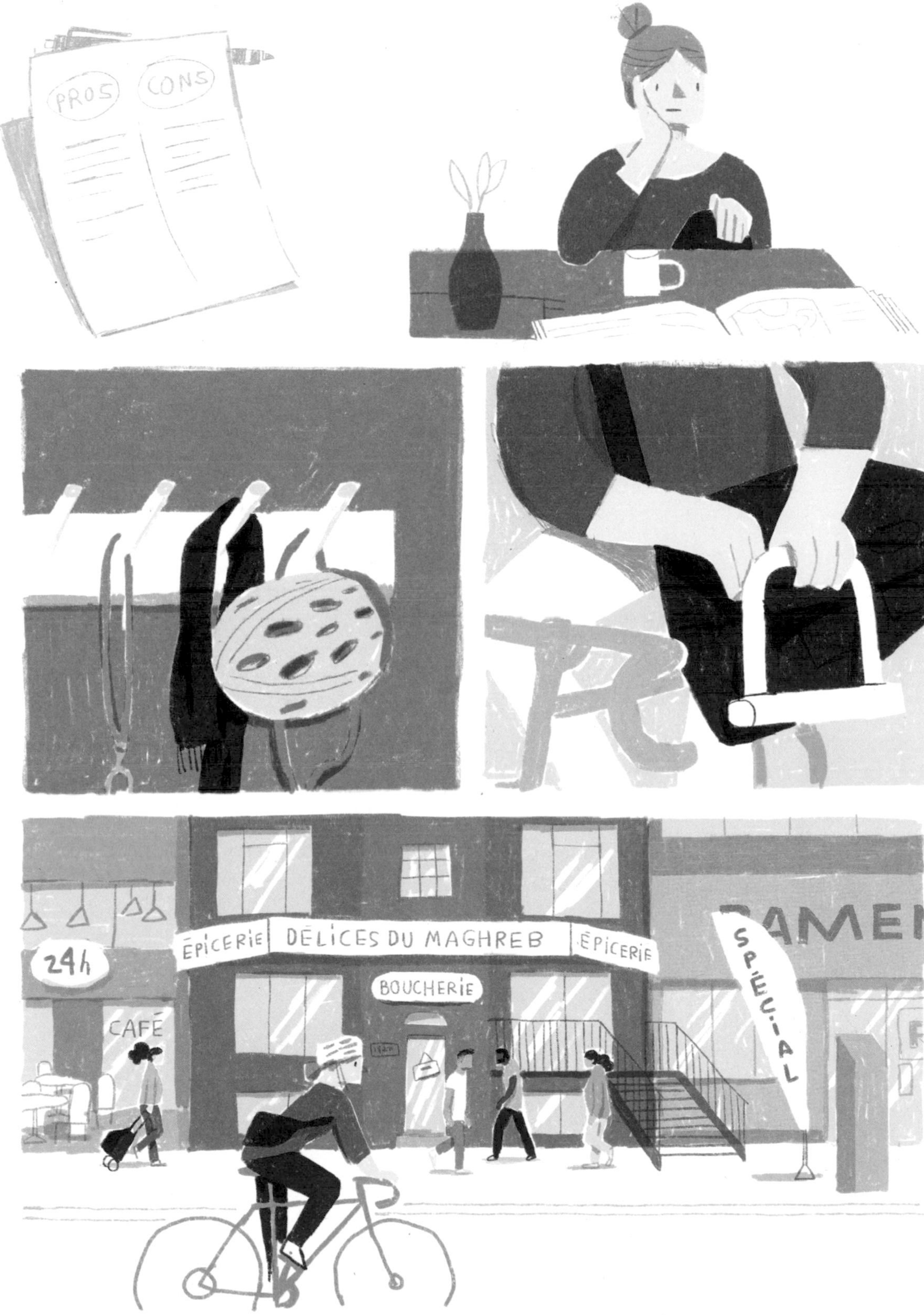
PROS
CONS
ÉPICERIE
DÉLICES DU MAGHREB
ÉPICERIE
24h
BOUCHERIE
CAFÉ
SPÉCIAL

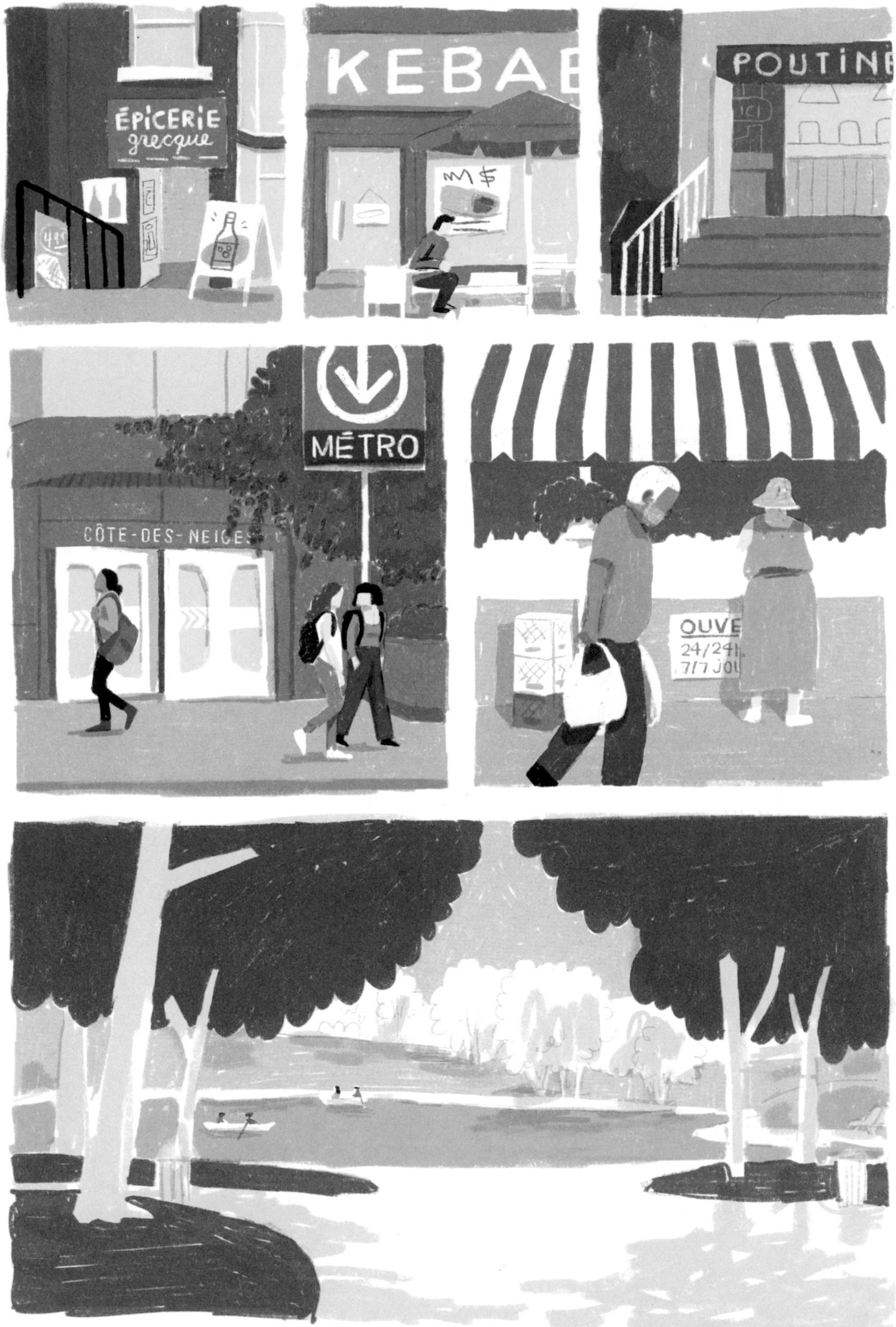
ÉPICERIE
grecque
KEBA
POUTINE
MÉTRO
CÔTE-DES-NEIGES
OUVE
24/24
7/7 JOU

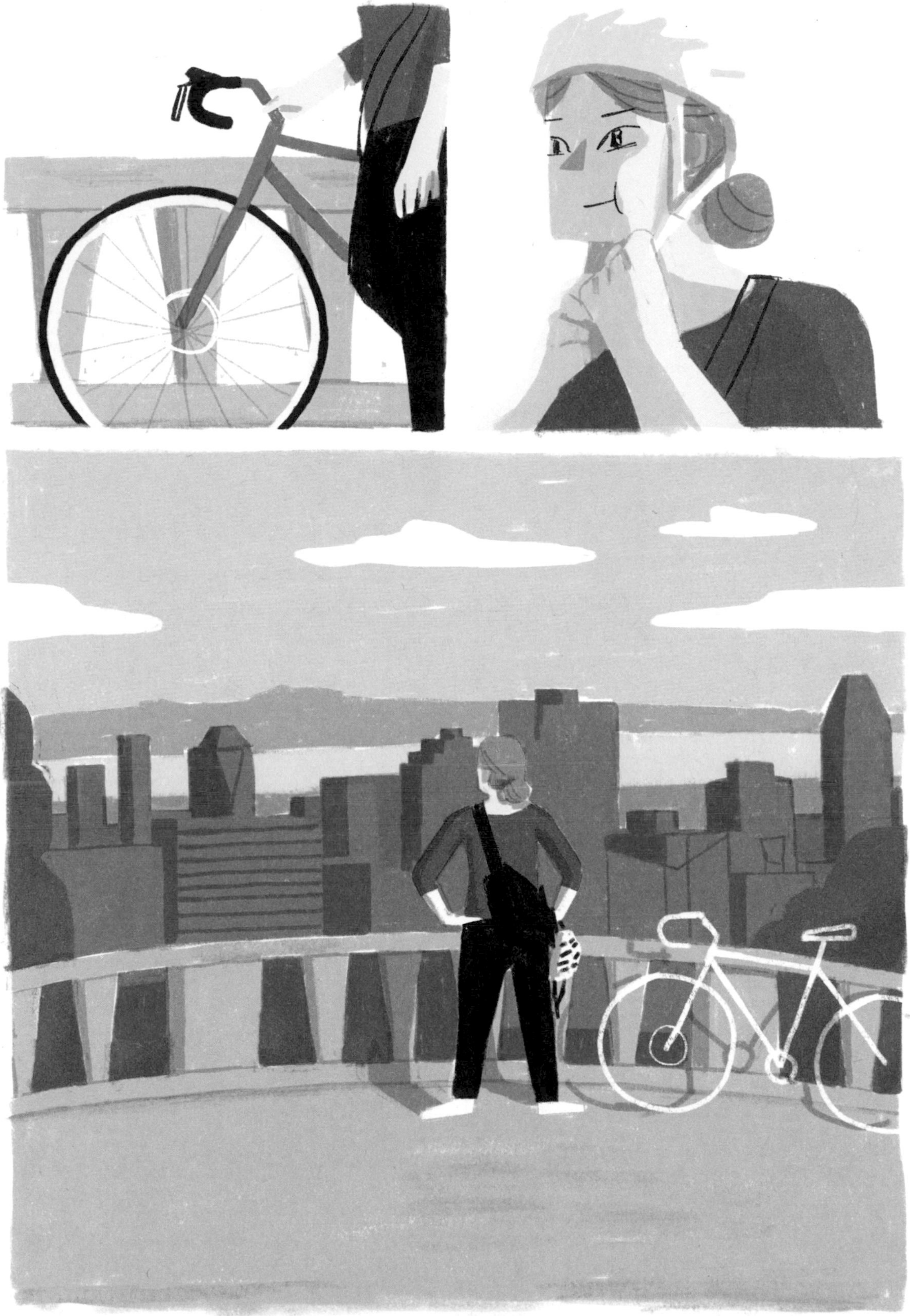

SIMONE
ENTERS POLITICS

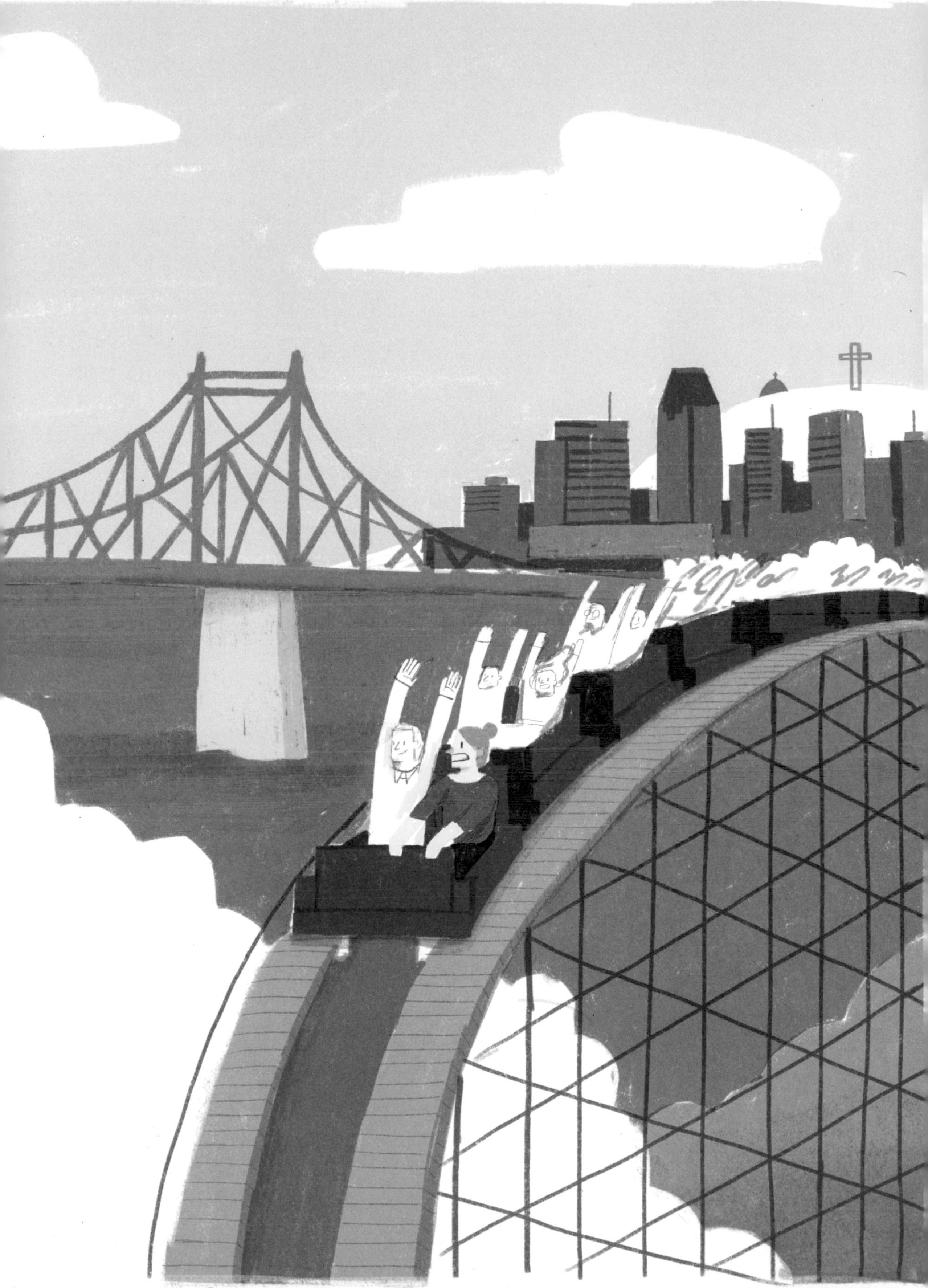

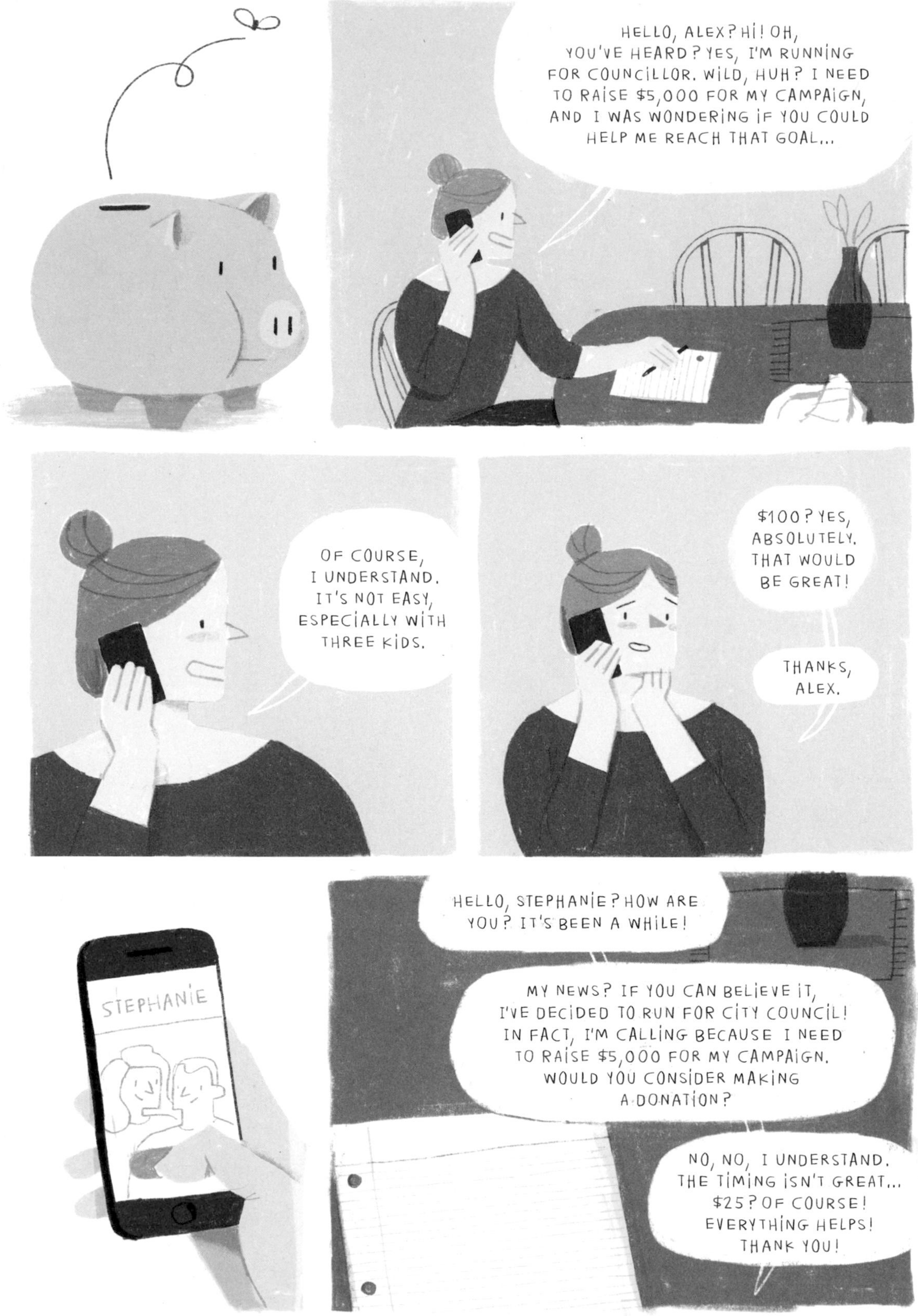

HELLO, ALEX? HI! OH, YOU'VE HEARD? YES, I'M RUNNING FOR COUNCILLOR. WILD, HUH? I NEED TO RAISE $5,000 FOR MY CAMPAIGN, AND I WAS WONDERING IF YOU COULD HELP ME REACH THAT GOAL...
OF COURSE, I UNDERSTAND. IT'S NOT EASY, ESPECIALLY WITH THREE KIDS.
$100? YES, ABSOLUTELY. THAT WOULD BE GREAT!
THANKS, ALEX.
STEPHANIE
HELLO, STEPHANIE? HOW ARE YOU? IT'S BEEN A WHILE!
MY NEWS? IF YOU CAN BELIEVE IT, I'VE DECIDED TO RUN FOR CITY COUNCIL! IN FACT, I'M CALLING BECAUSE I NEED TO RAISE $5,000 FOR MY CAMPAIGN. WOULD YOU CONSIDER MAKING A DONATION?
NO, NO, I UNDERSTAND. THE TIMING ISN'T GREAT... $25? OF COURSE! EVERYTHING HELPS! THANK YOU!

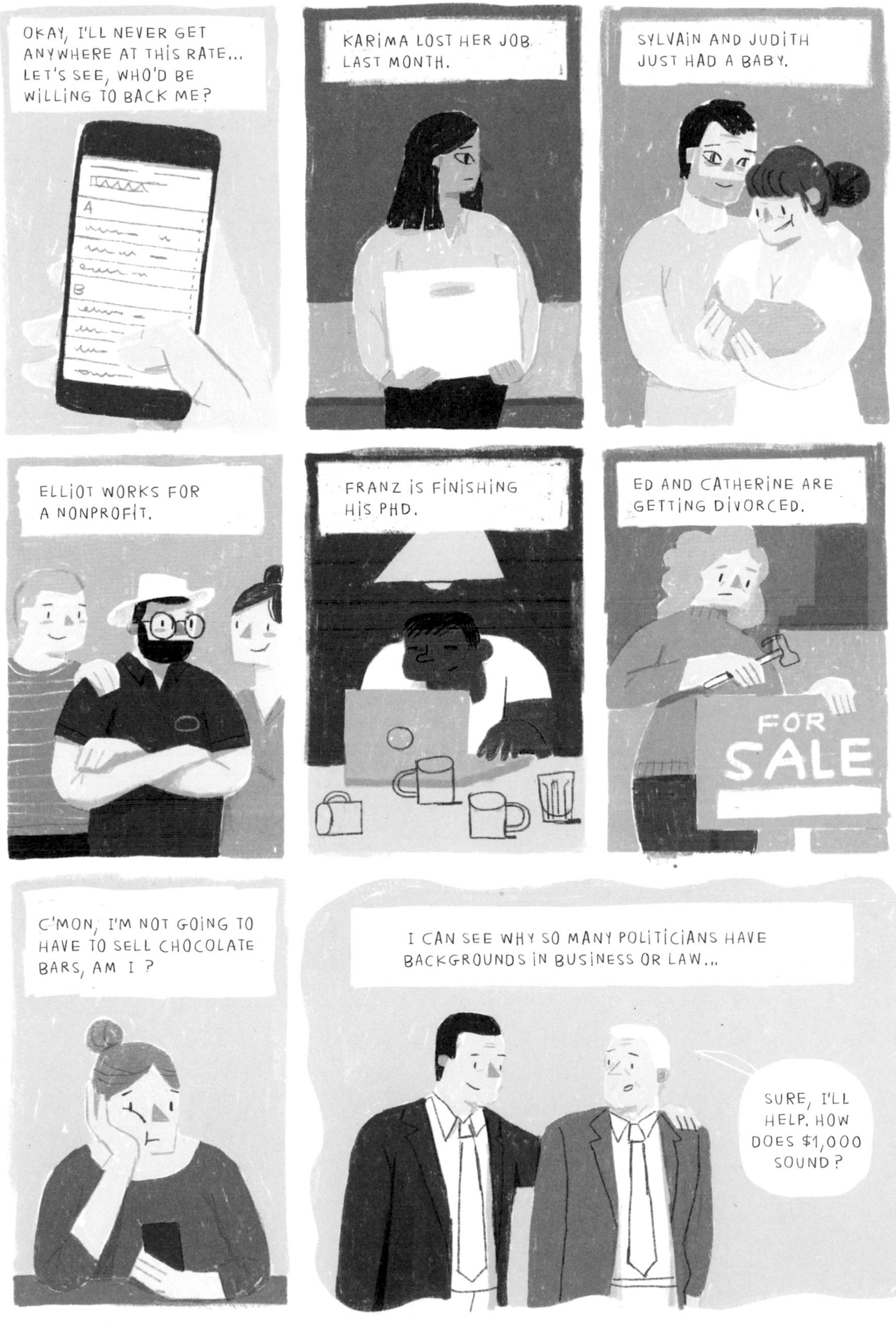
OKAY, I'LL NEVER GET ANYWHERE AT THIS RATE... LET'S SEE, WHO'D BE WILLING TO BACK ME?
KARIMA LOST HER JOB LAST MONTH.
SYLVAIN AND JUDITH JUST HAD A BABY.
ELLIOT WORKS FOR A NONPROFIT.
FRANZ IS FINISHING HIS PHD.
ED AND CATHERINE ARE GETTING DIVORCED.
FOR SALE
C'MON, I'M NOT GOING TO HAVE TO SELL CHOCOLATE BARS, AM I ?
I CAN SEE WHY SO MANY POLITICIANS HAVE BACKGROUNDS IN BUSINESS OR LAW...
SURE, I'LL HELP. HOW DOES $1,000 SOUND?

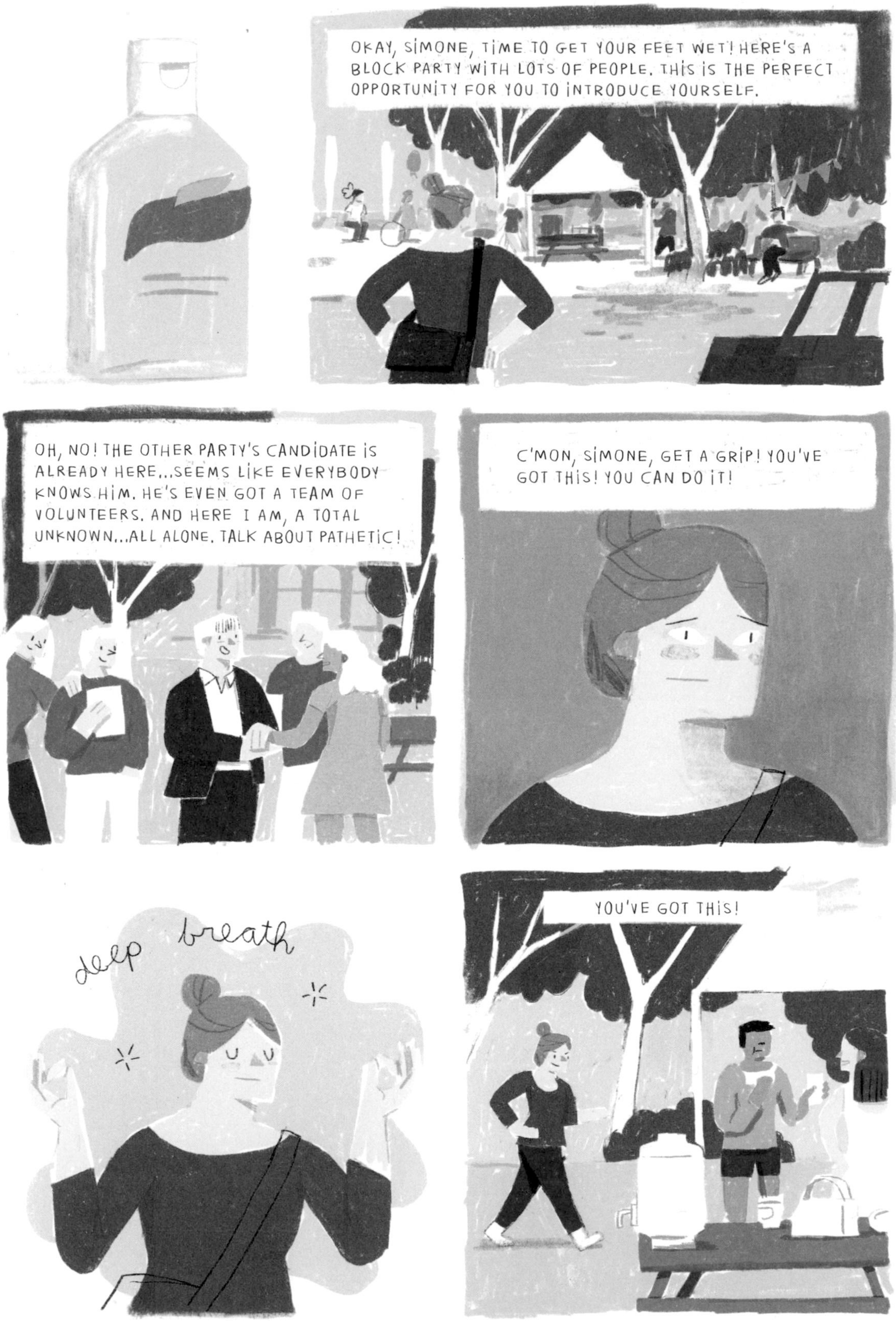
OKAY, SIMONE, TIME TO GET YOUR FEET WET! HERE'S A BLOCK PARTY WITH LOTS OF PEOPLE. THIS IS THE PERFECT OPPORTUNITY FOR YOU TO INTRODUCE YOURSELF.
OH, NO! THE OTHER PARTY'S CANDIDATE IS ALREADY HERE...SEEMS LIKE EVERYBODY KNOWS HIM. HE'S EVEN GOT A TEAM OF VOLUNTEERS. AND HERE I AM, A TOTAL UNKNOWN...ALL ALONE. TALK ABOUT PATHETIC!
C'MON, SIMONE, GET A GRIP! YOU'VE GOT THIS! YOU CAN DO IT!
deep breath
YOU'VE GOT THIS!

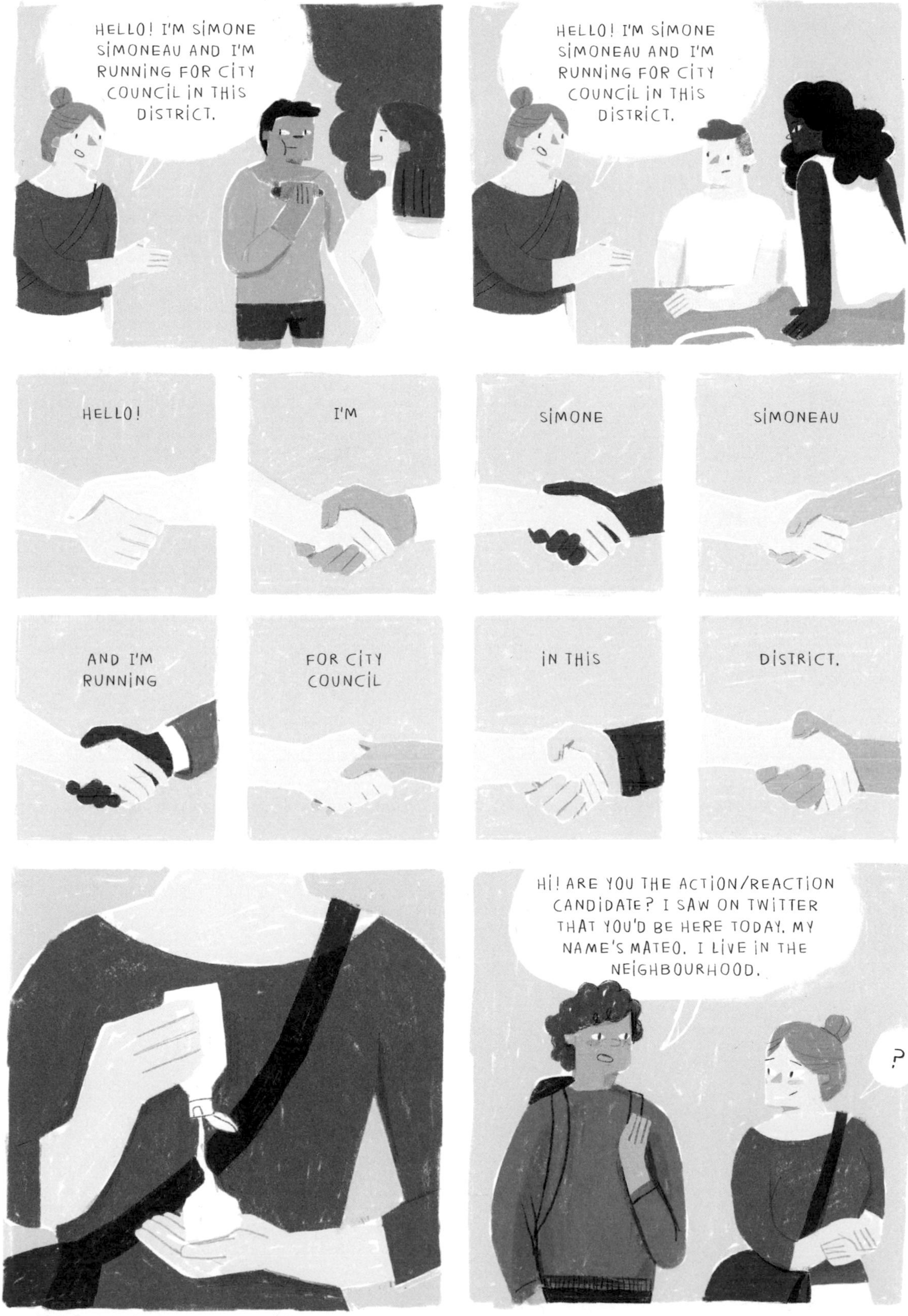
HELLO! I'M SIMONE SIMONEAU AND I'M RUNNING FOR CITY COUNCIL IN THIS DISTRICT.
HELLO! I'M SIMONE SIMONEAU AND I'M RUNNING FOR CITY COUNCIL IN THIS DISTRICT.
HELLO!
I'M
SIMONE
SIMONEAU
AND I'M RUNNING
FOR CITY COUNCIL
IN THIS
DISTRICT.
HI! ARE YOU THE ACTION/REACTION CANDIDATE? I SAW ON TWITTER THAT YOU'D BE HERE TODAY. MY NAME'S MATEO. I LIVE IN THE NEIGHBOURHOOD.
?

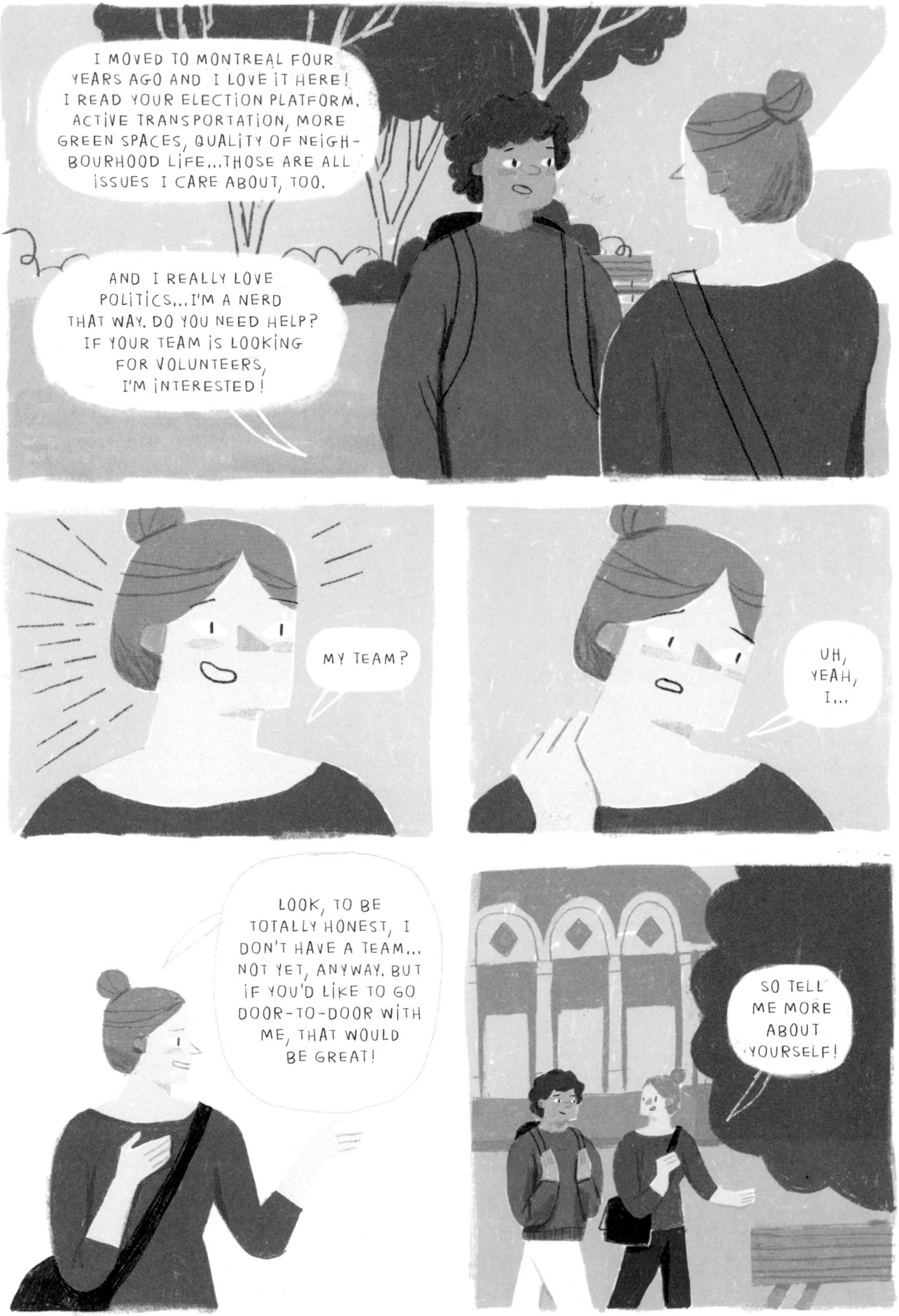
I MOVED TO MONTREAL FOUR YEARS AGO AND I LOVE IT HERE! I READ YOUR ELECTION PLATFORM. ACTIVE TRANSPORTATION, MORE GREEN SPACES, QUALITY OF NEIGHBOURHOOD LIFE...THOSE ARE ALL ISSUES I CARE ABOUT, TOO.
AND I REALLY LOVE POLITICS...I'M A NERD THAT WAY. DO YOU NEED HELP? IF YOUR TEAM IS LOOKING FOR VOLUNTEERS, I'M INTERESTED!
MY TEAM?
UH, YEAH, I...
LOOK, TO BE TOTALLY HONEST, I DON'T HAVE A TEAM... NOT YET, ANYWAY. BUT IF YOU'D LIKE TO GO DOOR-TO-DOOR WITH ME, THAT WOULD BE GREAT!
SO TELL ME MORE ABOUT YOURSELF!

I'M FROM MEXICO. I CAME HERE TO STUDY AND DECIDED TO STAY. I WORK AT UBISOFT. IT'S A COOL COMPANY. I LIVE RIGHT NEARBY, ON FULLUM STREET. THIS NEIGHBOURHOOD IS NICE AND CENTRAL, THAT'S WHAT I LIKE ABOUT IT. I LIKE THE PEOPLE, TOO. THEY'RE A REAL MIX...YOUNG, OLD, SOME DOWN-AND-OUTS, FAMILIES, STUDENTS... SOMETIMES I MISS MY FAMILY BUT...

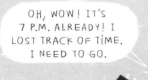

OH, WOW! IT'S 7 P.M. ALREADY! I LOST TRACK OF TIME. I NEED TO GO.

LET'S BE IN TOUCH THIS WEEK TO START KNOCKING ON DOORS!

YOU BET!

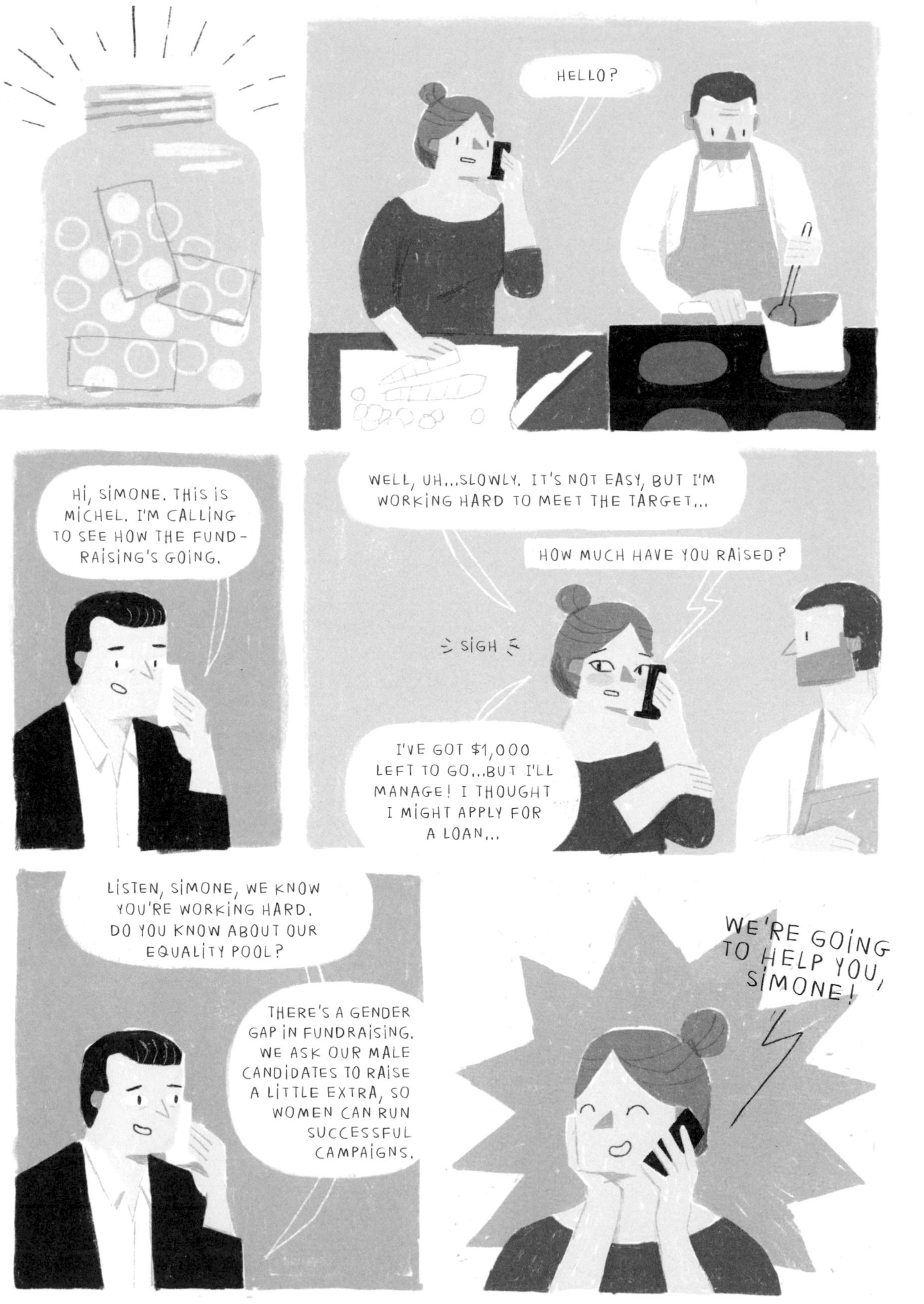
HELLO?
Hi, SIMONE. THIS IS MICHEL. I'M CALLING TO SEE HOW THE FUND-RAISING'S GOING.
WELL, UH...SLOWLY. IT'S NOT EASY, BUT I'M WORKING HARD TO MEET THE TARGET...
HOW MUCH HAVE YOU RAISED?
SIGH
I'VE GOT $1,000 LEFT TO GO...BUT I'LL MANAGE! I THOUGHT I MIGHT APPLY FOR A LOAN...
LISTEN, SIMONE, WE KNOW YOU'RE WORKING HARD. DO YOU KNOW ABOUT OUR EQUALITY POOL?
THERE'S A GENDER GAP IN FUNDRAISING. WE ASK OUR MALE CANDIDATES TO RAISE A LITTLE EXTRA, SO WOMEN CAN RUN SUCCESSFUL CAMPAIGNS.
WE'RE GOING TO HELP YOU, SIMONE!

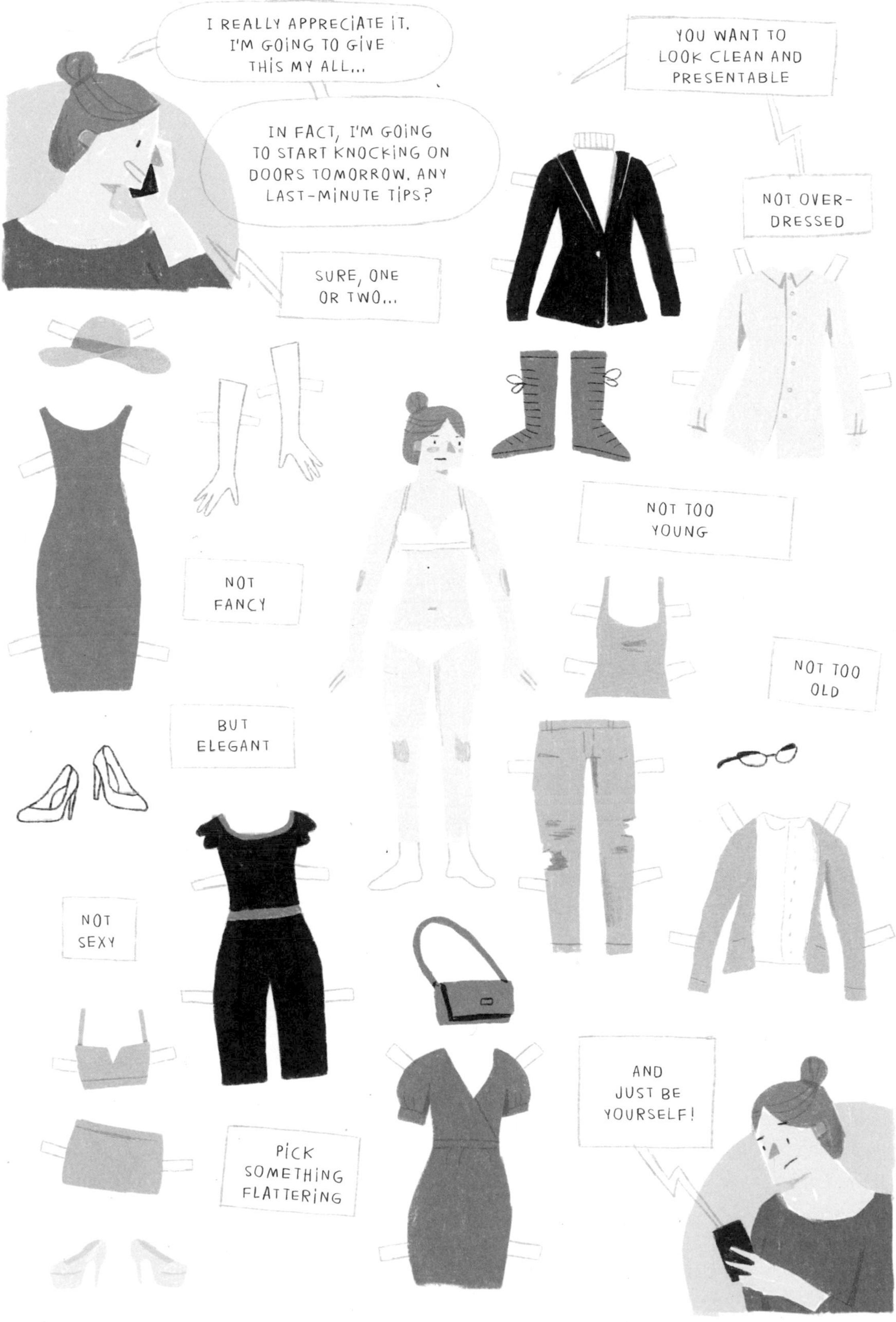
I REALLY APPRECIATE IT. I'M GOING TO GIVE THIS MY ALL...
IN FACT, I'M GOING TO START KNOCKING ON DOORS TOMORROW. ANY LAST-MINUTE TIPS?
SURE, ONE OR TWO...
YOU WANT TO LOOK CLEAN AND PRESENTABLE
NOT OVER-DRESSED
NOT TOO YOUNG
NOT FANCY
NOT TOO OLD
BUT ELEGANT
NOT SEXY
PICK SOMETHING FLATTERING
AND JUST BE YOURSELF!

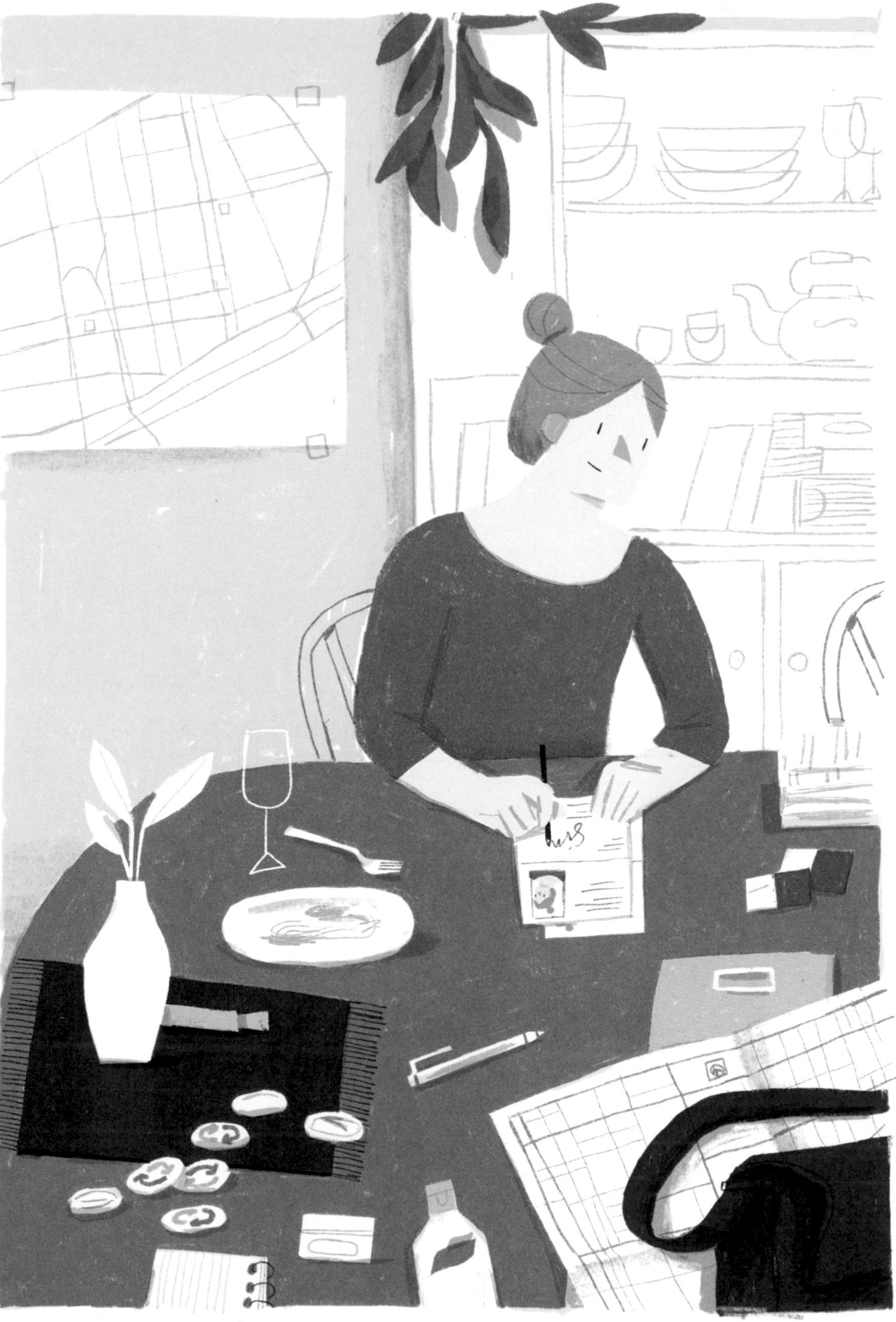

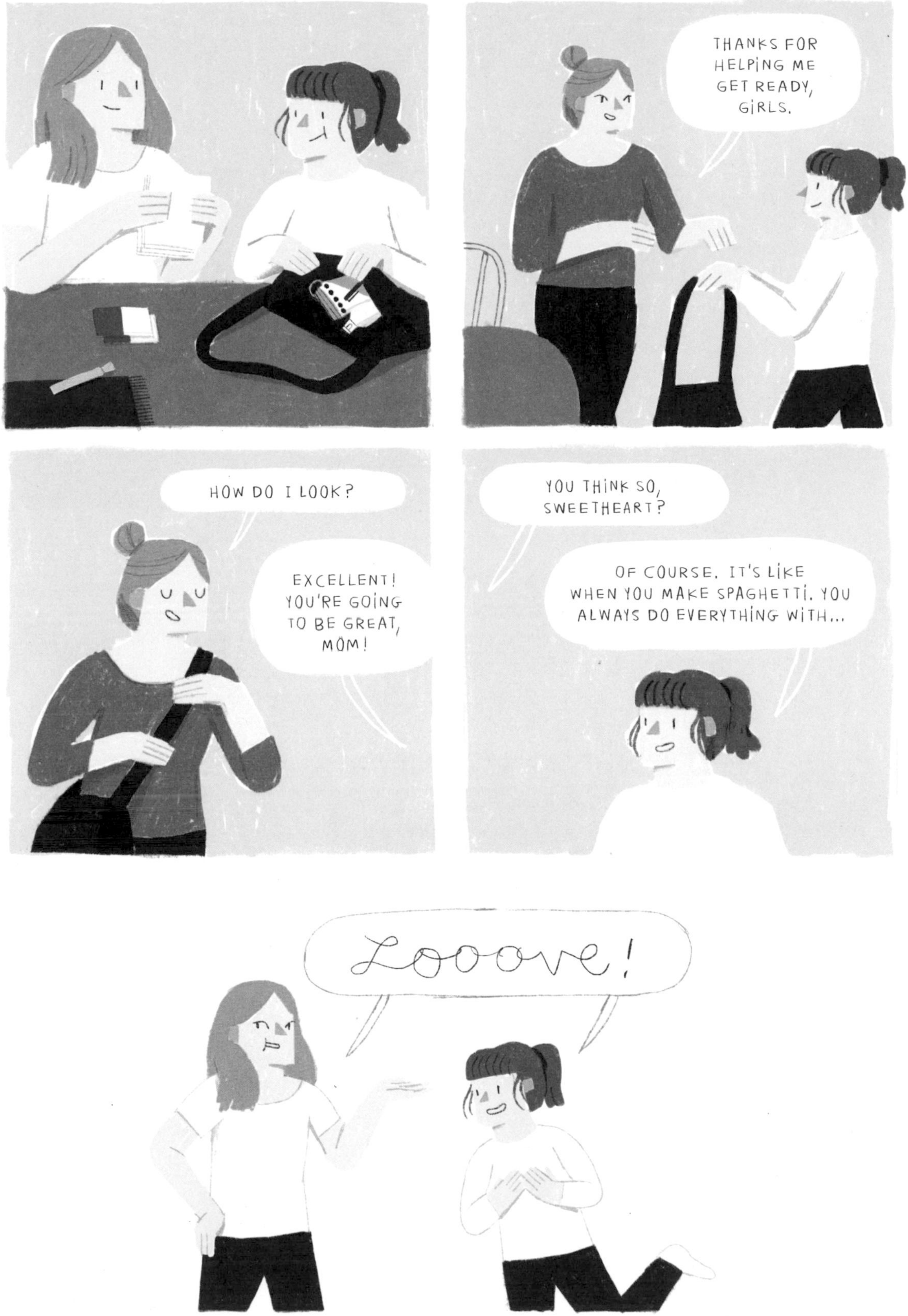
THANKS FOR HELPING ME GET READY, GIRLS.
HOW DO I LOOK?
EXCELLENT! YOU'RE GOING TO BE GREAT, MOM!
YOU THINK SO, SWEETHEART?
OF COURSE. IT'S LIKE WHEN YOU MAKE SPAGHETTI. YOU ALWAYS DO EVERYTHING WITH...
Looove!

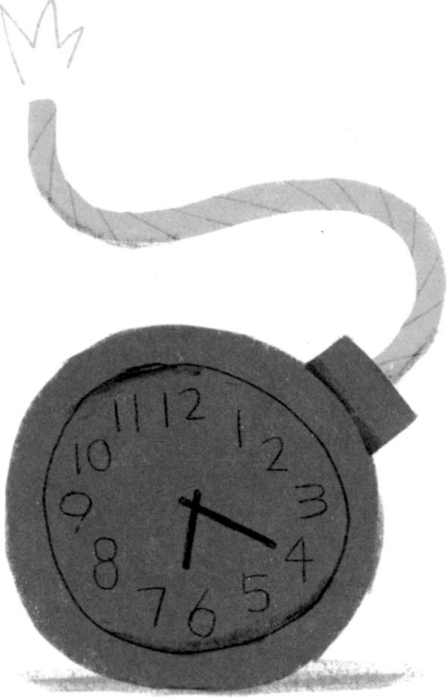

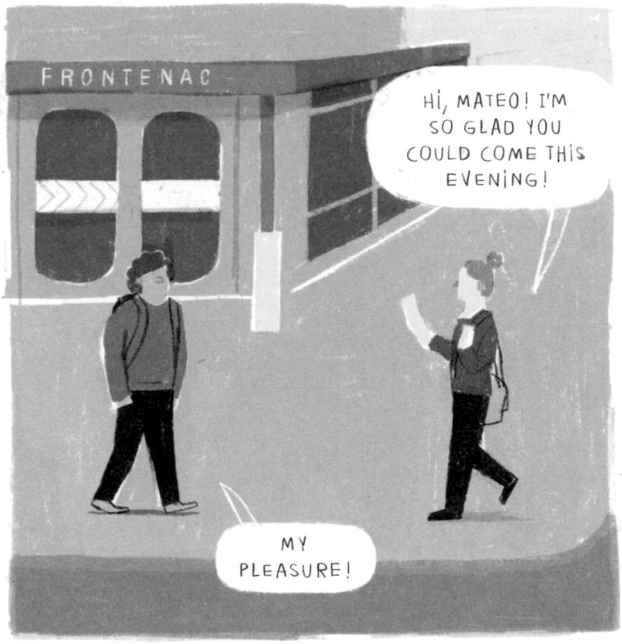
FRONTENAC
HI, MATEO! I'M SO GLAD YOU COULD COME THIS EVENING!
MY PLEASURE!

PORTRAIT OF A VOLUNTEER

MATEO

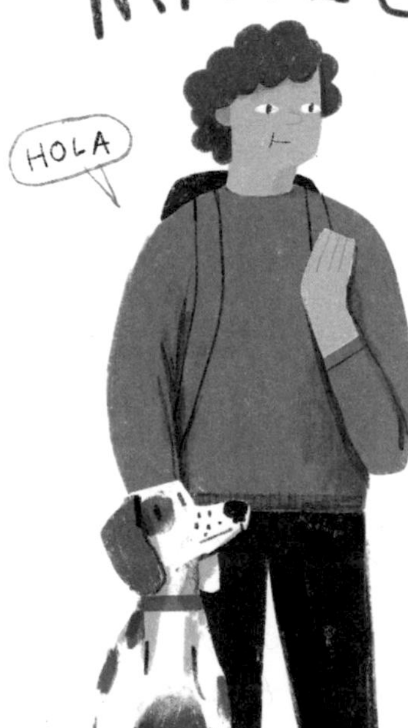
HOLA

INHERITED A DOG NAMED PERNOD AFTER HIS GREAT UNCLE DIED LAST YEAR.

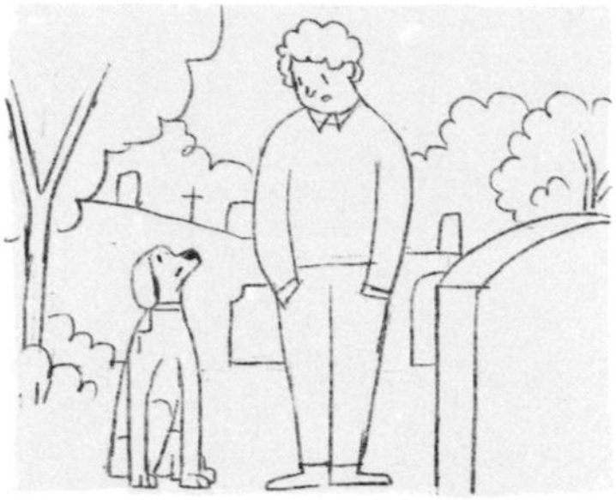

LOVES BAGELS, ESPECIALLY ROSEMARY SEA SALT ONES.

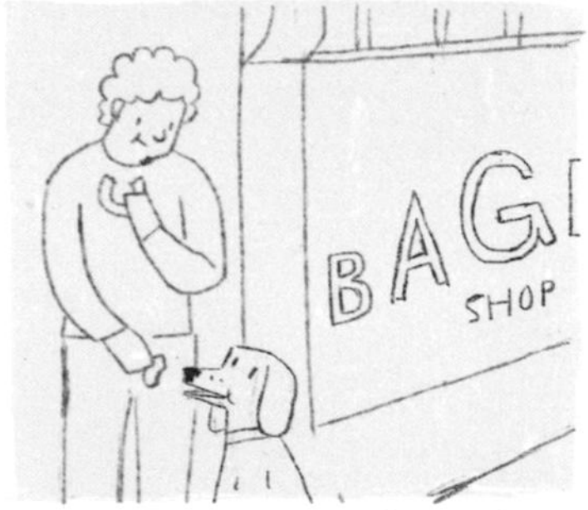
SHOP

ALWAYS CHOOSES THE LONGEST LINE AT THE CHECKOUT SO HE CAN READ THE TABLOID HEADLINES.

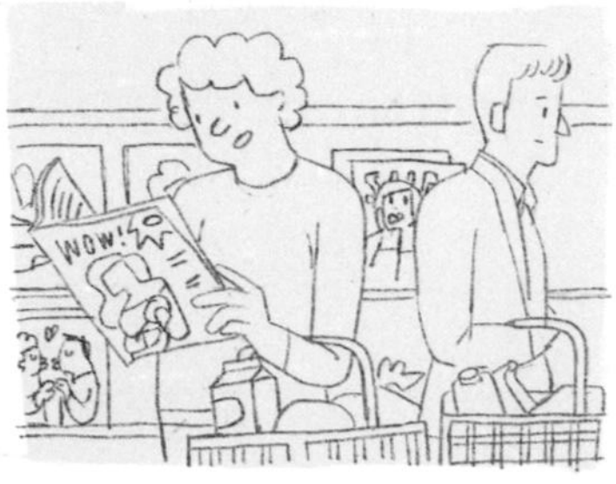
WOW!

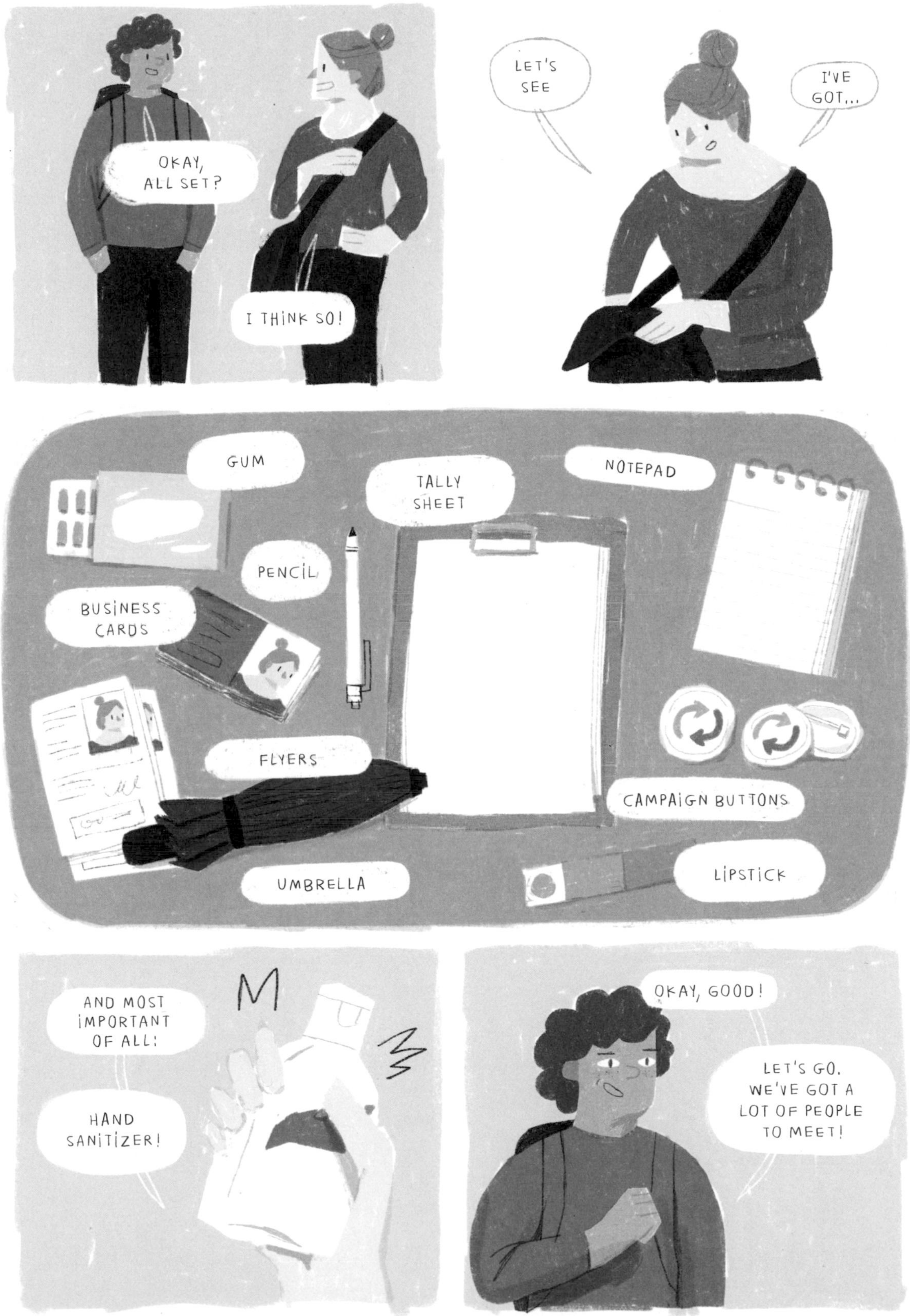
OKAY, ALL SET?
I THINK SO!
LET'S SEE
I'VE GOT...
GUM
TALLY SHEET
NOTEPAD
PENCIL
BUSINESS CARDS
FLYERS
CAMPAIGN BUTTONS
UMBRELLA
LIPSTICK
AND MOST IMPORTANT OF ALL:
HAND SANITIZER!
M
OKAY, GOOD!
LET'S GO. WE'VE GOT A LOT OF PEOPLE TO MEET!

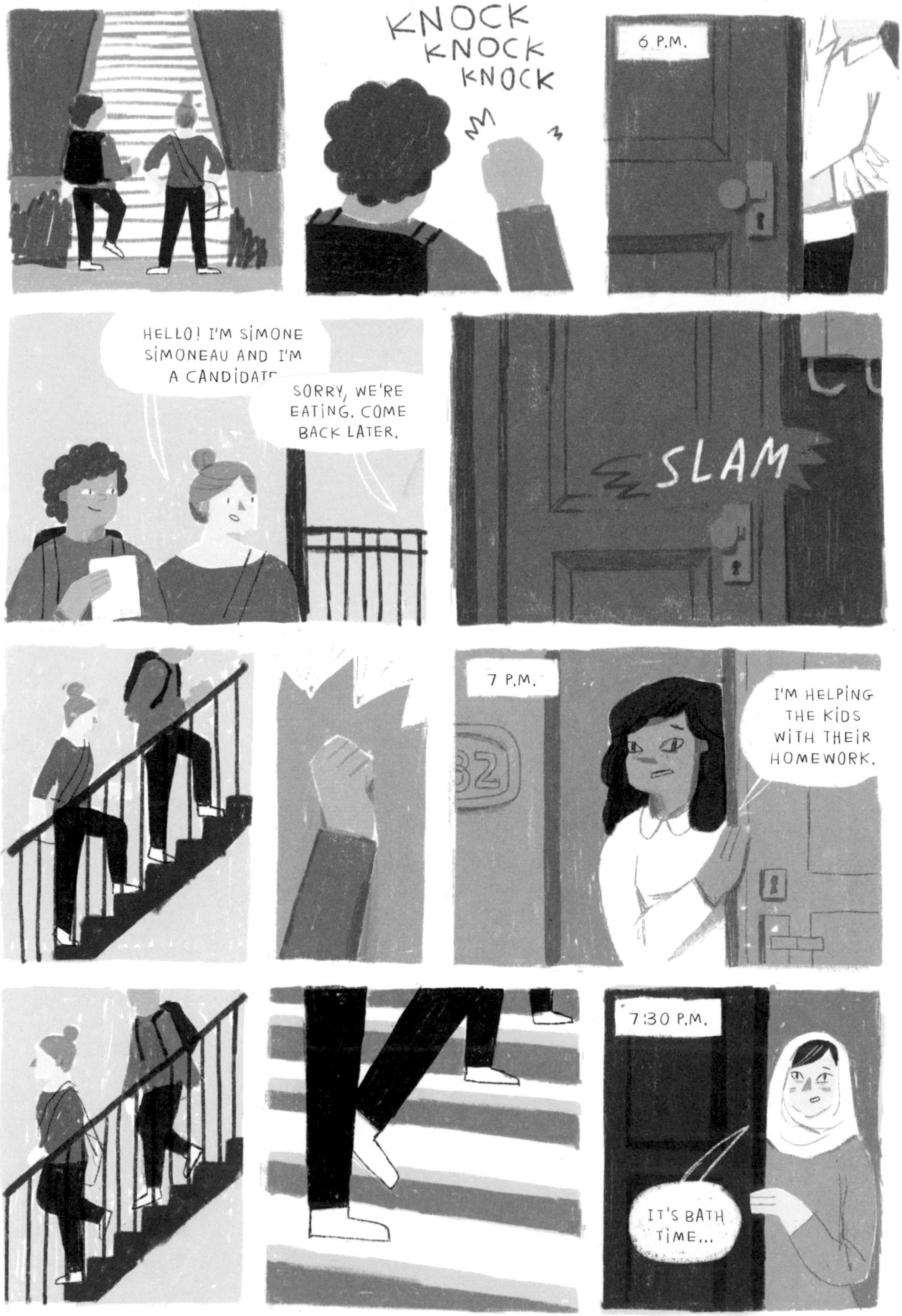
KNOCK KNOCK KNOCK
6 P.M.
HELLO! I'M SIMONE SIMONEAU AND I'M A CANDIDATE
SORRY, WE'RE EATING. COME BACK LATER.
SLAM
7 P.M.
I'M HELPING THE KIDS WITH THEIR HOMEWORK.
7:30 P.M.
IT'S BATH TIME...

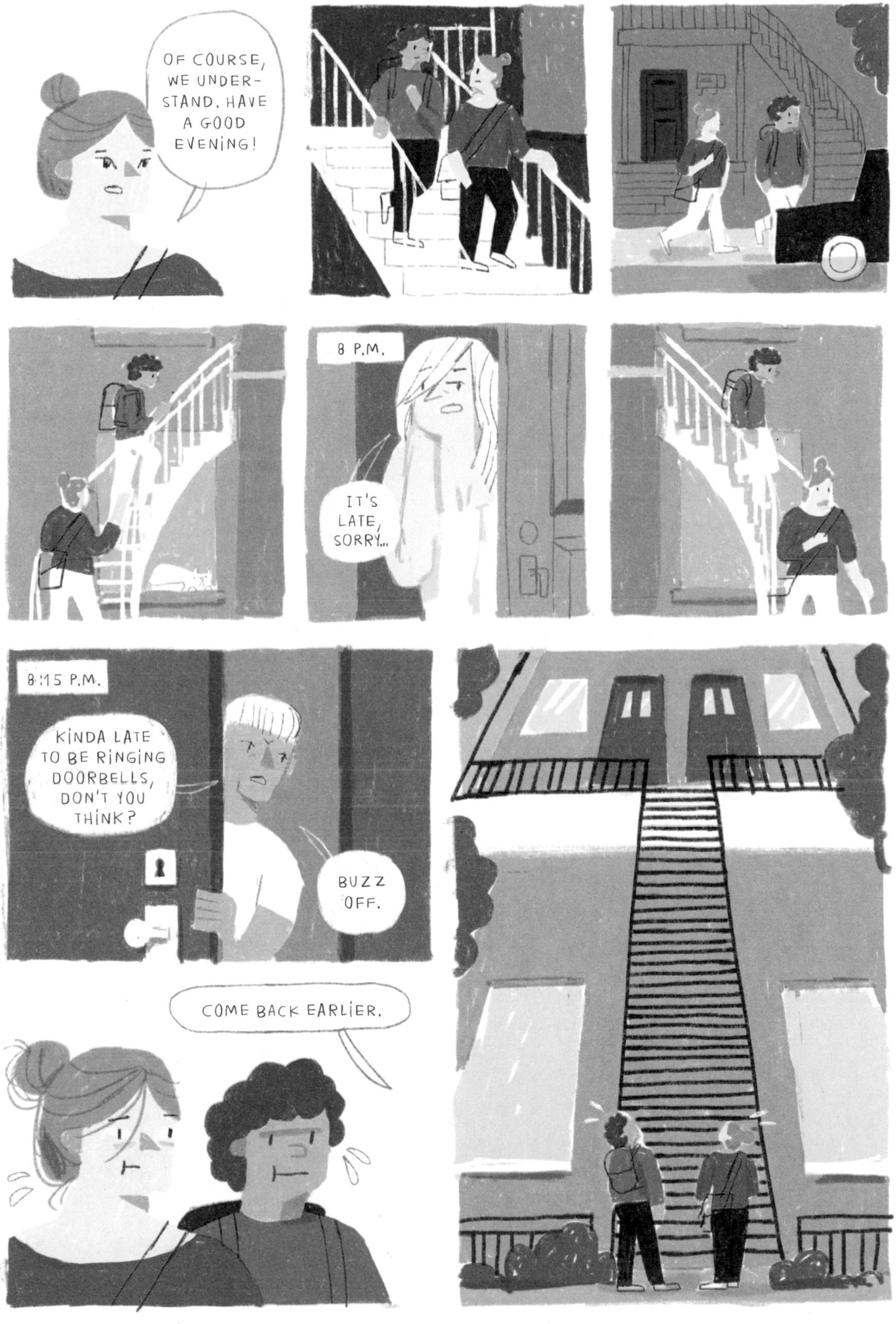
OF COURSE, WE UNDER-STAND. HAVE A GOOD EVENING!
8 P.M.
IT'S LATE, SORRY...
8:15 P.M.
KINDA LATE TO BE RINGING DOORBELLS, DON'T YOU THINK?
BUZZ OFF.
COME BACK EARLIER.

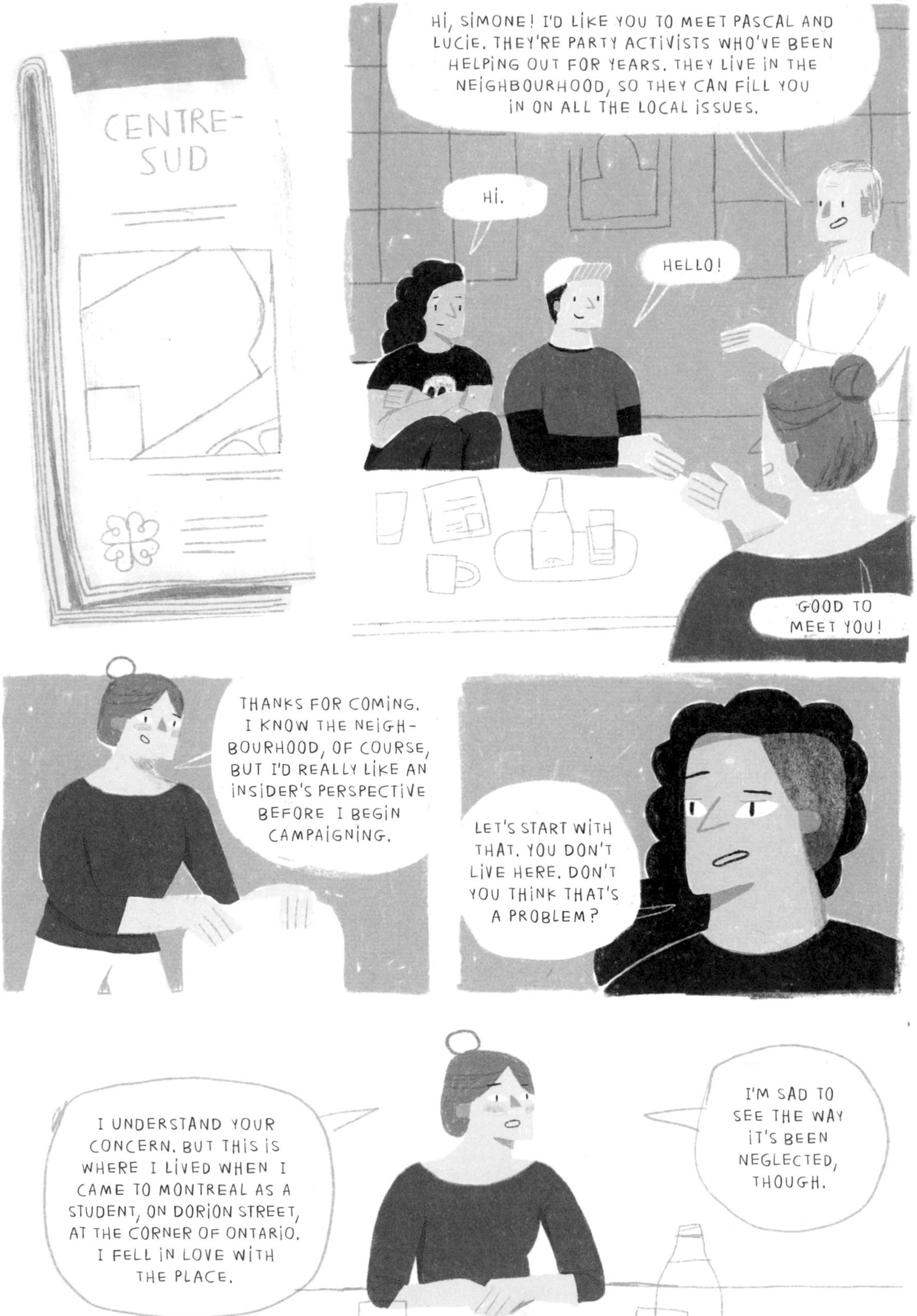
CENTRE-SUD
HI, SIMONE! I'D LIKE YOU TO MEET PASCAL AND LUCIE. THEY'RE PARTY ACTIVISTS WHO'VE BEEN HELPING OUT FOR YEARS. THEY LIVE IN THE NEIGHBOURHOOD, SO THEY CAN FILL YOU IN ON ALL THE LOCAL ISSUES.
HI.
HELLO!
GOOD TO MEET YOU!
THANKS FOR COMING. I KNOW THE NEIGHBOURHOOD, OF COURSE, BUT I'D REALLY LIKE AN INSIDER'S PERSPECTIVE BEFORE I BEGIN CAMPAIGNING.
LET'S START WITH THAT. YOU DON'T LIVE HERE. DON'T YOU THINK THAT'S A PROBLEM?
I UNDERSTAND YOUR CONCERN. BUT THIS IS WHERE I LIVED WHEN I CAME TO MONTREAL AS A STUDENT, ON DORION STREET, AT THE CORNER OF ONTARIO. I FELL IN LOVE WITH THE PLACE.
I'M SAD TO SEE THE WAY IT'S BEEN NEGLECTED, THOUGH.

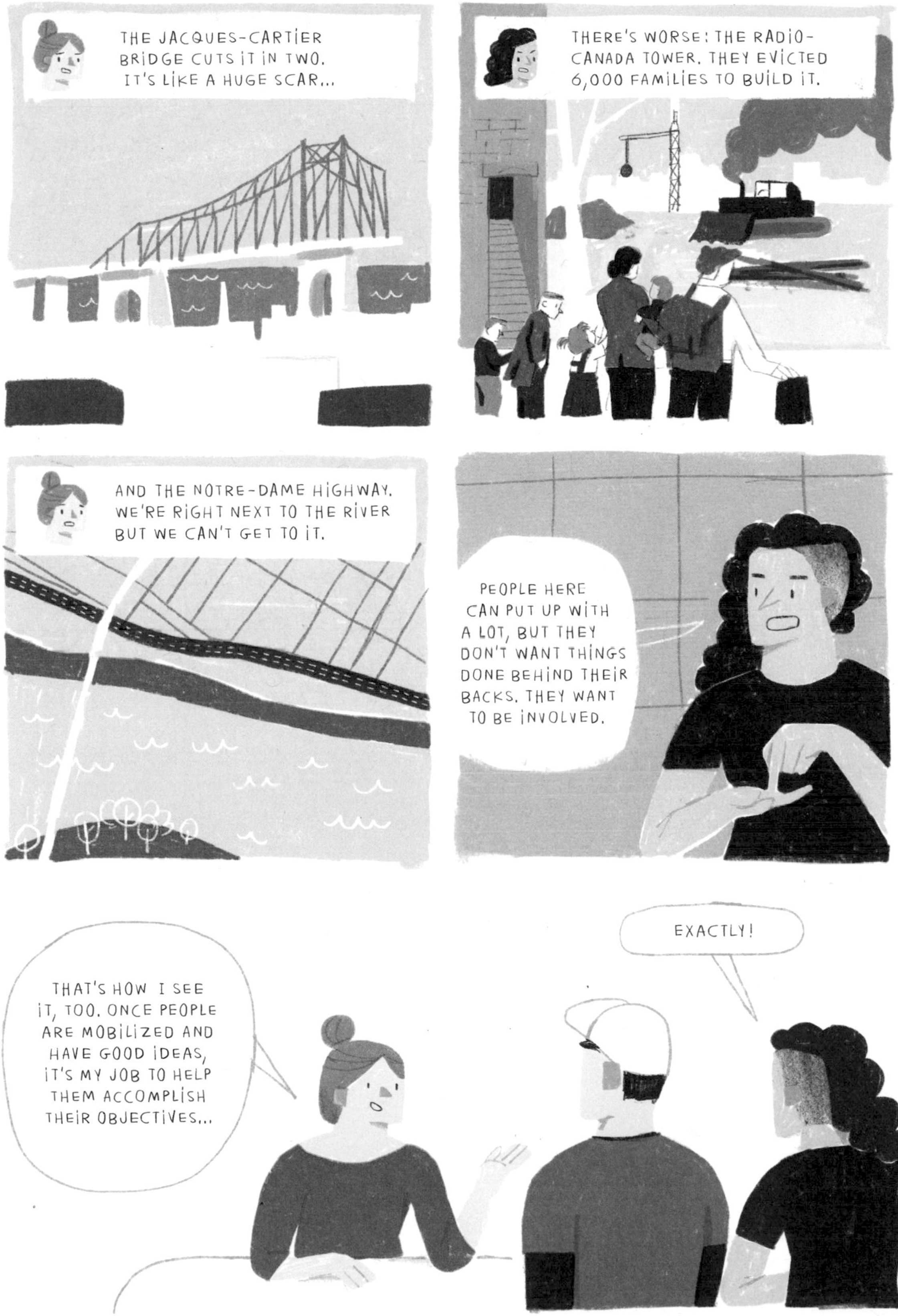
THE JACQUES-CARTIER BRIDGE CUTS IT IN TWO. IT'S LIKE A HUGE SCAR...
THERE'S WORSE: THE RADIO-CANADA TOWER. THEY EVICTED 6,000 FAMILIES TO BUILD IT.
AND THE NOTRE-DAME HIGHWAY. WE'RE RIGHT NEXT TO THE RIVER BUT WE CAN'T GET TO IT.
PEOPLE HERE CAN PUT UP WITH A LOT, BUT THEY DON'T WANT THINGS DONE BEHIND THEIR BACKS. THEY WANT TO BE INVOLVED.
THAT'S HOW I SEE IT, TOO. ONCE PEOPLE ARE MOBILIZED AND HAVE GOOD IDEAS, IT'S MY JOB TO HELP THEM ACCOMPLISH THEIR OBJECTIVES...
EXACTLY!

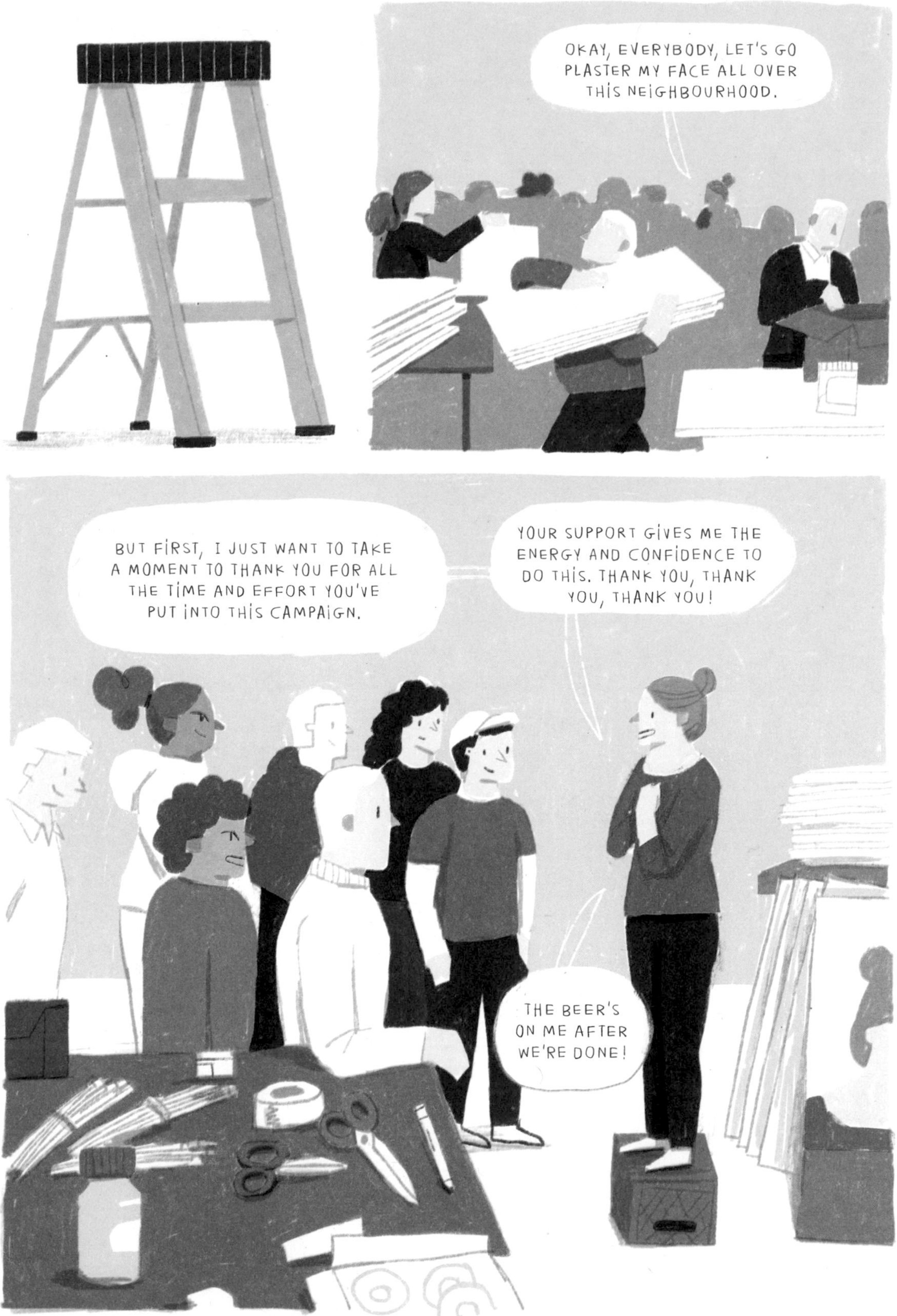
OKAY, EVERYBODY, LET'S GO PLASTER MY FACE ALL OVER THIS NEIGHBOURHOOD.
BUT FIRST, I JUST WANT TO TAKE A MOMENT TO THANK YOU FOR ALL THE TIME AND EFFORT YOU'VE PUT INTO THIS CAMPAIGN.
YOUR SUPPORT GIVES ME THE ENERGY AND CONFIDENCE TO DO THIS. THANK YOU, THANK YOU, THANK YOU!
THE BEER'S ON ME AFTER WE'RE DONE!

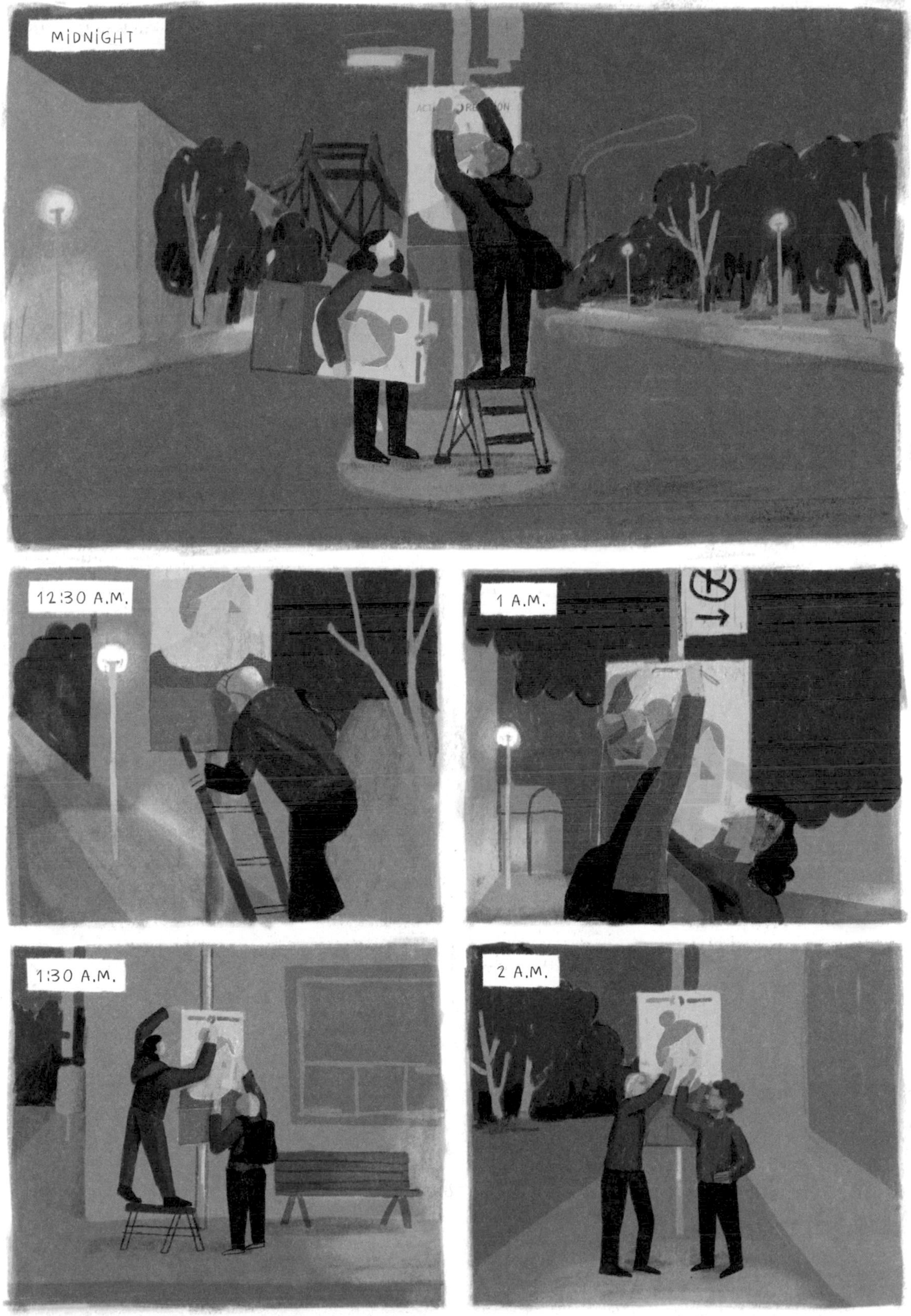
MIDNIGHT
12:30 A.M.
1 A.M.
1:30 A.M.
2 A.M.

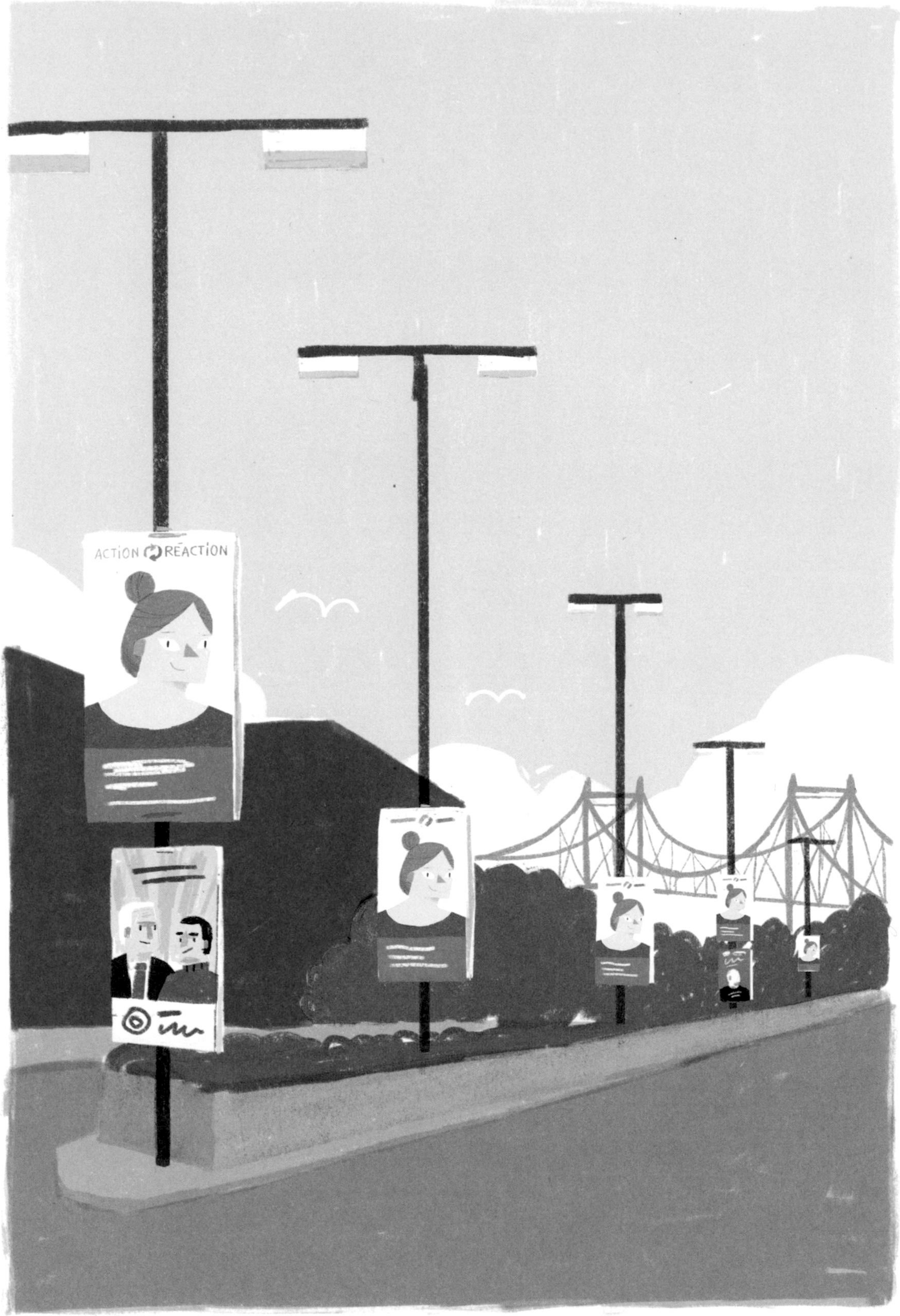
ACTION REACTION

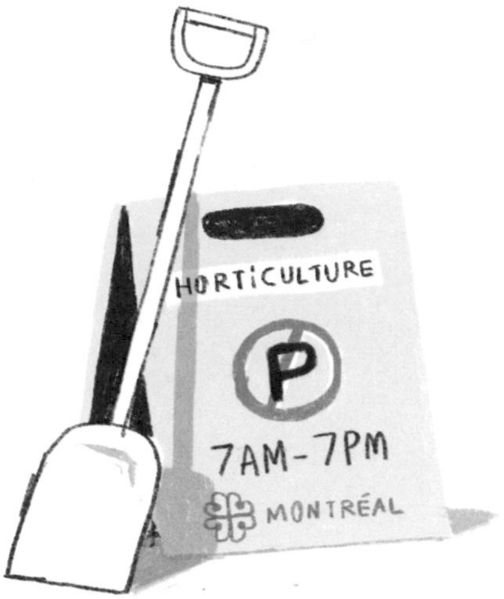
HORTICULTURE
7AM-7PM
MONTRÉAL

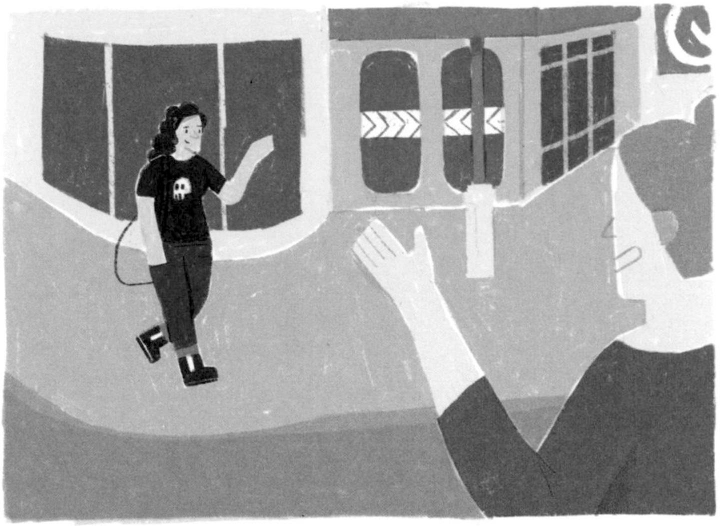

PORTRAIT OF A VOLUNTEER

LUCIE

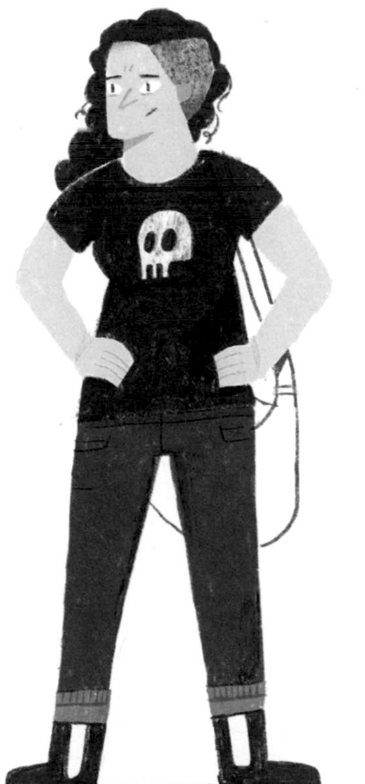

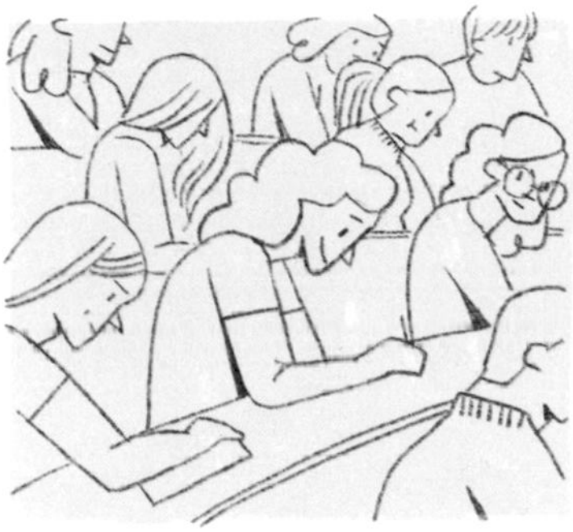

STUDYING POLI SCI AND FEMINIST STUDIES.

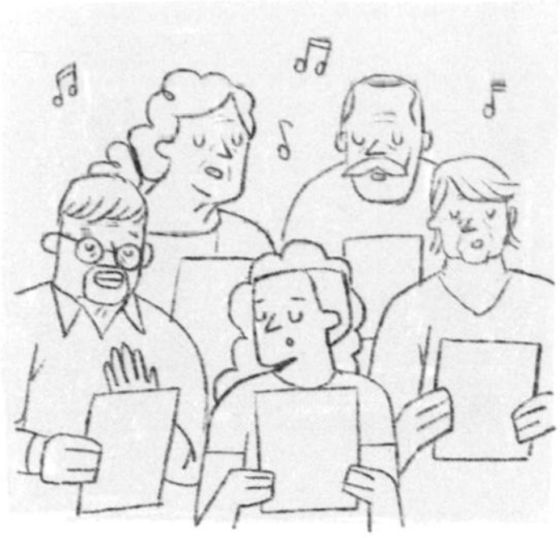

SINGS IN A CHOIR WITH SENIORS TO RELAX.

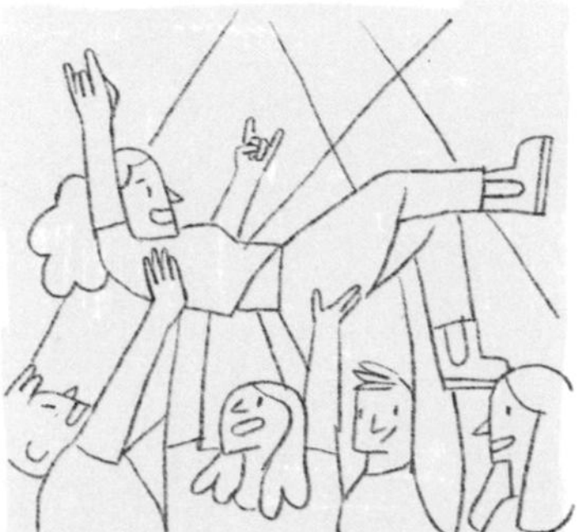

LETS OFF STEAM AT METAL SHOWS.

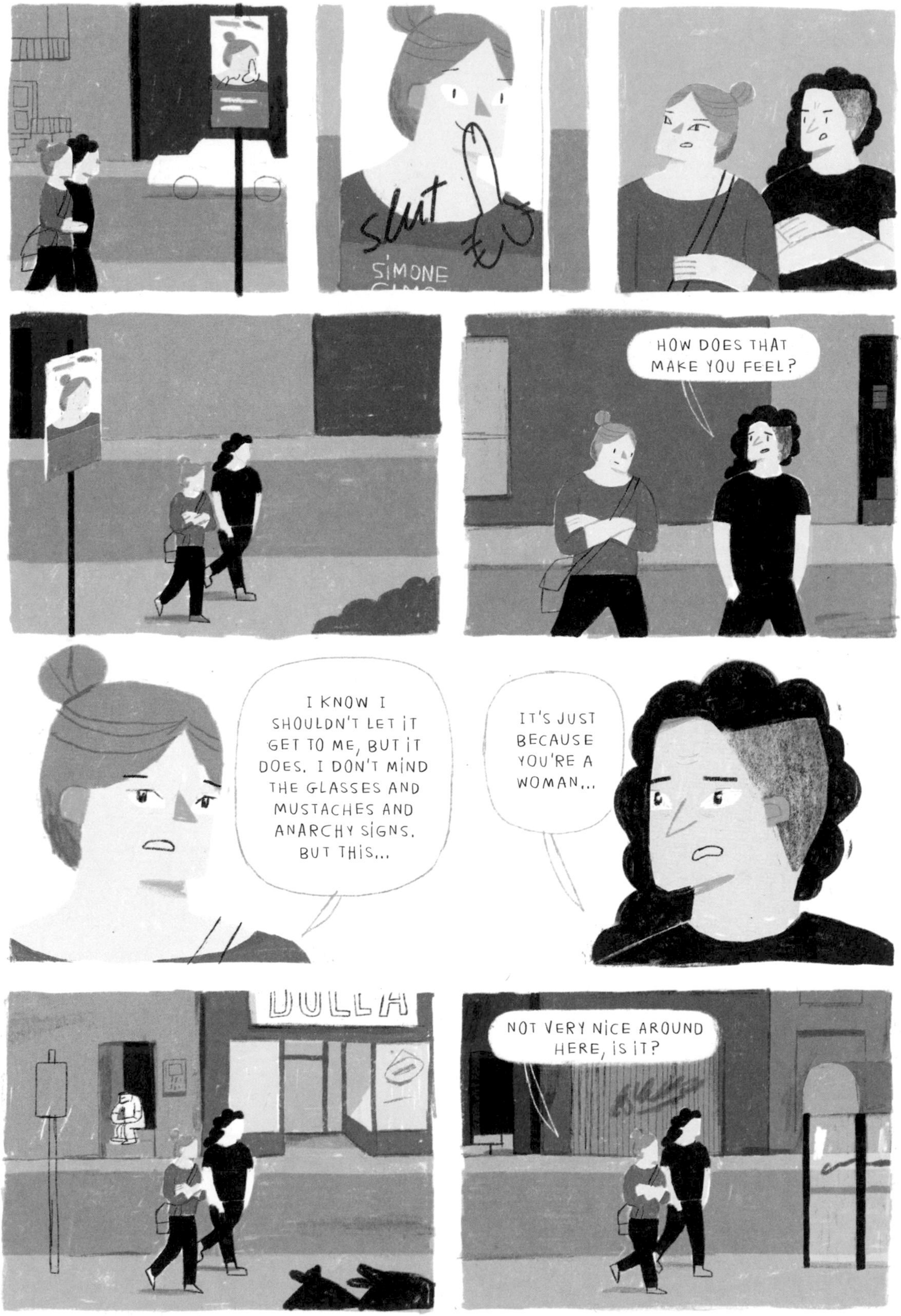
slut
SIMONE
HOW DOES THAT MAKE YOU FEEL?
I KNOW I SHOULDN'T LET IT GET TO ME, BUT IT DOES. I DON'T MIND THE GLASSES AND MUSTACHES AND ANARCHY SIGNS. BUT THIS...
IT'S JUST BECAUSE YOU'RE A WOMAN...
DOLLA
NOT VERY NICE AROUND HERE, IS IT?

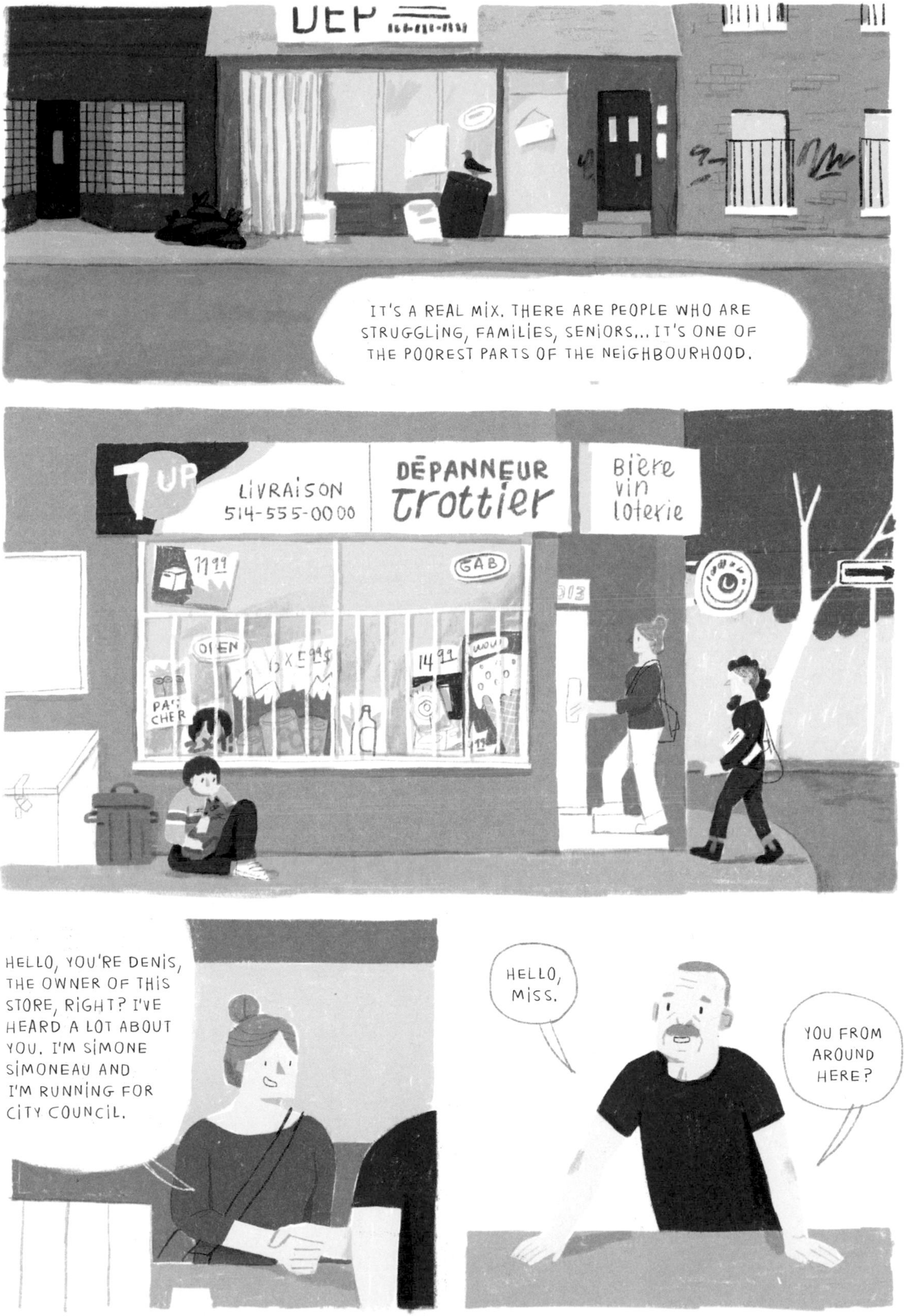
IT'S A REAL MIX. THERE ARE PEOPLE WHO ARE STRUGGLING, FAMILIES, SENIORS... IT'S ONE OF THE POOREST PARTS OF THE NEIGHBOURHOOD.
7 UP
LIVRAISON
514-555-0000
DÉPANNEUR
Trottier
Bière
vin
loterie
GAB
OPEN
HELLO, YOU'RE DENIS, THE OWNER OF THIS STORE, RIGHT? I'VE HEARD A LOT ABOUT YOU. I'M SIMONE SIMONEAU AND I'M RUNNING FOR CITY COUNCIL.
HELLO, MISS.
YOU FROM AROUND HERE?

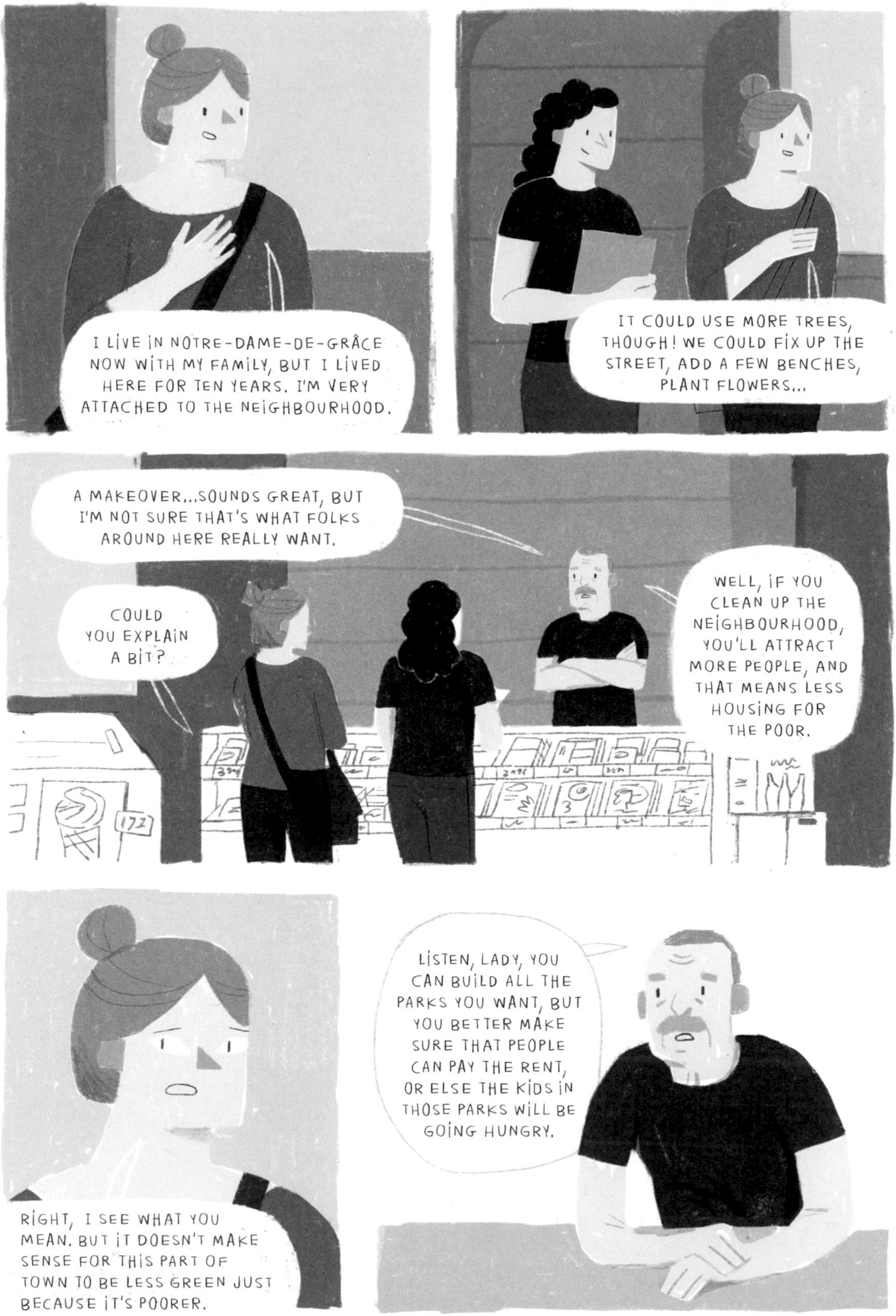
I LIVE IN NOTRE-DAME-DE-GRÂCE NOW WITH MY FAMILY, BUT I LIVED HERE FOR TEN YEARS. I'M VERY ATTACHED TO THE NEIGHBOURHOOD.
IT COULD USE MORE TREES, THOUGH! WE COULD FIX UP THE STREET, ADD A FEW BENCHES, PLANT FLOWERS...
A MAKEOVER...SOUNDS GREAT, BUT I'M NOT SURE THAT'S WHAT FOLKS AROUND HERE REALLY WANT.
COULD YOU EXPLAIN A BIT?
WELL, IF YOU CLEAN UP THE NEIGHBOURHOOD, YOU'LL ATTRACT MORE PEOPLE, AND THAT MEANS LESS HOUSING FOR THE POOR.
LISTEN, LADY, YOU CAN BUILD ALL THE PARKS YOU WANT, BUT YOU BETTER MAKE SURE THAT PEOPLE CAN PAY THE RENT, OR ELSE THE KIDS IN THOSE PARKS WILL BE GOING HUNGRY.
RIGHT, I SEE WHAT YOU MEAN. BUT IT DOESN'T MAKE SENSE FOR THIS PART OF TOWN TO BE LESS GREEN JUST BECAUSE IT'S POORER.

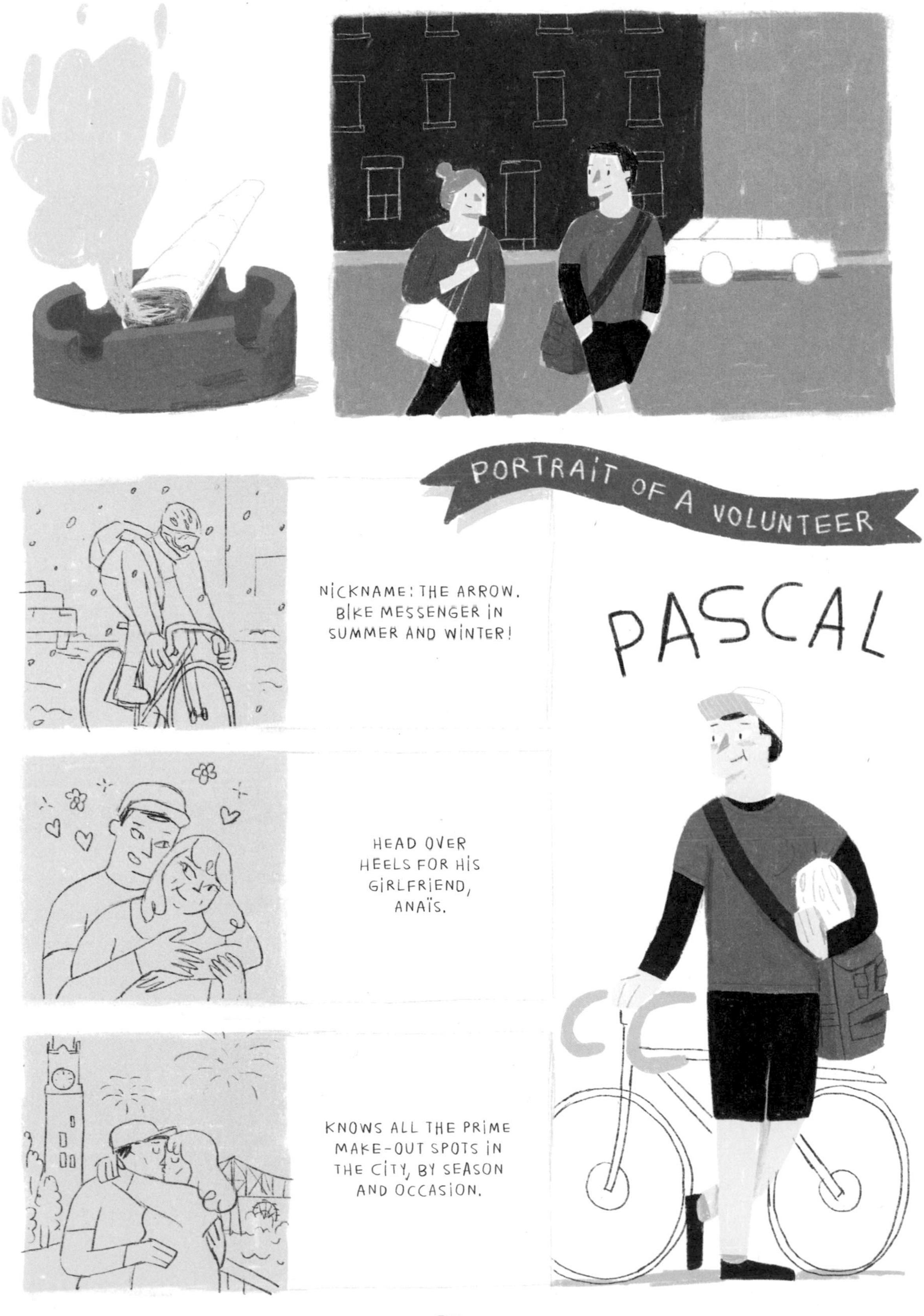
PORTRAIT OF A VOLUNTEER
PASCAL
NICKNAME: THE ARROW. BIKE MESSENGER IN SUMMER AND WINTER!
HEAD OVER HEELS FOR HIS GIRLFRIEND, ANAÏS.
KNOWS ALL THE PRIME MAKE-OUT SPOTS IN THE CITY, BY SEASON AND OCCASION.

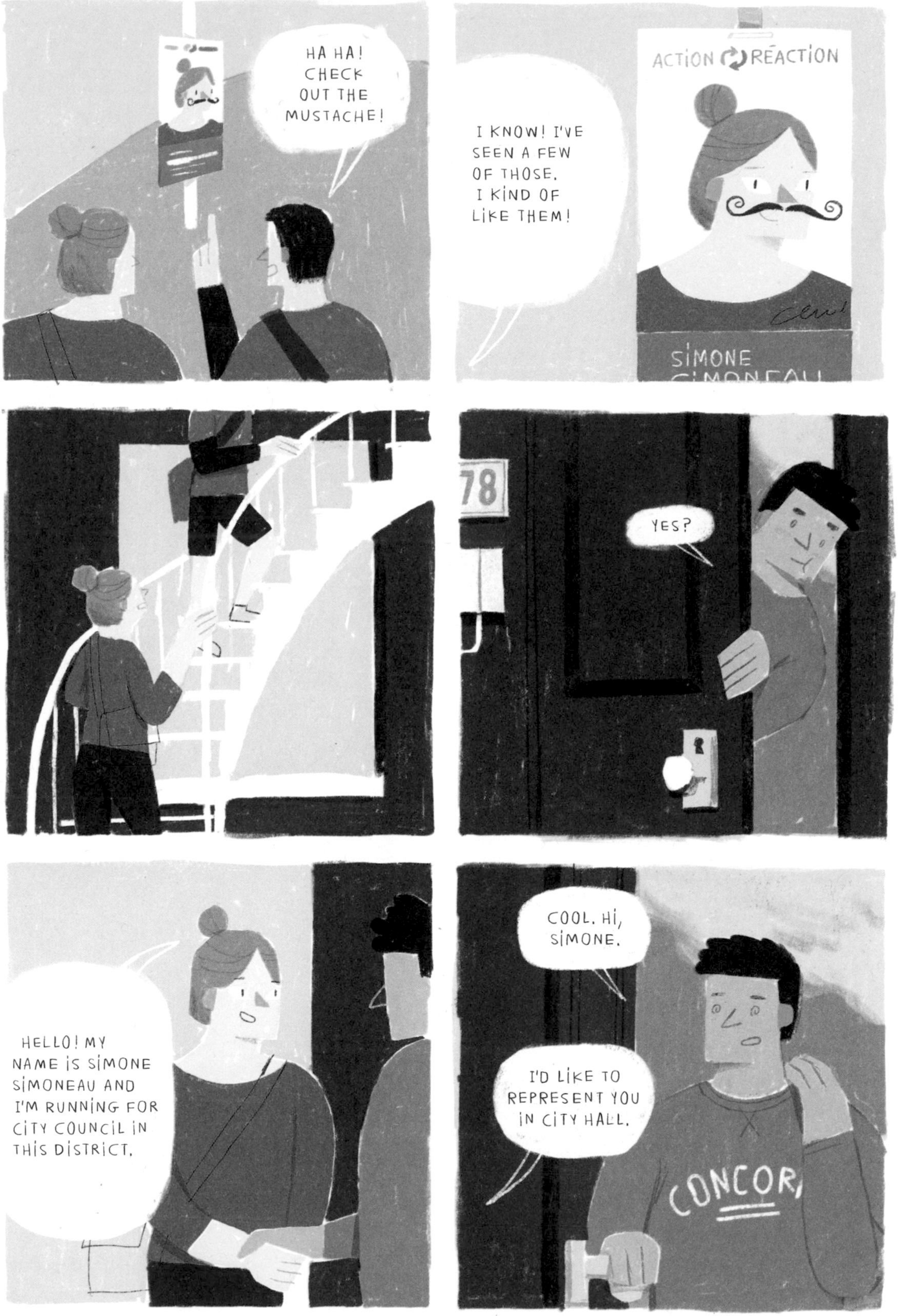
HA HA! CHECK OUT THE MUSTACHE!
I KNOW! I'VE SEEN A FEW OF THOSE. I KIND OF LIKE THEM!
ACTION RÉACTION
SIMONE
YES?
HELLO! MY NAME IS SIMONE SIMONEAU AND I'M RUNNING FOR CITY COUNCIL IN THIS DISTRICT.
COOL. HI, SIMONE.
I'D LIKE TO REPRESENT YOU IN CITY HALL.

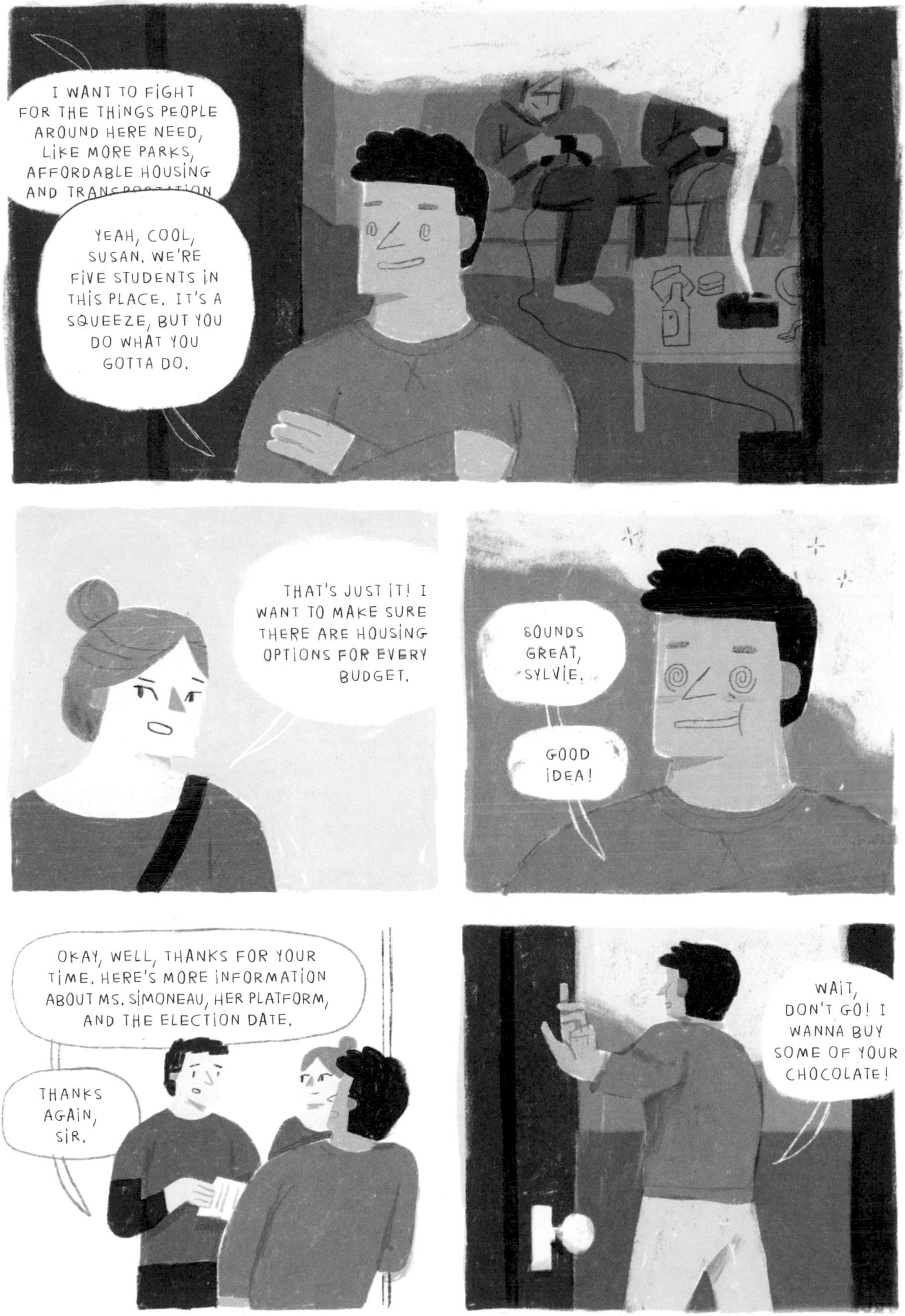
I WANT TO FIGHT FOR THE THINGS PEOPLE AROUND HERE NEED, LIKE MORE PARKS, AFFORDABLE HOUSING AND TRANS
YEAH, COOL, SUSAN. WE'RE FIVE STUDENTS IN THIS PLACE. IT'S A SQUEEZE, BUT YOU DO WHAT YOU GOTTA DO.
THAT'S JUST IT! I WANT TO MAKE SURE THERE ARE HOUSING OPTIONS FOR EVERY BUDGET.
SOUNDS GREAT, SYLVIE.
GOOD IDEA!
OKAY, WELL, THANKS FOR YOUR TIME. HERE'S MORE INFORMATION ABOUT MS. SIMONEAU, HER PLATFORM, AND THE ELECTION DATE.
THANKS AGAIN, SIR.
WAIT, DON'T GO! I WANNA BUY SOME OF YOUR CHOCOLATE!

BEEEP
5:00 AM
BEEEP

RADIO INTERVIEW THIS MORNING.

HUGO IS OUT OF TOWN...

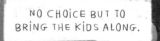

NO CHOICE BUT TO BRING THE KIDS ALONG.

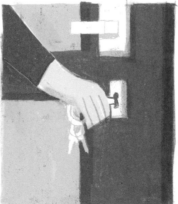

TAXI

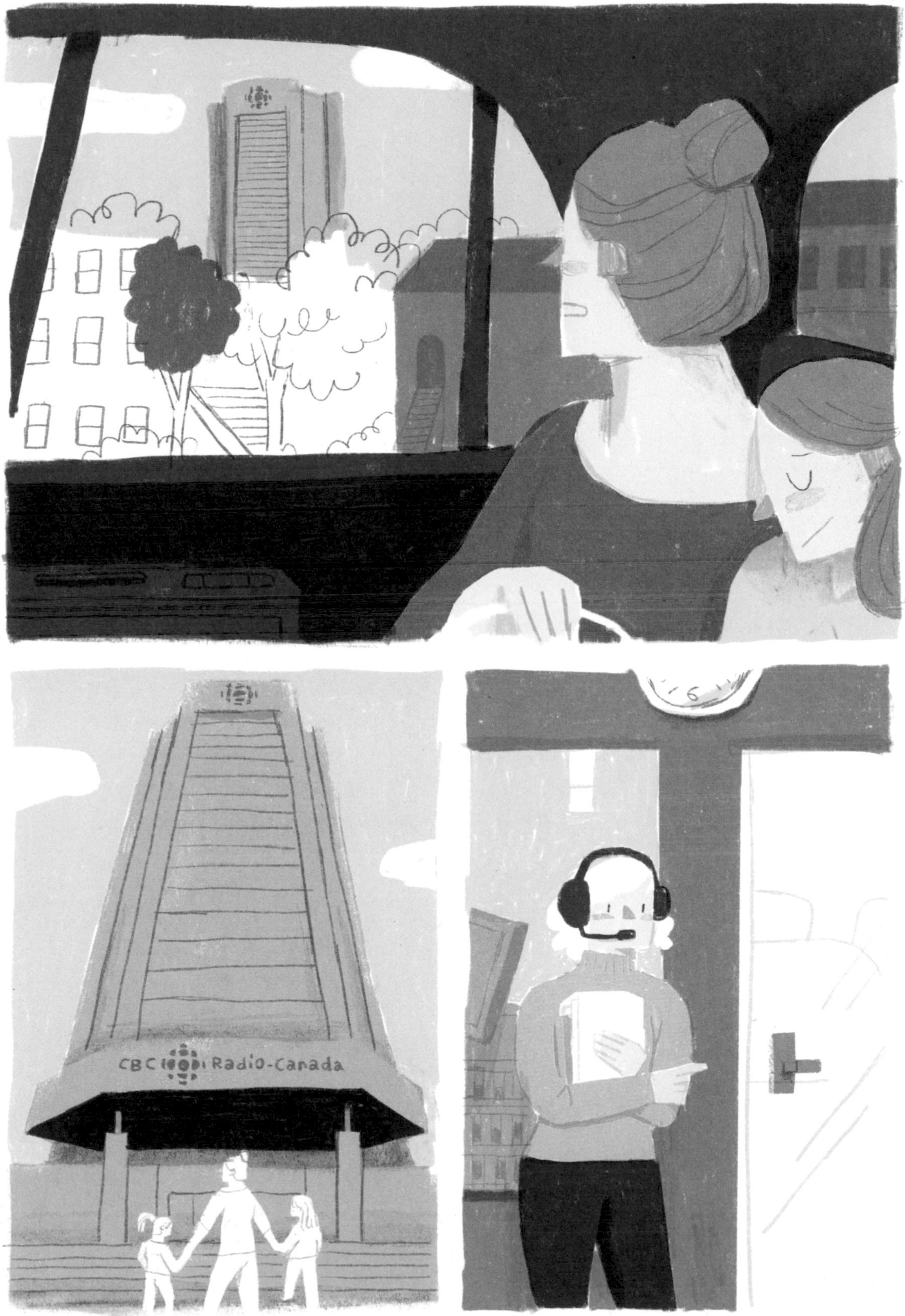
CBC Radio-Canada

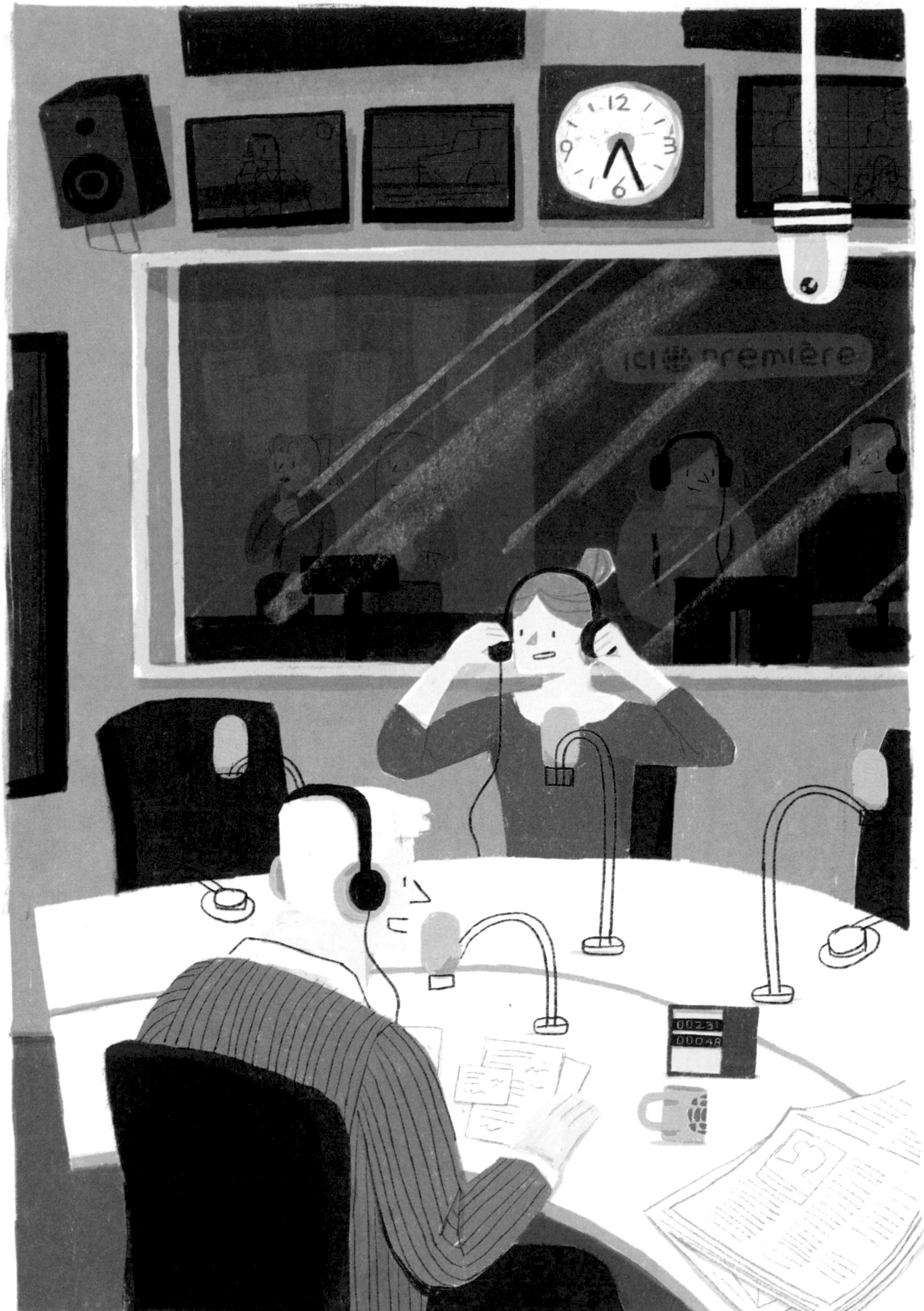
ICI première
00231
00048

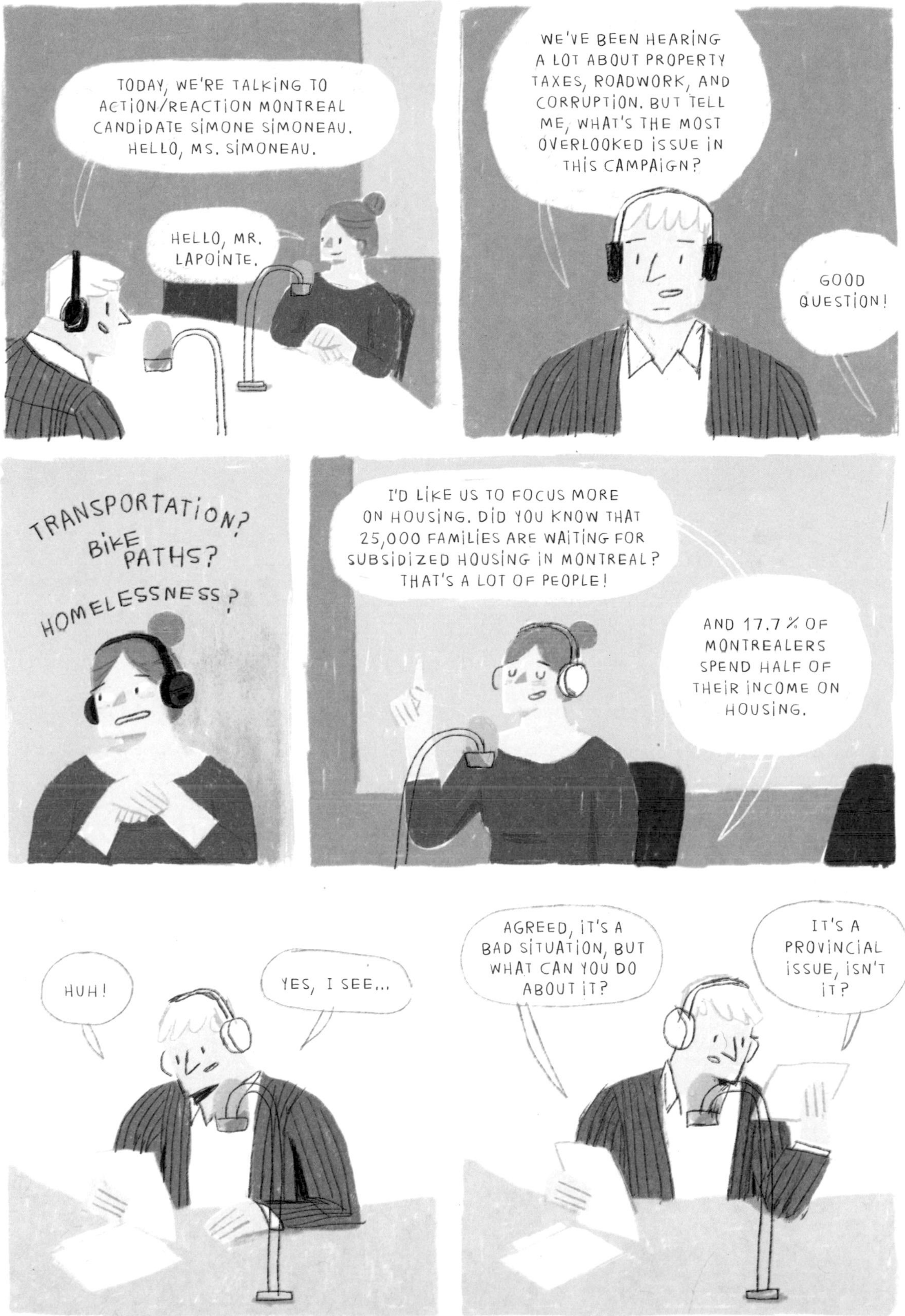
TODAY, WE'RE TALKING TO ACTION/REACTION MONTREAL CANDIDATE SIMONE SIMONEAU. HELLO, MS. SIMONEAU.
HELLO, MR. LAPOINTE.
WE'VE BEEN HEARING A LOT ABOUT PROPERTY TAXES, ROADWORK, AND CORRUPTION. BUT TELL ME, WHAT'S THE MOST OVERLOOKED ISSUE IN THIS CAMPAIGN?
GOOD QUESTION!
TRANSPORTATION?
BIKE PATHS?
HOMELESSNESS?
I'D LIKE US TO FOCUS MORE ON HOUSING. DID YOU KNOW THAT 25,000 FAMILIES ARE WAITING FOR SUBSIDIZED HOUSING IN MONTREAL? THAT'S A LOT OF PEOPLE!
AND 17.7% OF MONTREALERS SPEND HALF OF THEIR INCOME ON HOUSING.
HUH!
YES, I SEE...
AGREED, IT'S A BAD SITUATION, BUT WHAT CAN YOU DO ABOUT IT?
IT'S A PROVINCIAL ISSUE, ISN'T IT?

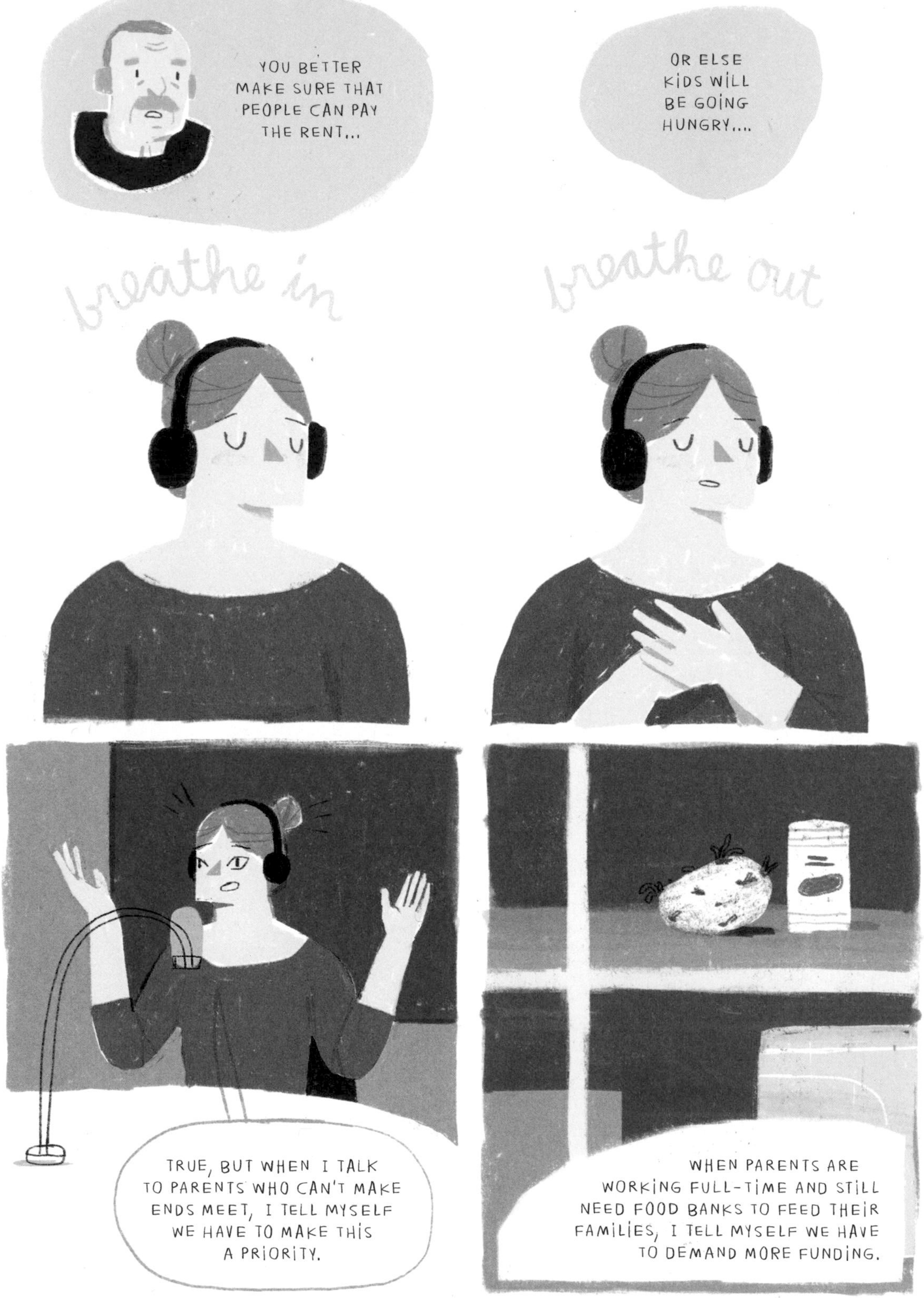
YOU BETTER MAKE SURE THAT PEOPLE CAN PAY THE RENT...
OR ELSE KIDS WILL BE GOING HUNGRY....
breathe in
breathe out
TRUE, BUT WHEN I TALK TO PARENTS WHO CAN'T MAKE ENDS MEET, I TELL MYSELF WE HAVE TO MAKE THIS A PRIORITY.
WHEN PARENTS ARE WORKING FULL-TIME AND STILL NEED FOOD BANKS TO FEED THEIR FAMILIES, I TELL MYSELF WE HAVE TO DEMAND MORE FUNDING.

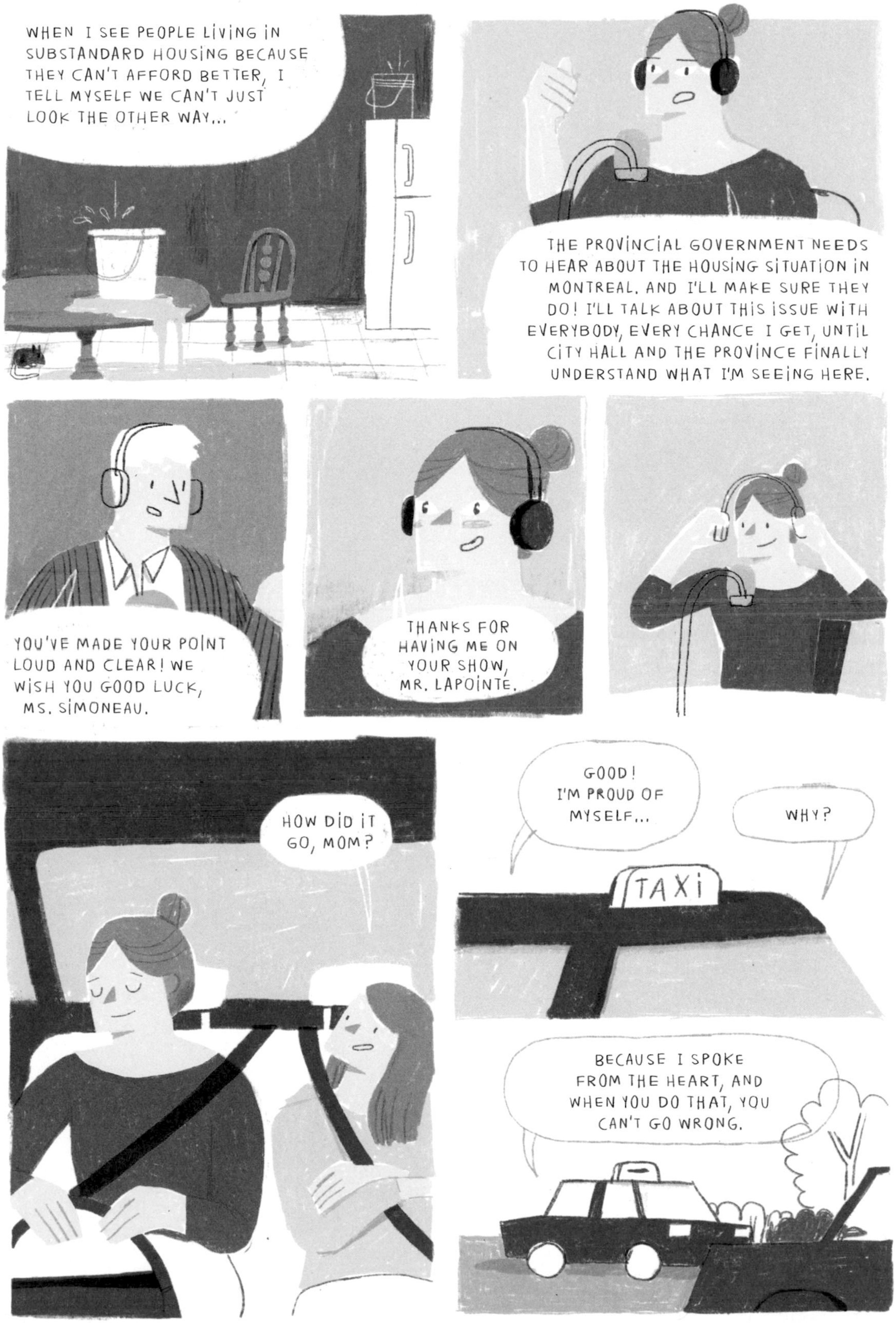
WHEN I SEE PEOPLE LIVING IN SUBSTANDARD HOUSING BECAUSE THEY CAN'T AFFORD BETTER, I TELL MYSELF WE CAN'T JUST LOOK THE OTHER WAY...
THE PROVINCIAL GOVERNMENT NEEDS TO HEAR ABOUT THE HOUSING SITUATION IN MONTREAL. AND I'LL MAKE SURE THEY DO! I'LL TALK ABOUT THIS ISSUE WITH EVERYBODY, EVERY CHANCE I GET, UNTIL CITY HALL AND THE PROVINCE FINALLY UNDERSTAND WHAT I'M SEEING HERE.
YOU'VE MADE YOUR POINT LOUD AND CLEAR! WE WISH YOU GOOD LUCK, MS. SIMONEAU.
THANKS FOR HAVING ME ON YOUR SHOW, MR. LAPOINTE.
HOW DID IT GO, MOM?
GOOD! I'M PROUD OF MYSELF...
WHY?
TAXI
BECAUSE I SPOKE FROM THE HEART, AND WHEN YOU DO THAT, YOU CAN'T GO WRONG.

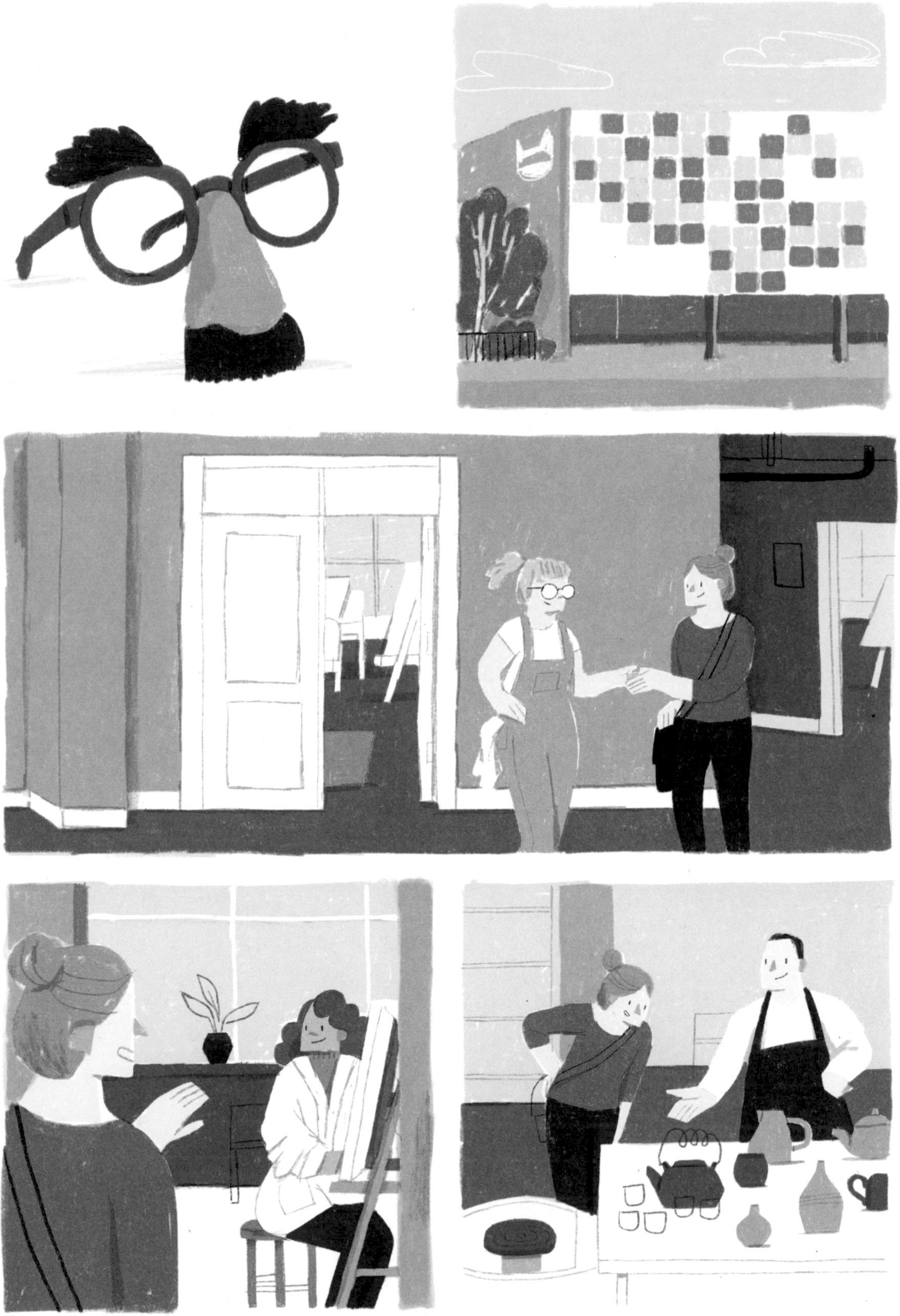

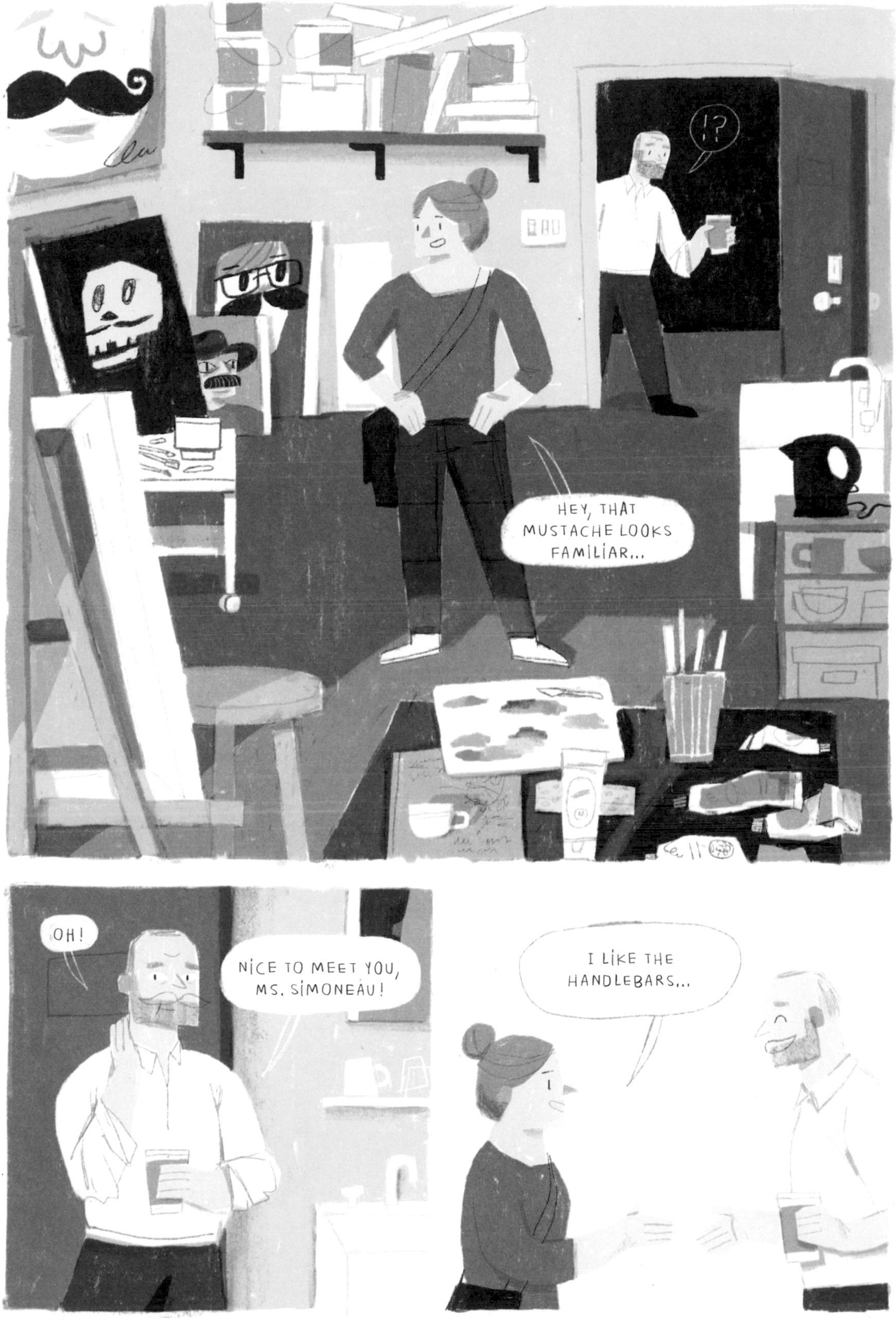
HEY, THAT MUSTACHE LOOKS FAMILIAR...
!?
OH!
NICE TO MEET YOU, MS. SIMONEAU!
I LIKE THE HANDLEBARS...

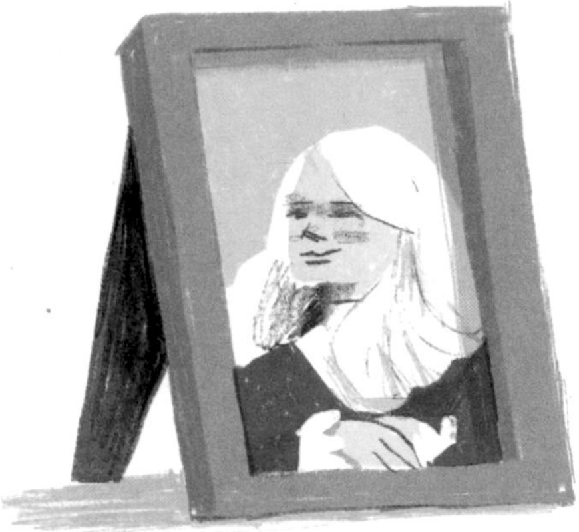

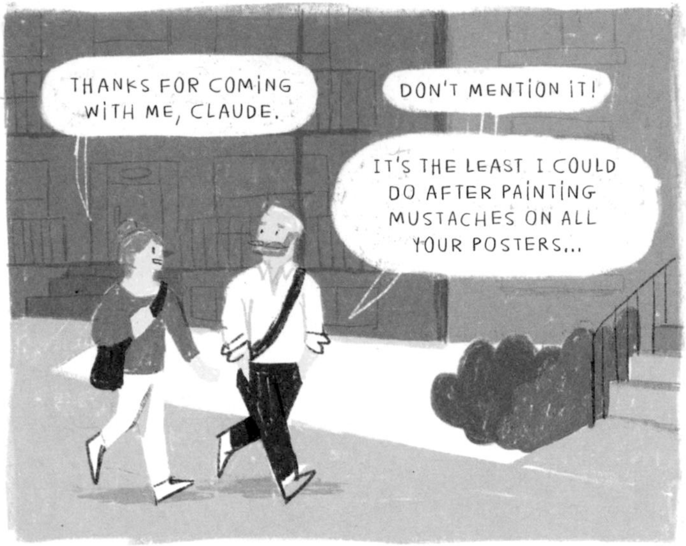
THANKS FOR COMING WITH ME, CLAUDE.
DON'T MENTION IT!
IT'S THE LEAST I COULD DO AFTER PAINTING MUSTACHES ON ALL YOUR POSTERS...

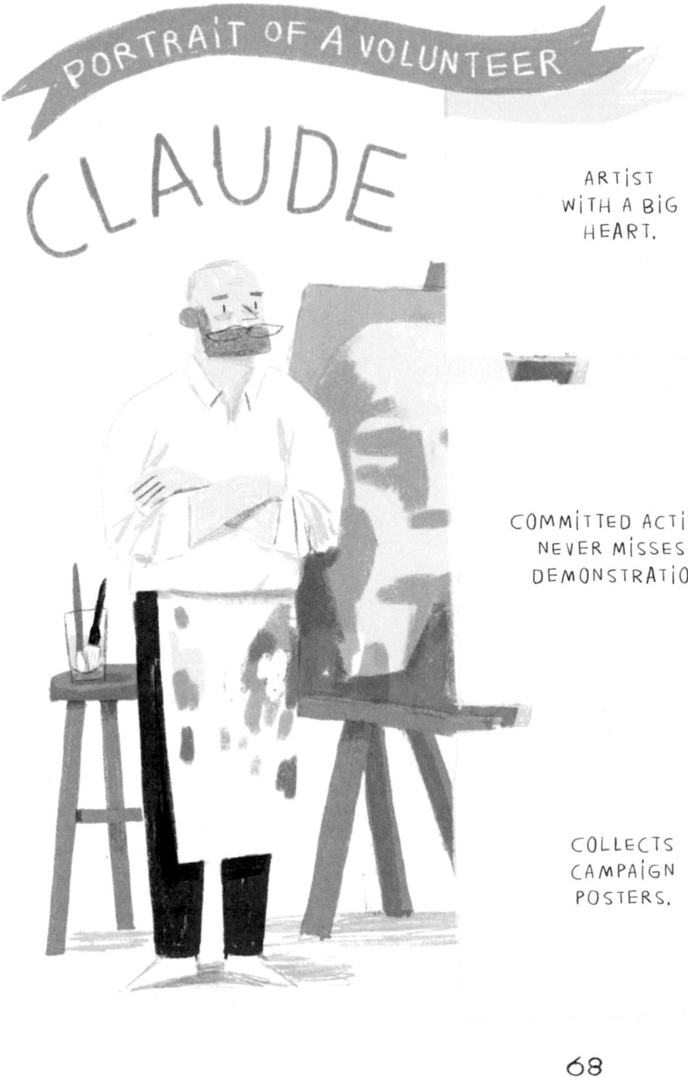
PORTRAIT OF A VOLUNTEER
CLAUDE

ARTIST WITH A BIG HEART.

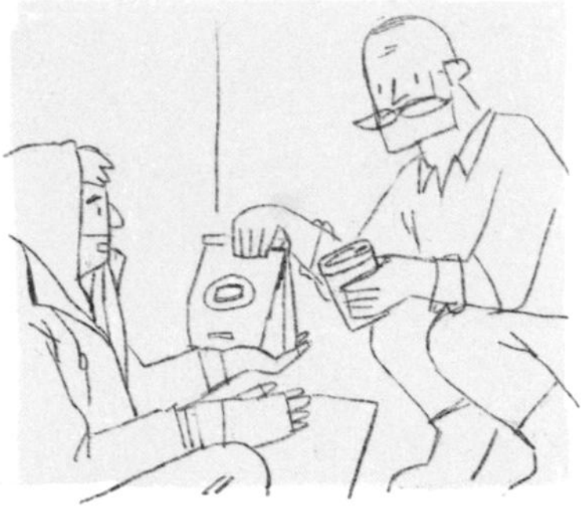

COMMITTED ACTIVIST. NEVER MISSES A DEMONSTRATION.

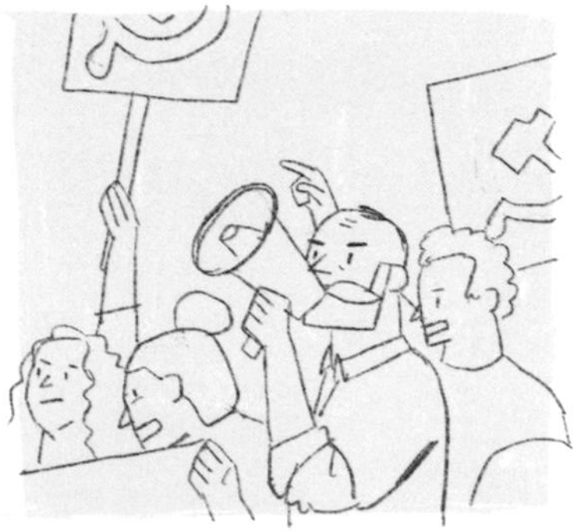

COLLECTS CAMPAIGN POSTERS.

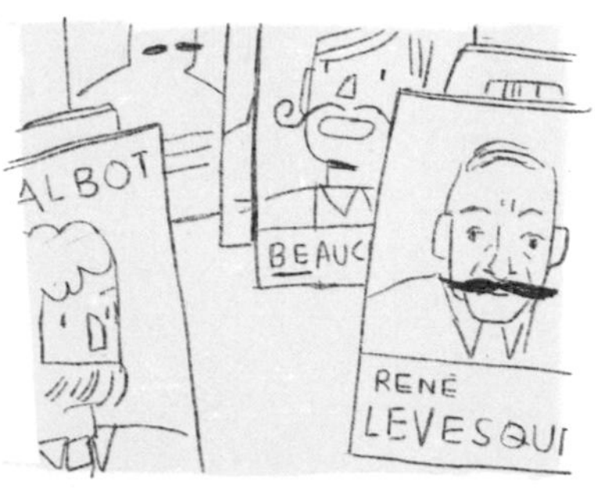
ALBOT
BEAUC
RENÉ
LEVESQU

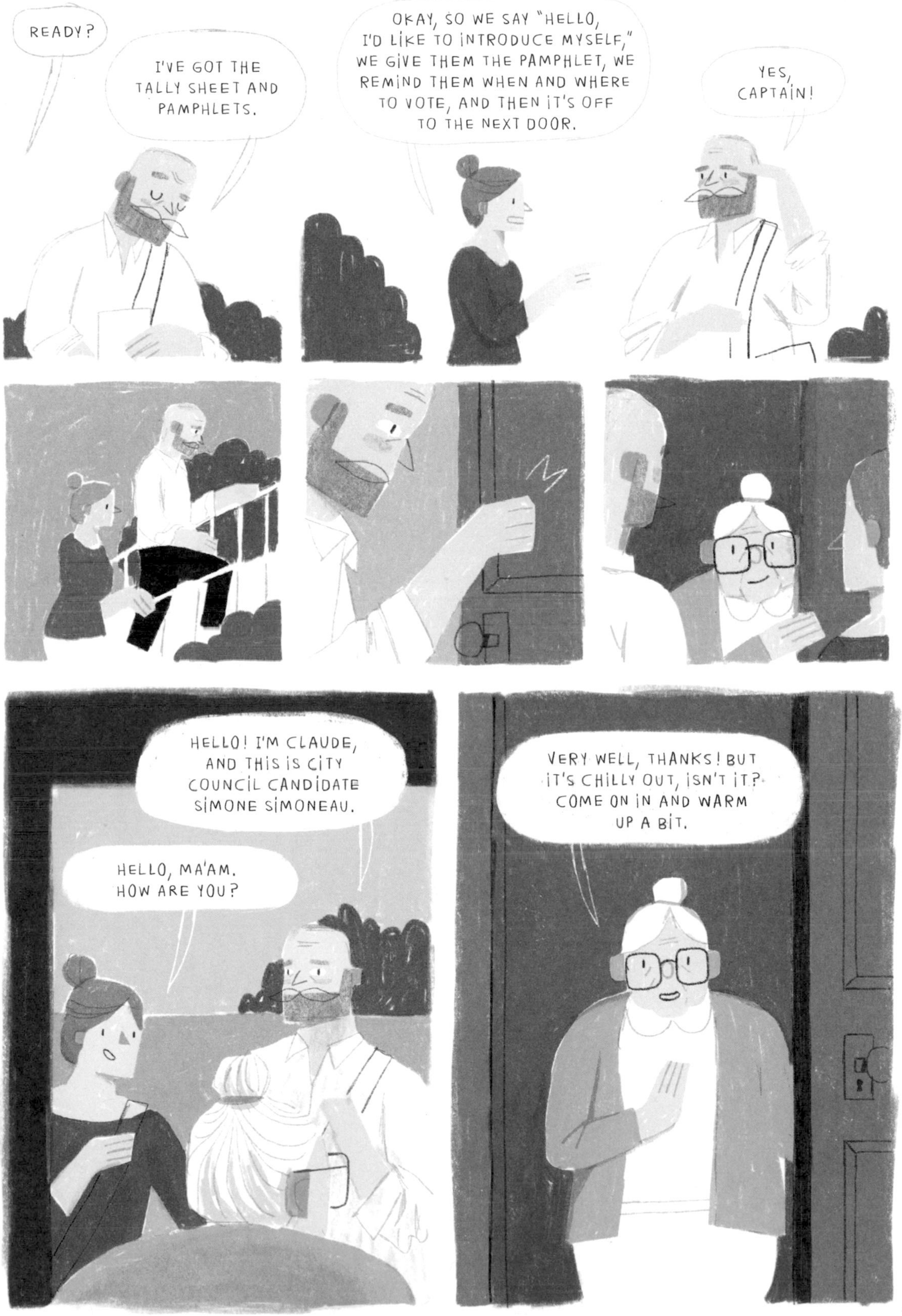
READY?
I'VE GOT THE TALLY SHEET AND PAMPHLETS.
OKAY, SO WE SAY "HELLO, I'D LIKE TO INTRODUCE MYSELF," WE GIVE THEM THE PAMPHLET, WE REMIND THEM WHEN AND WHERE TO VOTE, AND THEN IT'S OFF TO THE NEXT DOOR.
YES, CAPTAIN!
HELLO! I'M CLAUDE, AND THIS IS CITY COUNCIL CANDIDATE SIMONE SIMONEAU.
HELLO, MA'AM. HOW ARE YOU?
VERY WELL, THANKS! BUT IT'S CHILLY OUT, ISN'T IT? COME ON IN AND WARM UP A BIT.

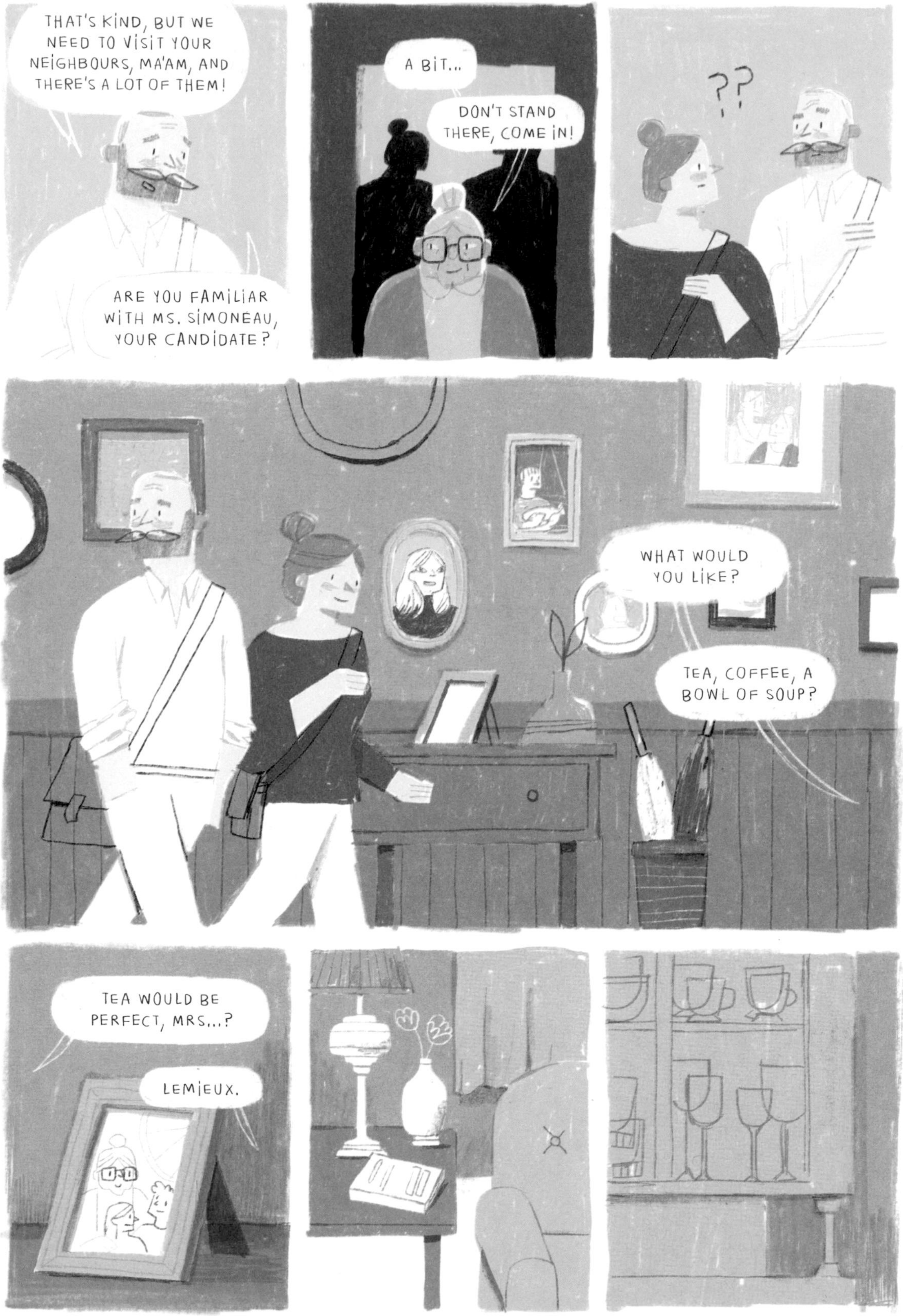
THAT'S KIND, BUT WE NEED TO VISIT YOUR NEIGHBOURS, MA'AM, AND THERE'S A LOT OF THEM!
ARE YOU FAMILIAR WITH MS. SIMONEAU, YOUR CANDIDATE?
A BIT...
DON'T STAND THERE, COME IN!
??
WHAT WOULD YOU LIKE?
TEA, COFFEE, A BOWL OF SOUP?
TEA WOULD BE PERFECT, MRS...?
LEMIEUX.

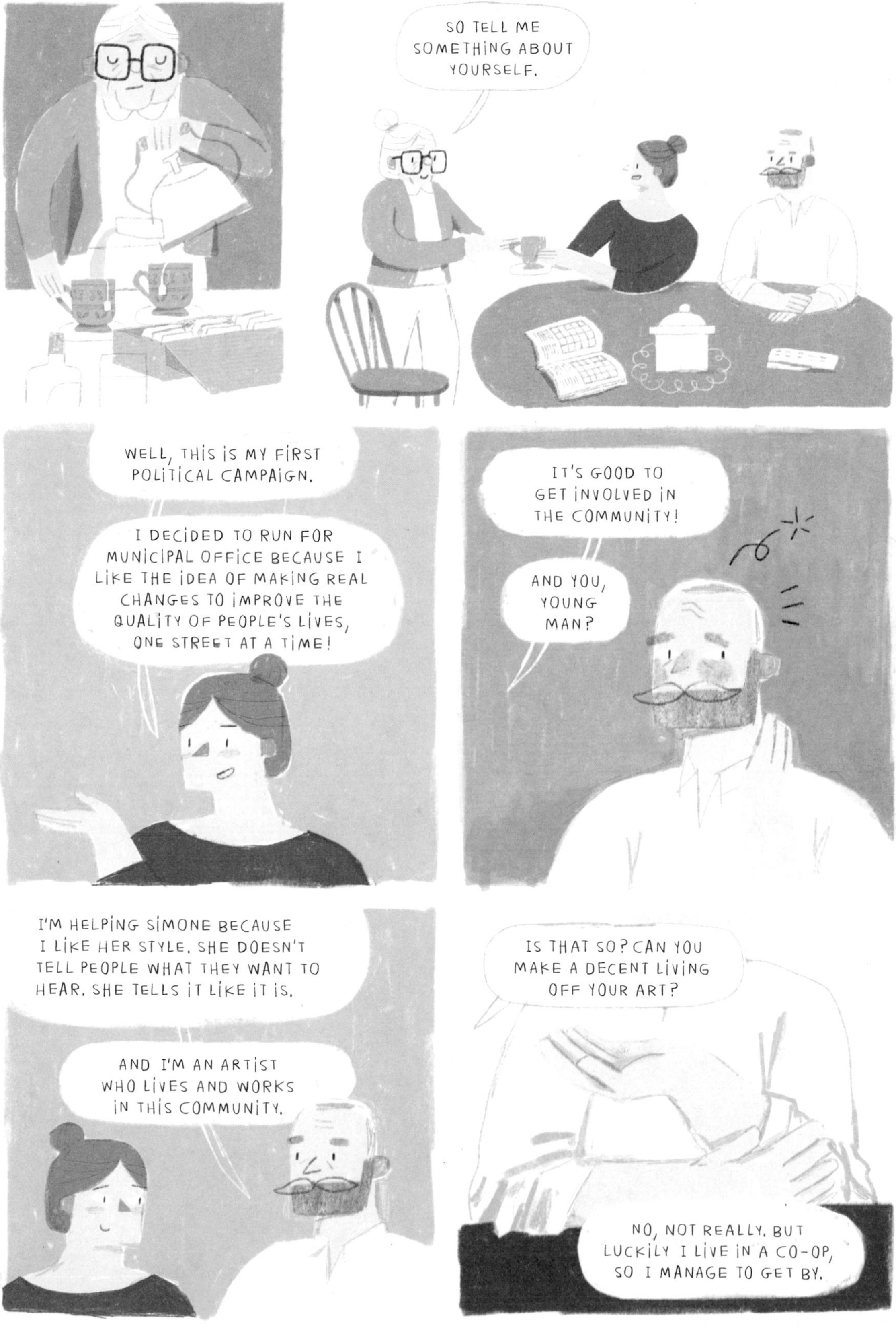

SO TELL ME SOMETHING ABOUT YOURSELF.
WELL, THIS IS MY FIRST POLITICAL CAMPAIGN.
I DECIDED TO RUN FOR MUNICIPAL OFFICE BECAUSE I LIKE THE IDEA OF MAKING REAL CHANGES TO IMPROVE THE QUALITY OF PEOPLE'S LIVES, ONE STREET AT A TIME!
IT'S GOOD TO GET INVOLVED IN THE COMMUNITY!
AND YOU, YOUNG MAN?
I'M HELPING SIMONE BECAUSE I LIKE HER STYLE. SHE DOESN'T TELL PEOPLE WHAT THEY WANT TO HEAR. SHE TELLS IT LIKE IT IS.
AND I'M AN ARTIST WHO LIVES AND WORKS IN THIS COMMUNITY.
IS THAT SO? CAN YOU MAKE A DECENT LIVING OFF YOUR ART?
NO, NOT REALLY. BUT LUCKILY I LIVE IN A CO-OP, SO I MANAGE TO GET BY.

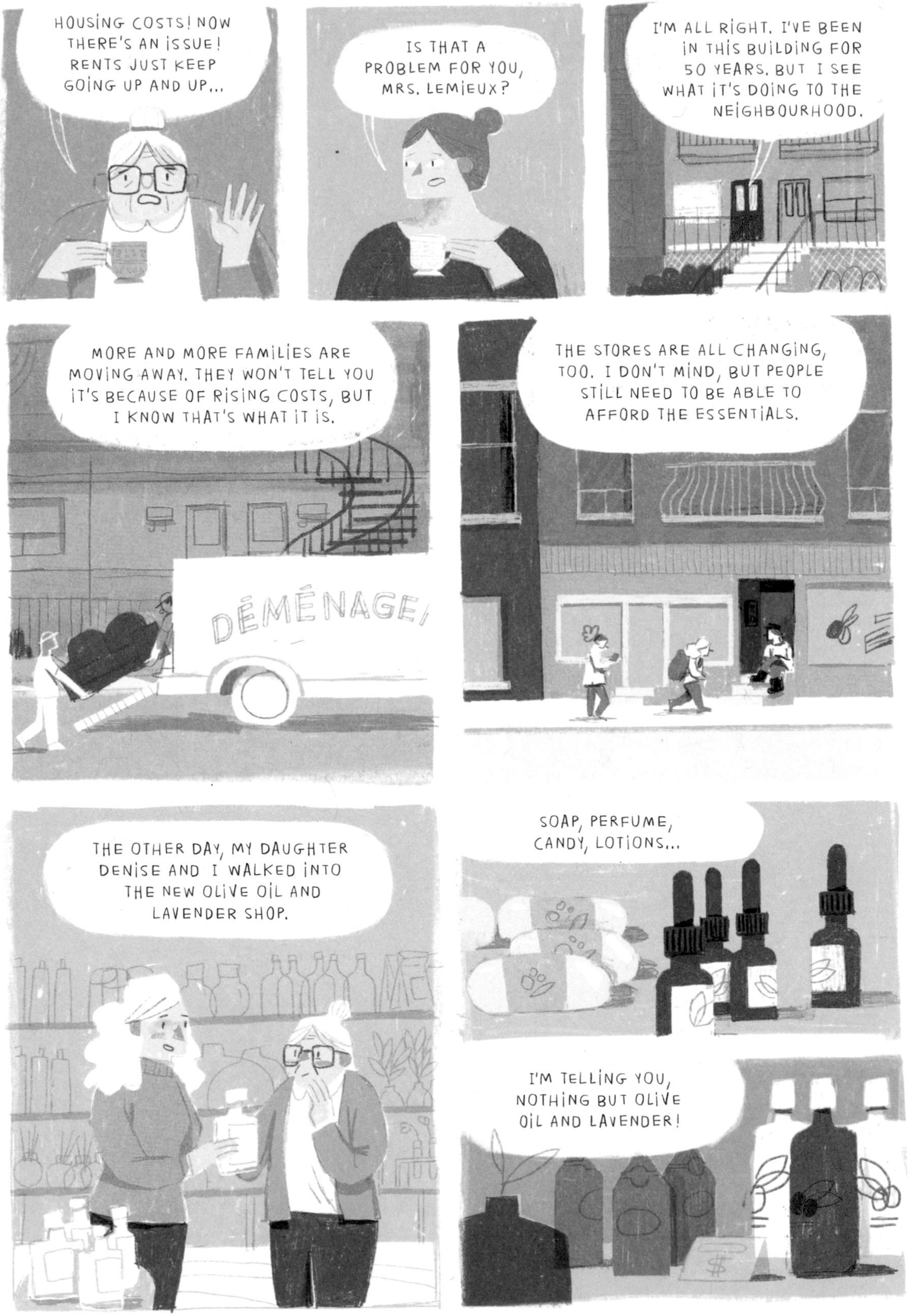
HOUSING COSTS! NOW THERE'S AN ISSUE! RENTS JUST KEEP GOING UP AND UP...
IS THAT A PROBLEM FOR YOU, MRS. LEMIEUX?
I'M ALL RIGHT. I'VE BEEN IN THIS BUILDING FOR 50 YEARS. BUT I SEE WHAT IT'S DOING TO THE NEIGHBOURHOOD.
MORE AND MORE FAMILIES ARE MOVING AWAY. THEY WON'T TELL YOU IT'S BECAUSE OF RISING COSTS, BUT I KNOW THAT'S WHAT IT IS.
DÉMÉNAGE
THE STORES ARE ALL CHANGING, TOO. I DON'T MIND, BUT PEOPLE STILL NEED TO BE ABLE TO AFFORD THE ESSENTIALS.
THE OTHER DAY, MY DAUGHTER DENISE AND I WALKED INTO THE NEW OLIVE OIL AND LAVENDER SHOP.
SOAP, PERFUME, CANDY, LOTIONS...
I'M TELLING YOU, NOTHING BUT OLIVE OIL AND LAVENDER!

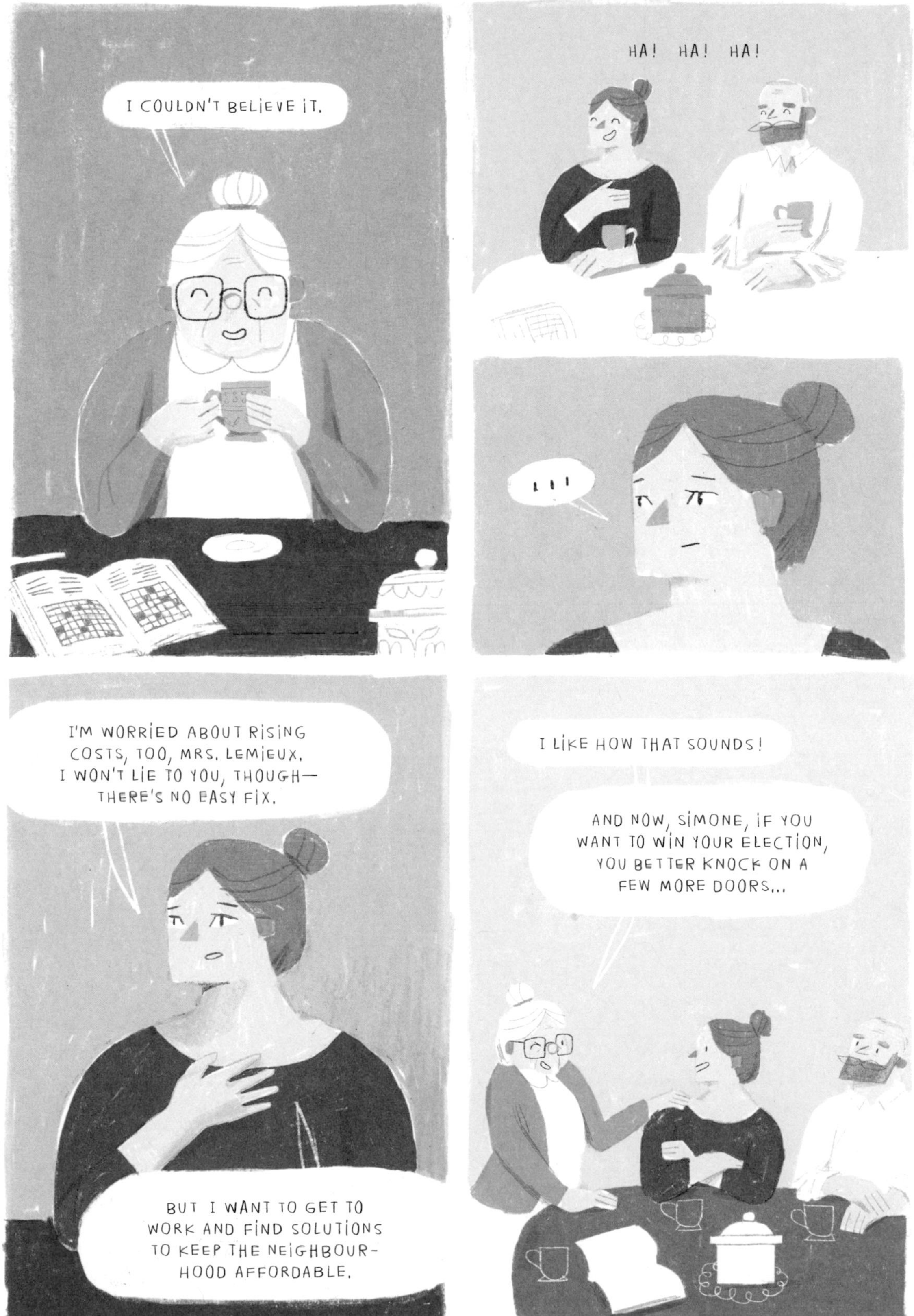
I COULDN'T BELIEVE IT.
HA! HA! HA!
...
I'M WORRIED ABOUT RISING COSTS, TOO, MRS. LEMIEUX. I WON'T LIE TO YOU, THOUGH— THERE'S NO EASY FIX.
BUT I WANT TO GET TO WORK AND FIND SOLUTIONS TO KEEP THE NEIGHBOURHOOD AFFORDABLE.
I LIKE HOW THAT SOUNDS!
AND NOW, SIMONE, IF YOU WANT TO WIN YOUR ELECTION, YOU BETTER KNOCK ON A FEW MORE DOORS...

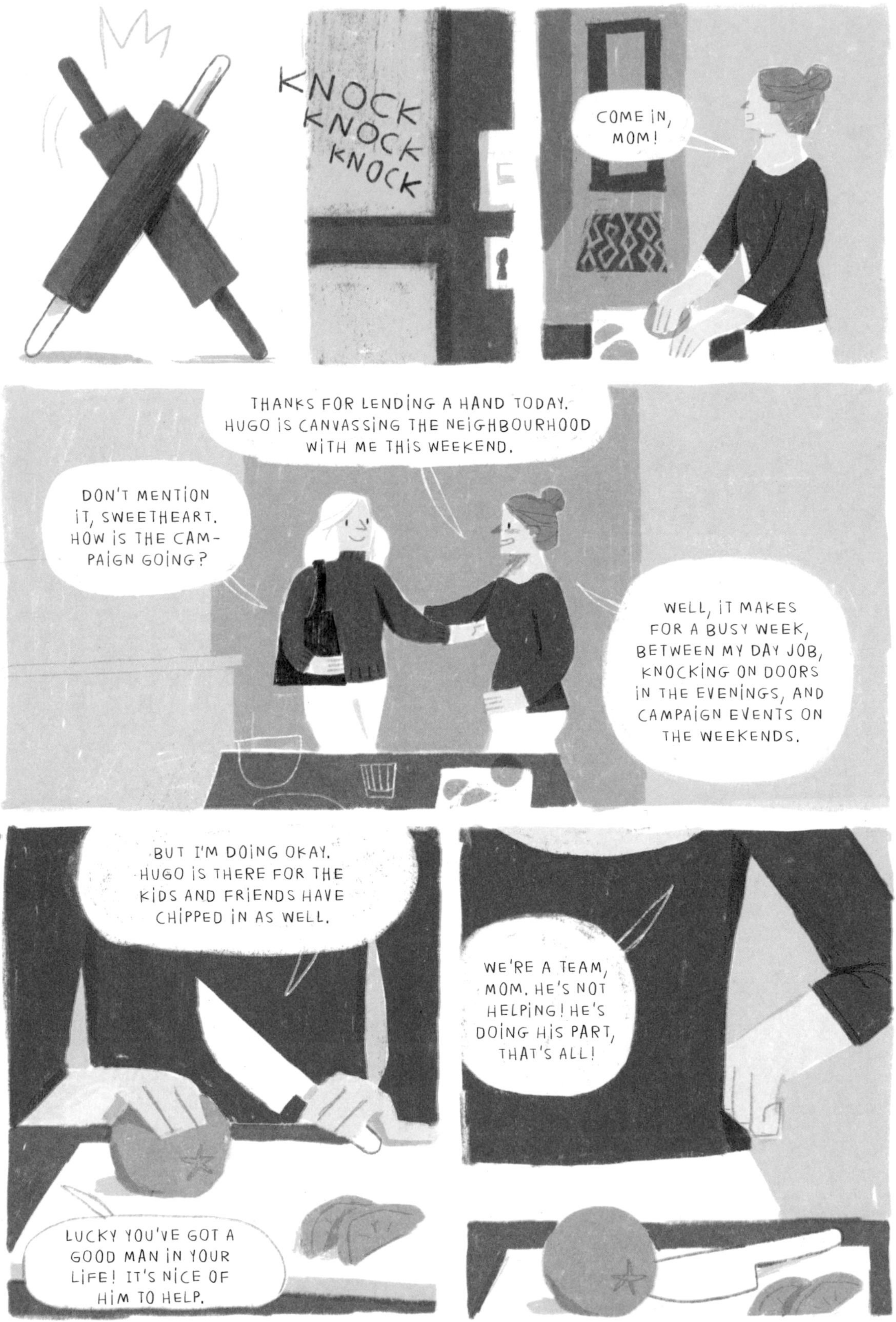
KNOCK KNOCK KNOCK
COME IN, MOM!
THANKS FOR LENDING A HAND TODAY. HUGO IS CANVASSING THE NEIGHBOURHOOD WITH ME THIS WEEKEND.
DON'T MENTION IT, SWEETHEART. HOW IS THE CAM-PAIGN GOING?
WELL, IT MAKES FOR A BUSY WEEK, BETWEEN MY DAY JOB, KNOCKING ON DOORS IN THE EVENINGS, AND CAMPAIGN EVENTS ON THE WEEKENDS.
BUT I'M DOING OKAY. HUGO IS THERE FOR THE KIDS AND FRIENDS HAVE CHIPPED IN AS WELL.
LUCKY YOU'VE GOT A GOOD MAN IN YOUR LIFE! IT'S NICE OF HIM TO HELP.
WE'RE A TEAM, MOM. HE'S NOT HELPING! HE'S DOING HIS PART, THAT'S ALL!

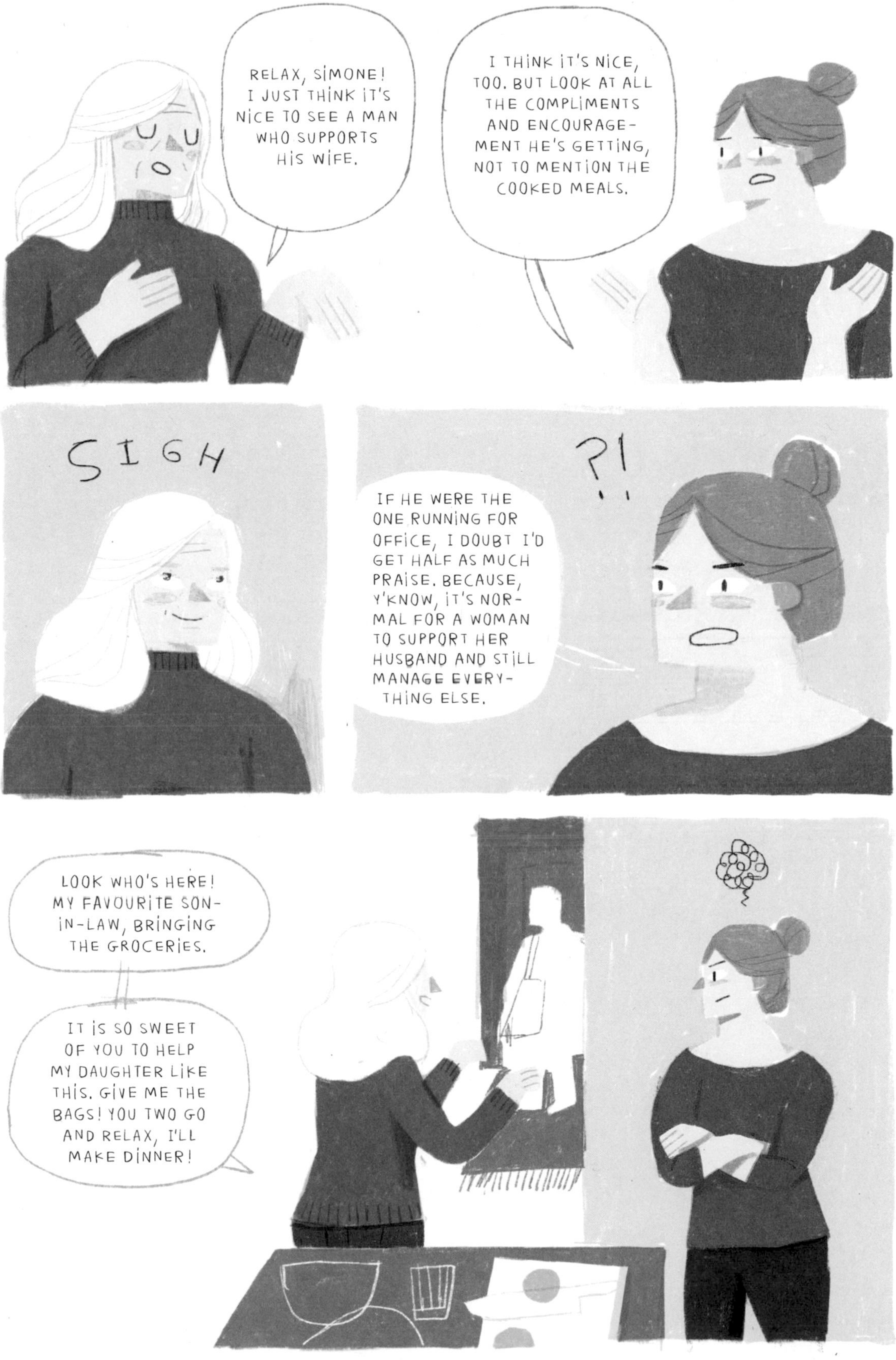
RELAX, SIMONE! I JUST THINK IT'S NICE TO SEE A MAN WHO SUPPORTS HIS WIFE.
I THINK IT'S NICE, TOO. BUT LOOK AT ALL THE COMPLIMENTS AND ENCOURAGE-MENT HE'S GETTING, NOT TO MENTION THE COOKED MEALS.
SIGH
?!
IF HE WERE THE ONE RUNNING FOR OFFICE, I DOUBT I'D GET HALF AS MUCH PRAISE. BECAUSE, Y'KNOW, IT'S NOR-MAL FOR A WOMAN TO SUPPORT HER HUSBAND AND STILL MANAGE EVERY-THING ELSE.
LOOK WHO'S HERE! MY FAVOURITE SON-IN-LAW, BRINGING THE GROCERIES.
IT IS SO SWEET OF YOU TO HELP MY DAUGHTER LIKE THIS. GIVE ME THE BAGS! YOU TWO GO AND RELAX, I'LL MAKE DINNER!

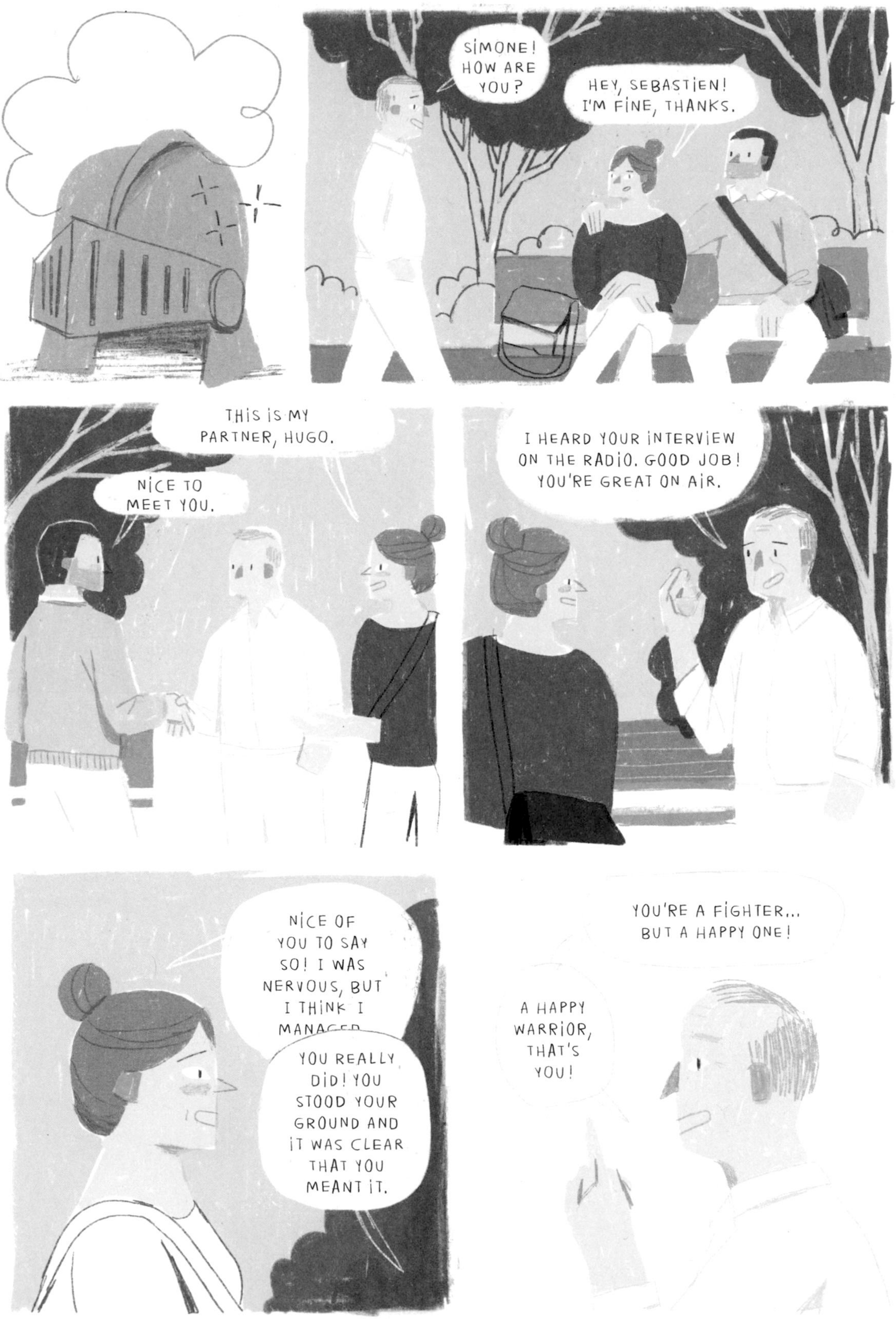
SIMONE! HOW ARE YOU?
HEY, SEBASTIEN! I'M FINE, THANKS.
THIS IS MY PARTNER, HUGO.
NICE TO MEET YOU.
I HEARD YOUR INTERVIEW ON THE RADIO. GOOD JOB! YOU'RE GREAT ON AIR.
NICE OF YOU TO SAY SO! I WAS NERVOUS, BUT I THINK I
YOU REALLY DID! YOU STOOD YOUR GROUND AND IT WAS CLEAR THAT YOU MEANT IT.
YOU'RE A FIGHTER... BUT A HAPPY ONE!
A HAPPY WARRIOR, THAT'S YOU!

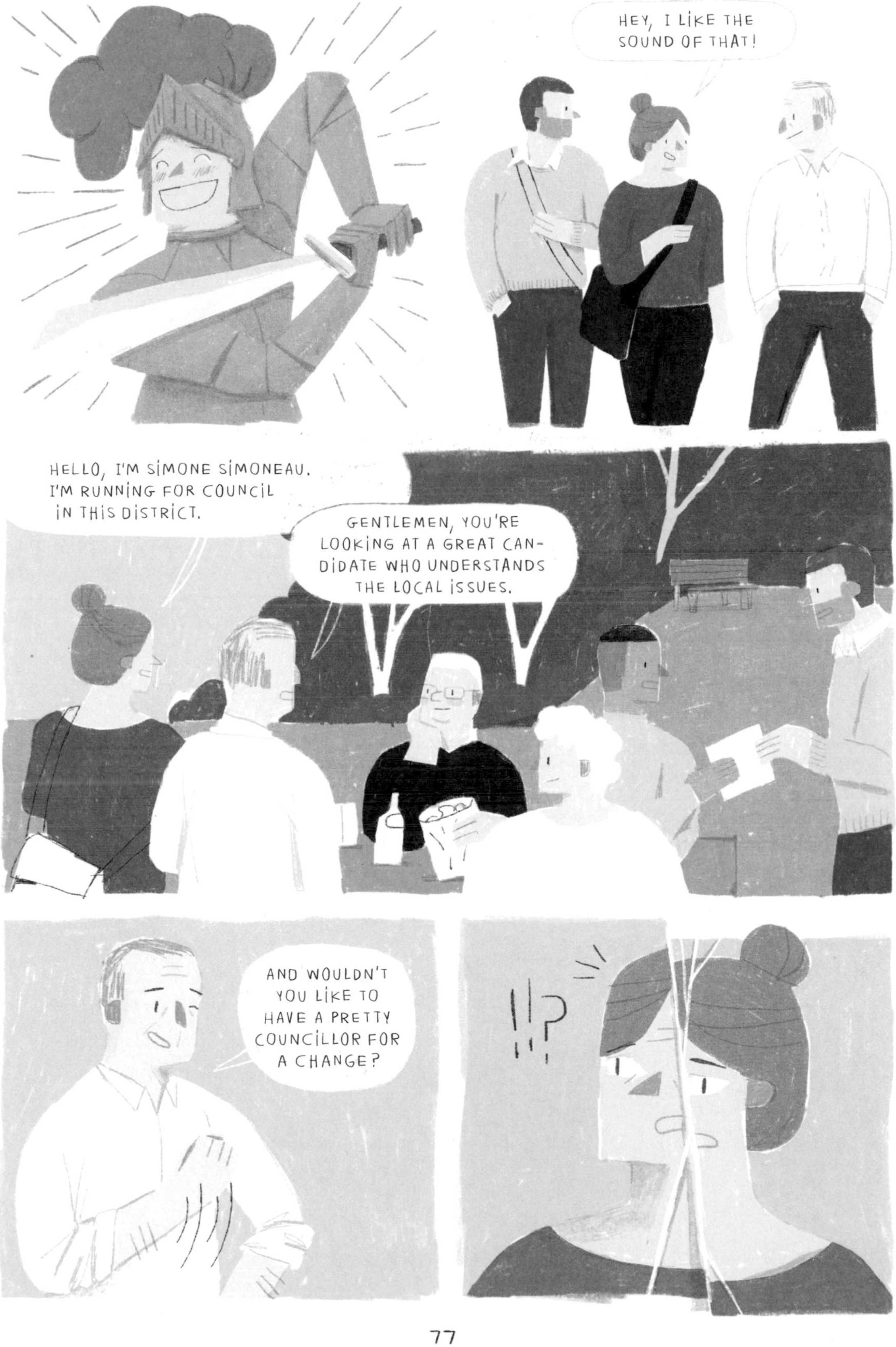

HEY, I LIKE THE SOUND OF THAT!
HELLO, I'M SIMONE SIMONEAU. I'M RUNNING FOR COUNCIL IN THIS DISTRICT.
GENTLEMEN, YOU'RE LOOKING AT A GREAT CAN-DIDATE WHO UNDERSTANDS THE LOCAL ISSUES.
AND WOULDN'T YOU LIKE TO HAVE A PRETTY COUNCILLOR FOR A CHANGE?
!!?

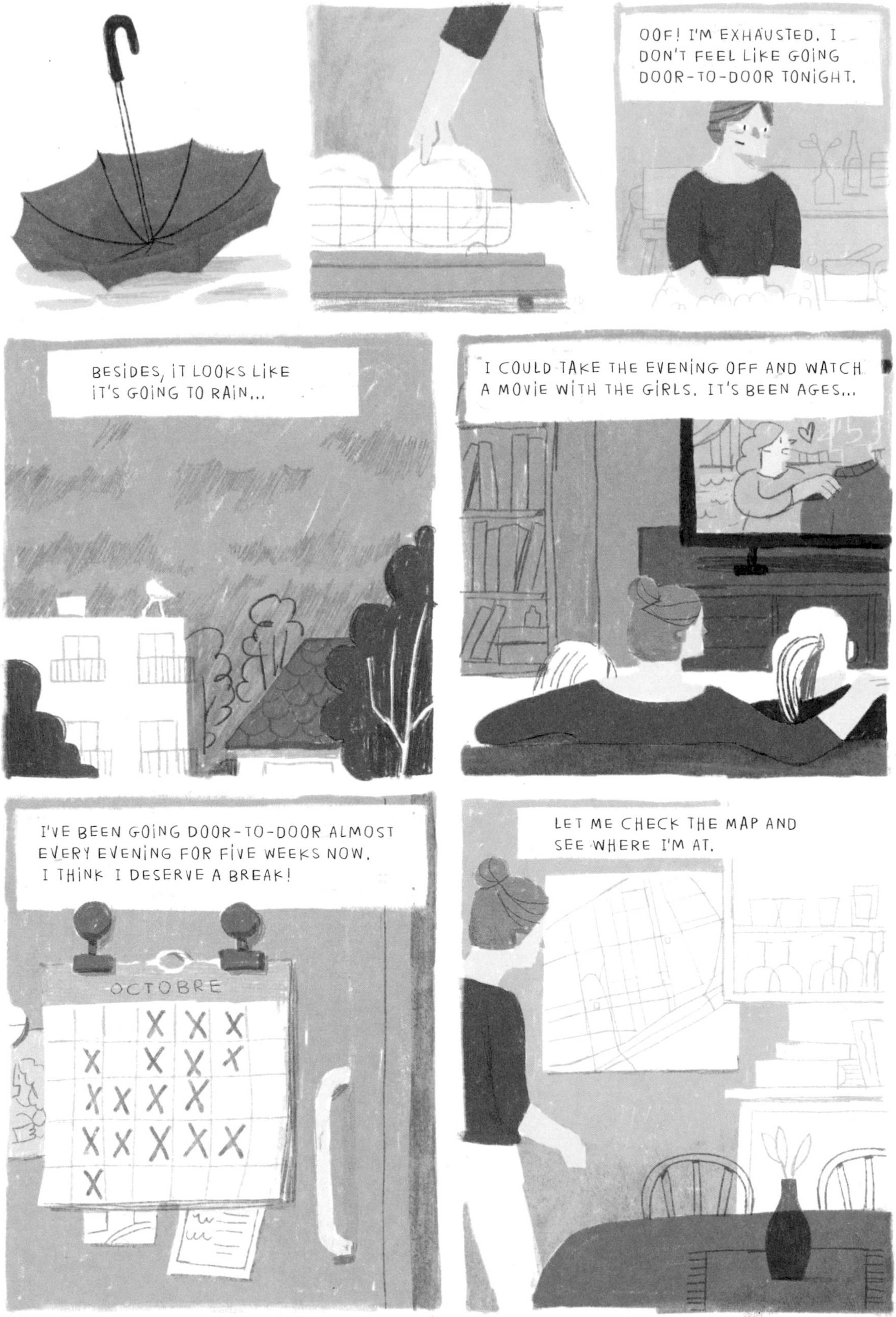
OOF! I'M EXHAUSTED. I DON'T FEEL LIKE GOING DOOR-TO-DOOR TONIGHT.
BESIDES, IT LOOKS LIKE IT'S GOING TO RAIN...
I COULD TAKE THE EVENING OFF AND WATCH A MOVIE WITH THE GIRLS. IT'S BEEN AGES...
I'VE BEEN GOING DOOR-TO-DOOR ALMOST EVERY EVENING FOR FIVE WEEKS NOW. I THINK I DESERVE A BREAK!
OCTOBRE
LET ME CHECK THE MAP AND SEE WHERE I'M AT.

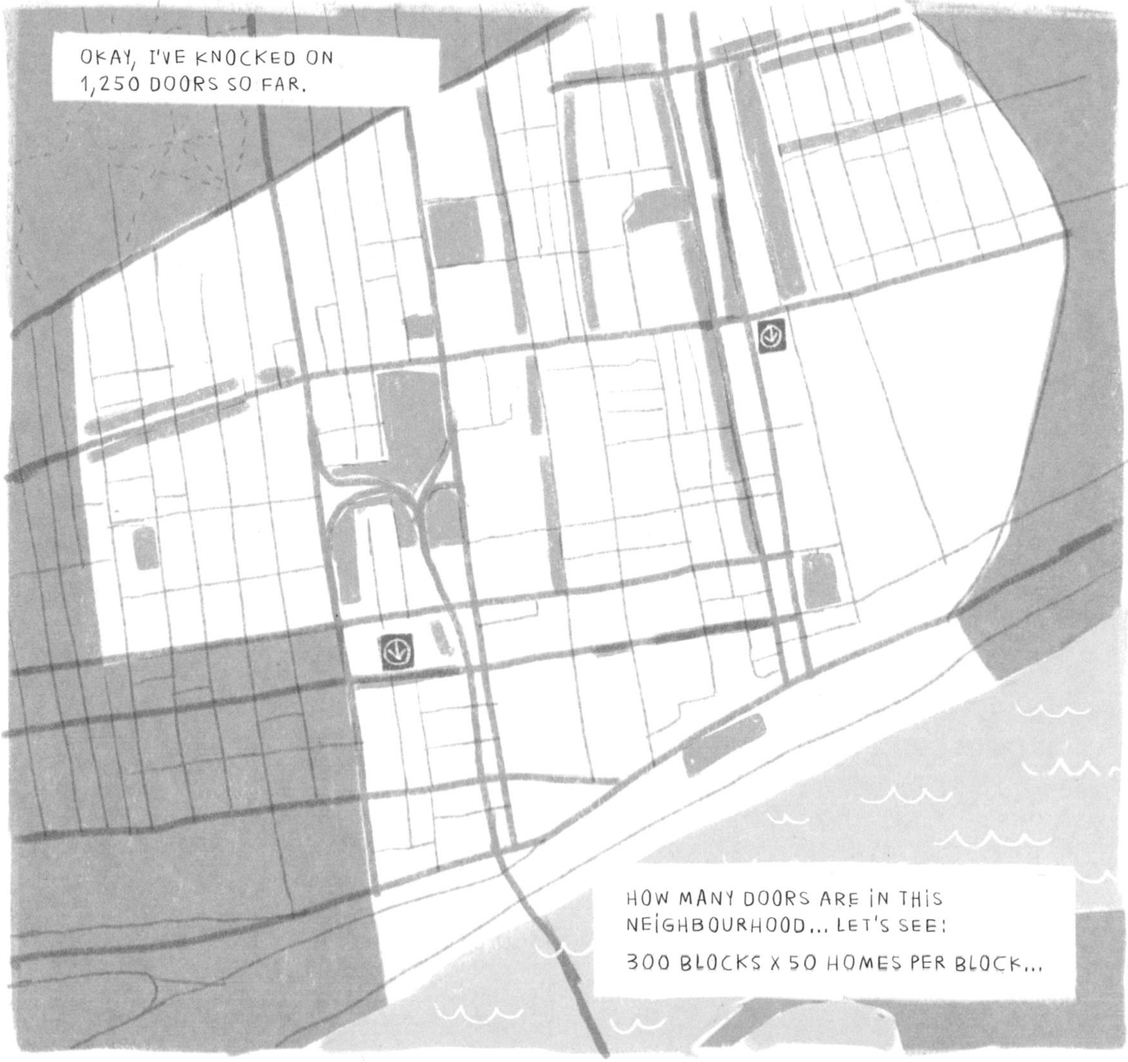
OKAY, I'VE KNOCKED ON 1,250 DOORS SO FAR.
HOW MANY DOORS ARE IN THIS NEIGHBOURHOOD... LET'S SEE:
300 BLOCKS X 50 HOMES PER BLOCK...

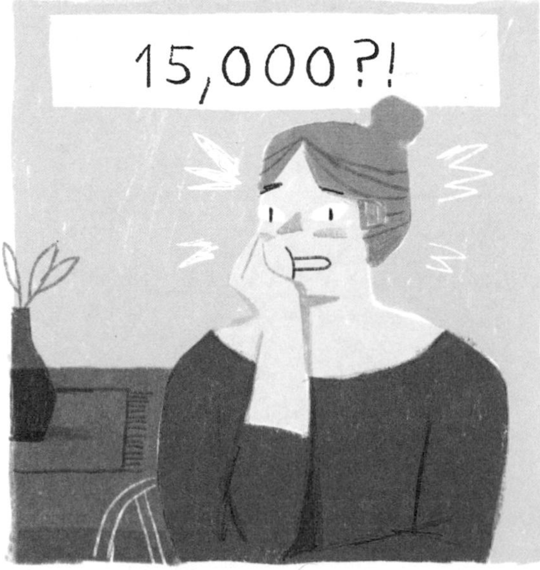
15,000?!

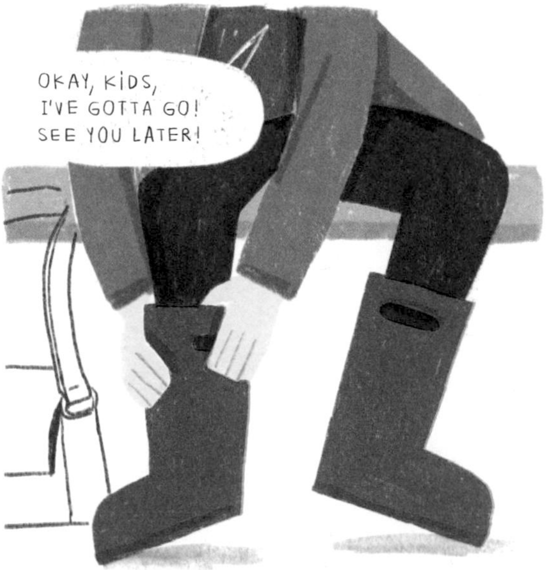
OKAY, KIDS, I'VE GOTTA GO! SEE YOU LATER!

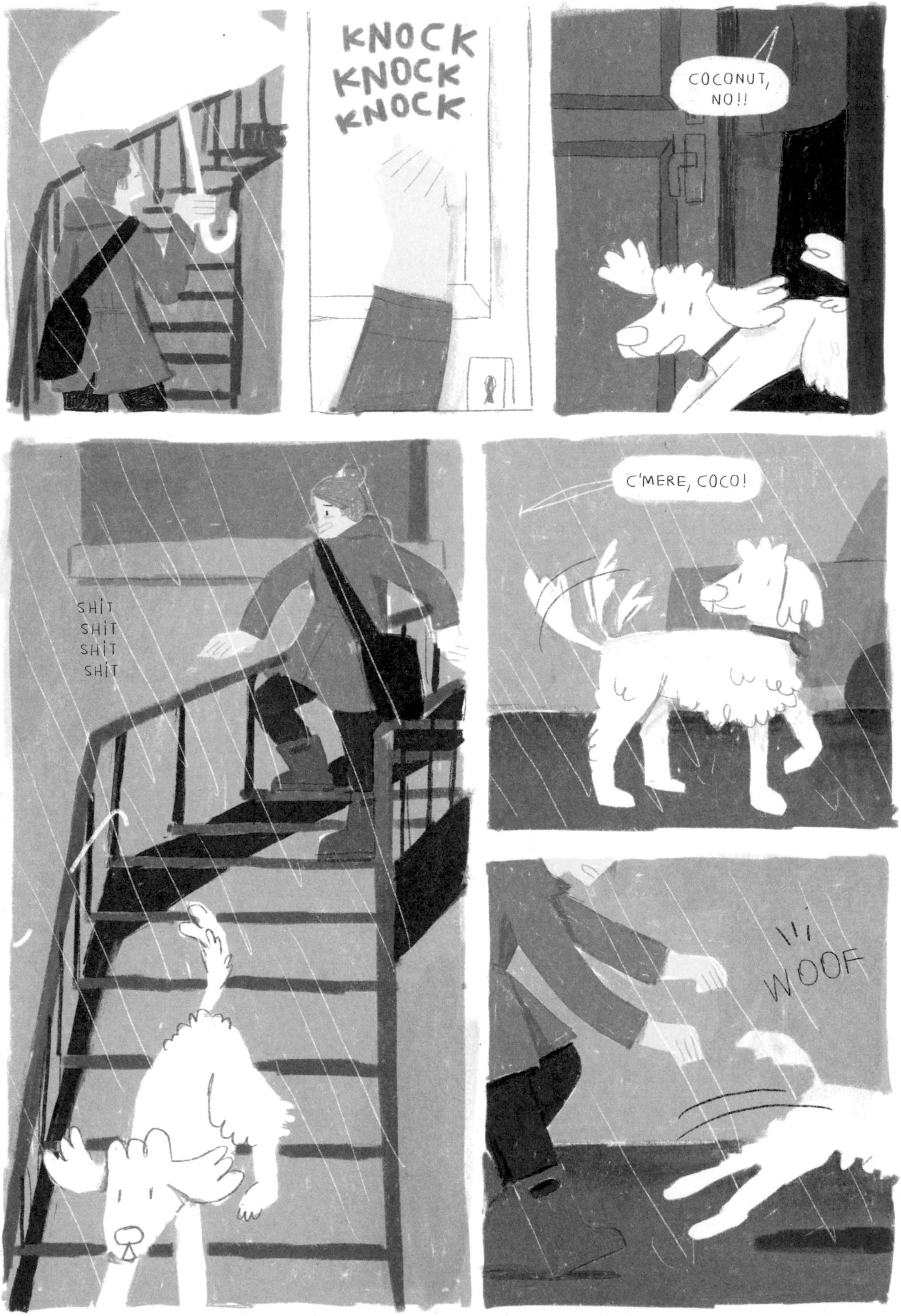
KNOCK
KNOCK
KNOCK
COCONUT, NO!!
SHIT
SHIT
SHIT
SHIT
C'MERE, COCO!
WOOF

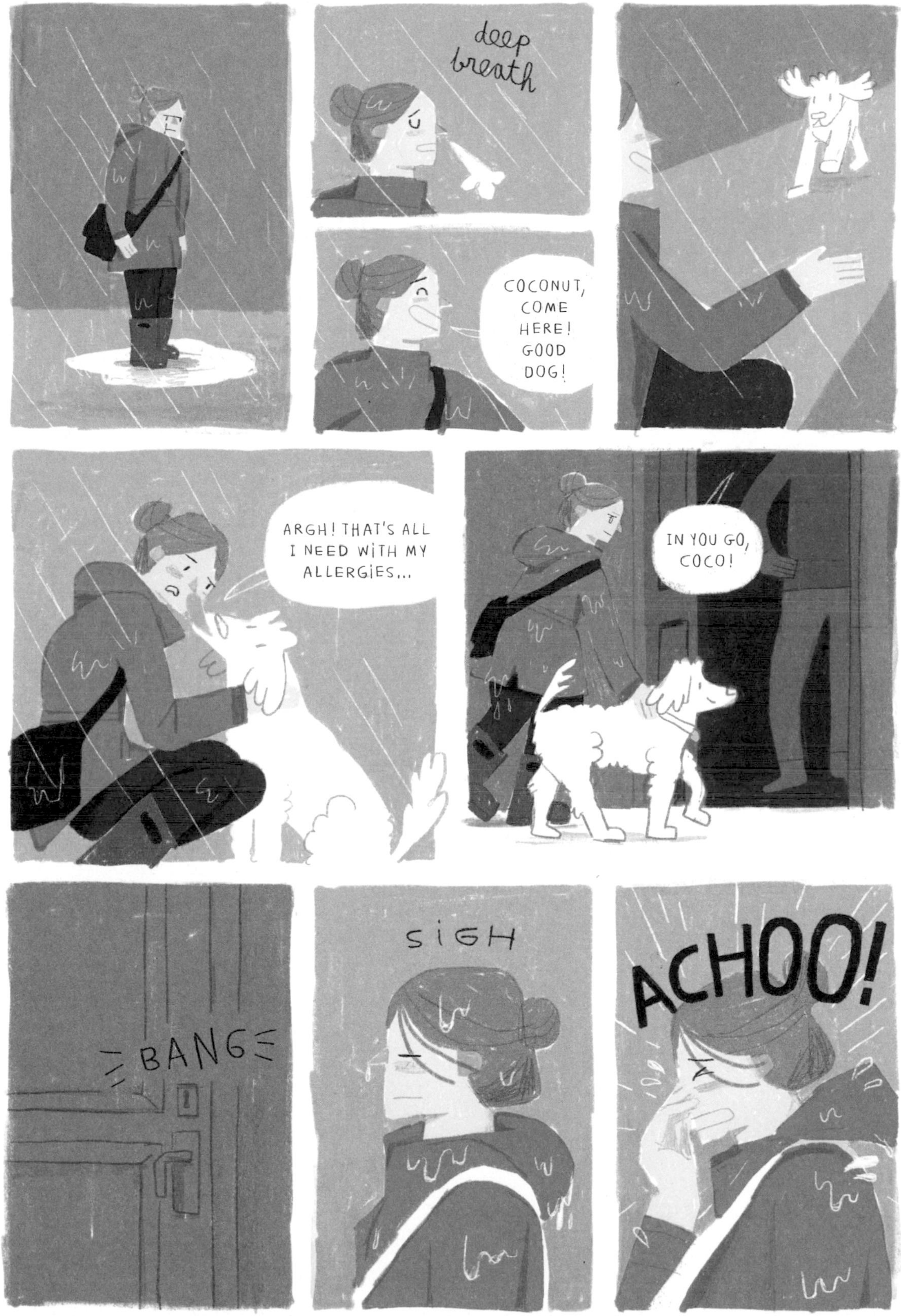
deep breath
COCONUT, COME HERE! GOOD DOG!
ARGH! THAT'S ALL I NEED WITH MY ALLERGIES...
IN YOU GO, COCO!
BANG
SIGH
ACHOO!

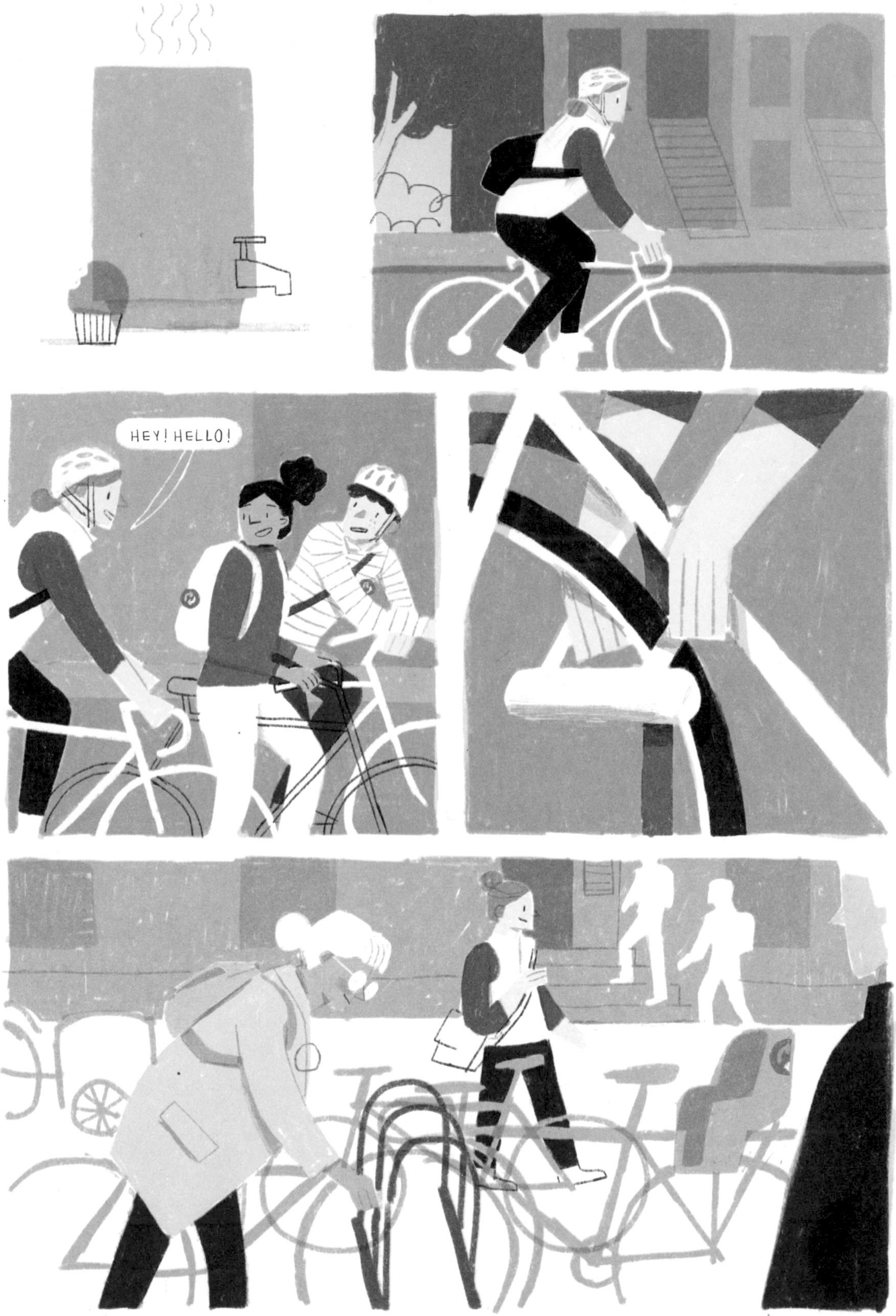
HEY! HELLO!

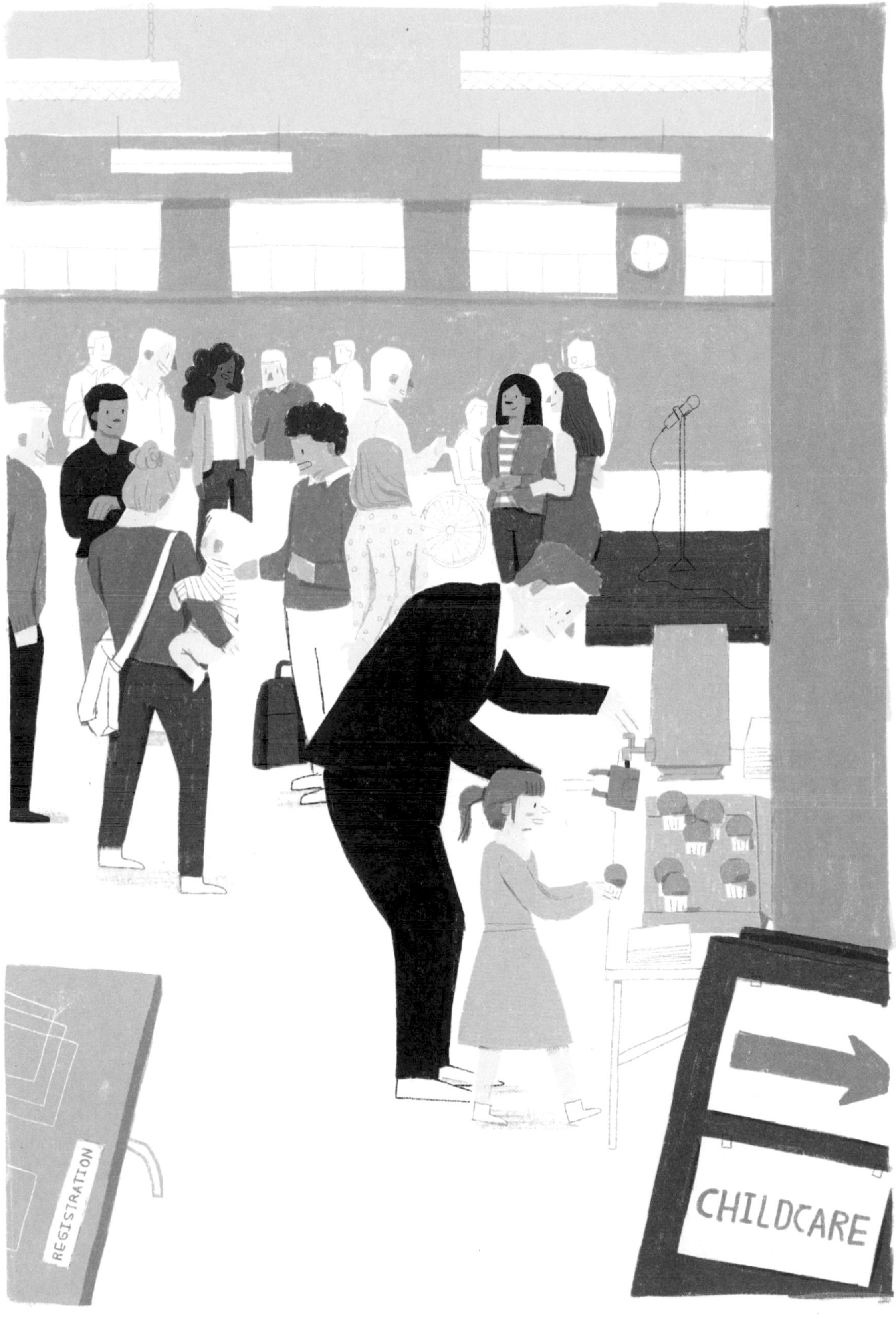

REGISTRATION
CHILDCARE

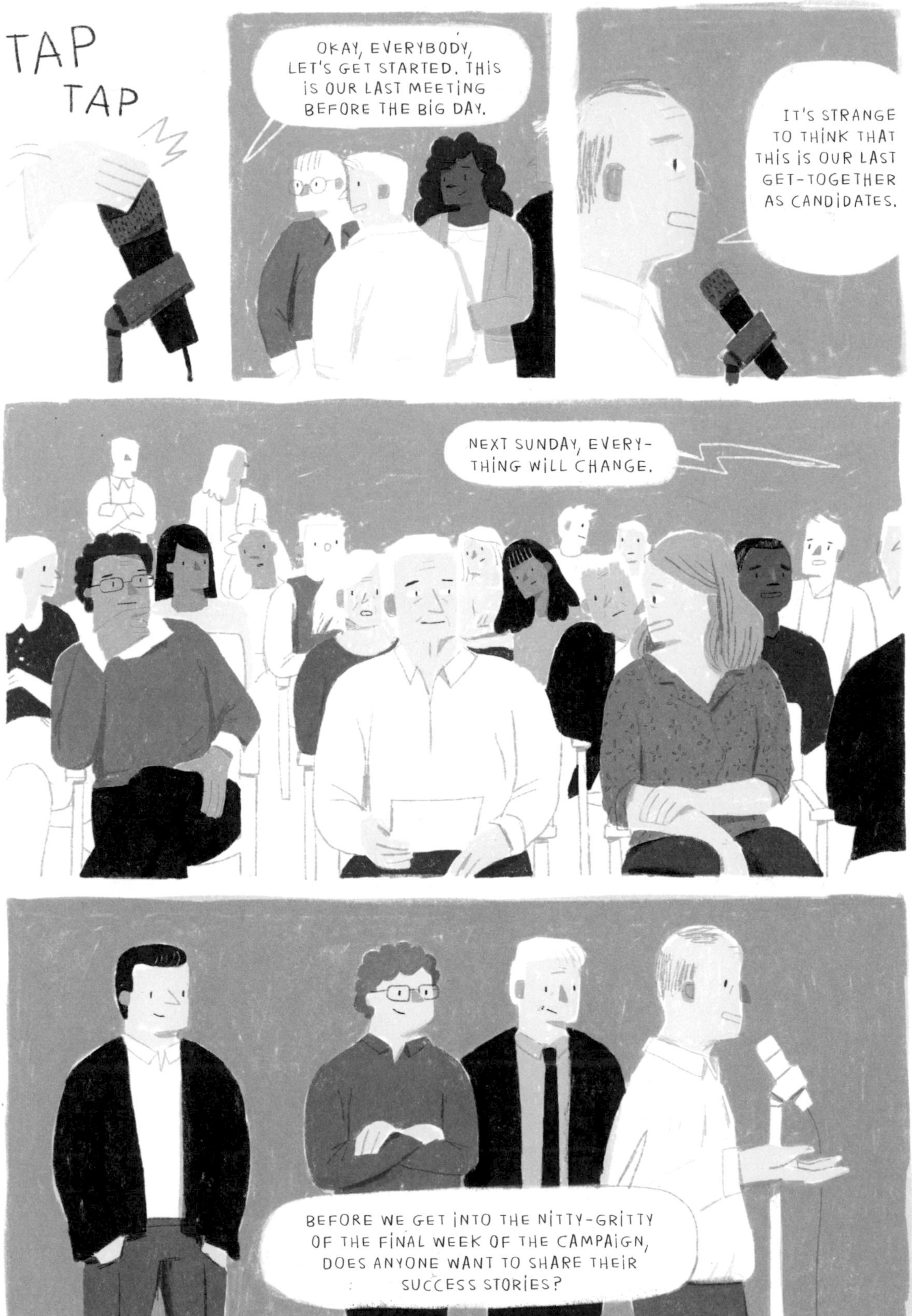
TAP
TAP
OKAY, EVERYBODY, LET'S GET STARTED. THIS IS OUR LAST MEETING BEFORE THE BIG DAY.
IT'S STRANGE TO THINK THAT THIS IS OUR LAST GET-TOGETHER AS CANDIDATES.
NEXT SUNDAY, EVERYTHING WILL CHANGE.
BEFORE WE GET INTO THE NITTY-GRITTY OF THE FINAL WEEK OF THE CAMPAIGN, DOES ANYONE WANT TO SHARE THEIR SUCCESS STORIES?

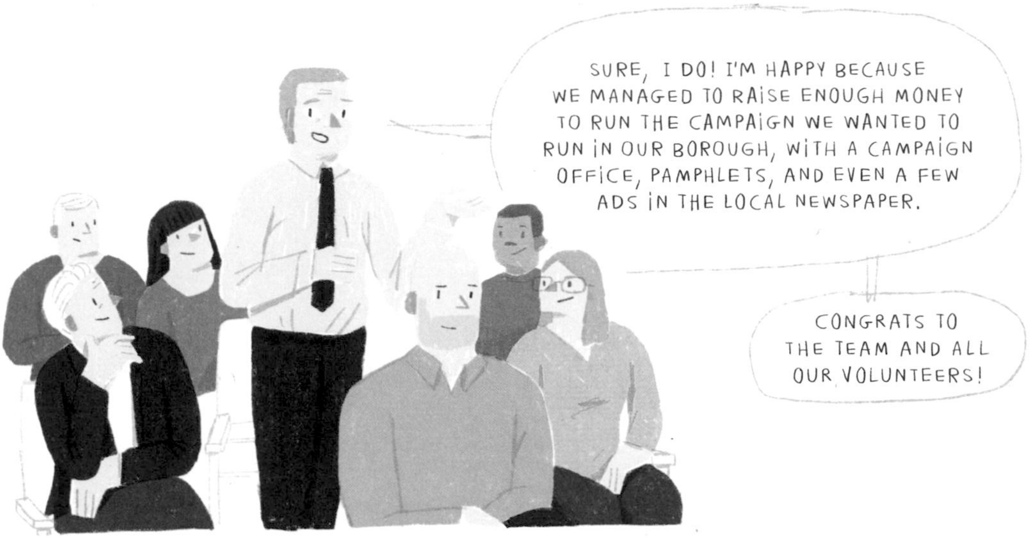
SURE, I DO! I'M HAPPY BECAUSE WE MANAGED TO RAISE ENOUGH MONEY TO RUN THE CAMPAIGN WE WANTED TO RUN IN OUR BOROUGH, WITH A CAMPAIGN OFFICE, PAMPHLETS, AND EVEN A FEW ADS IN THE LOCAL NEWSPAPER.
CONGRATS TO THE TEAM AND ALL OUR VOLUNTEERS!

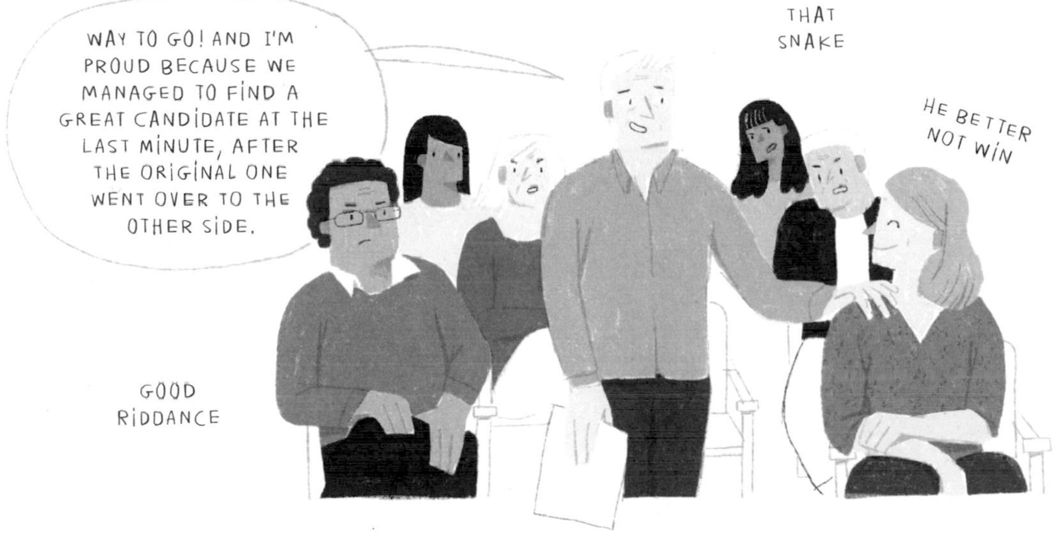
WAY TO GO! AND I'M PROUD BECAUSE WE MANAGED TO FIND A GREAT CANDIDATE AT THE LAST MINUTE, AFTER THE ORIGINAL ONE WENT OVER TO THE OTHER SIDE.
THAT SNAKE
HE BETTER NOT WIN
GOOD RIDDANCE

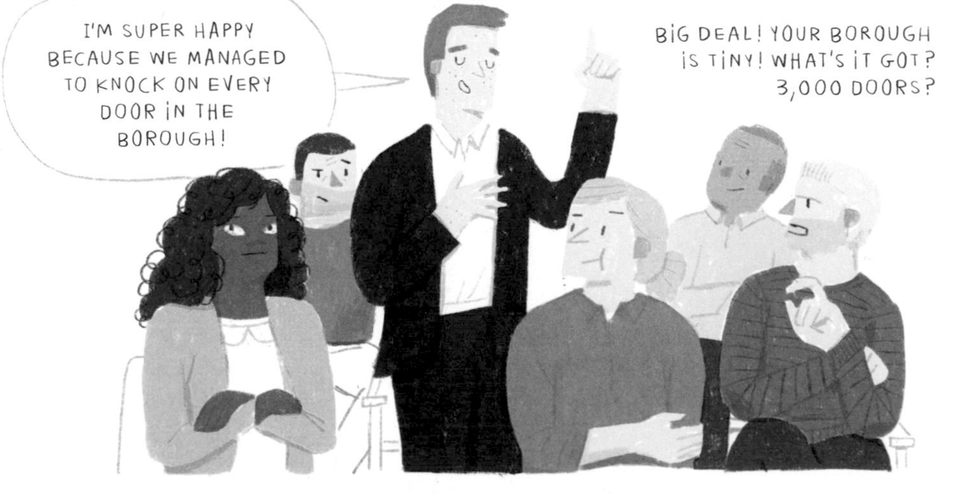
I'M SUPER HAPPY BECAUSE WE MANAGED TO KNOCK ON EVERY DOOR IN THE BOROUGH!
BIG DEAL! YOUR BOROUGH IS TINY! WHAT'S IT GOT? 3,000 DOORS?

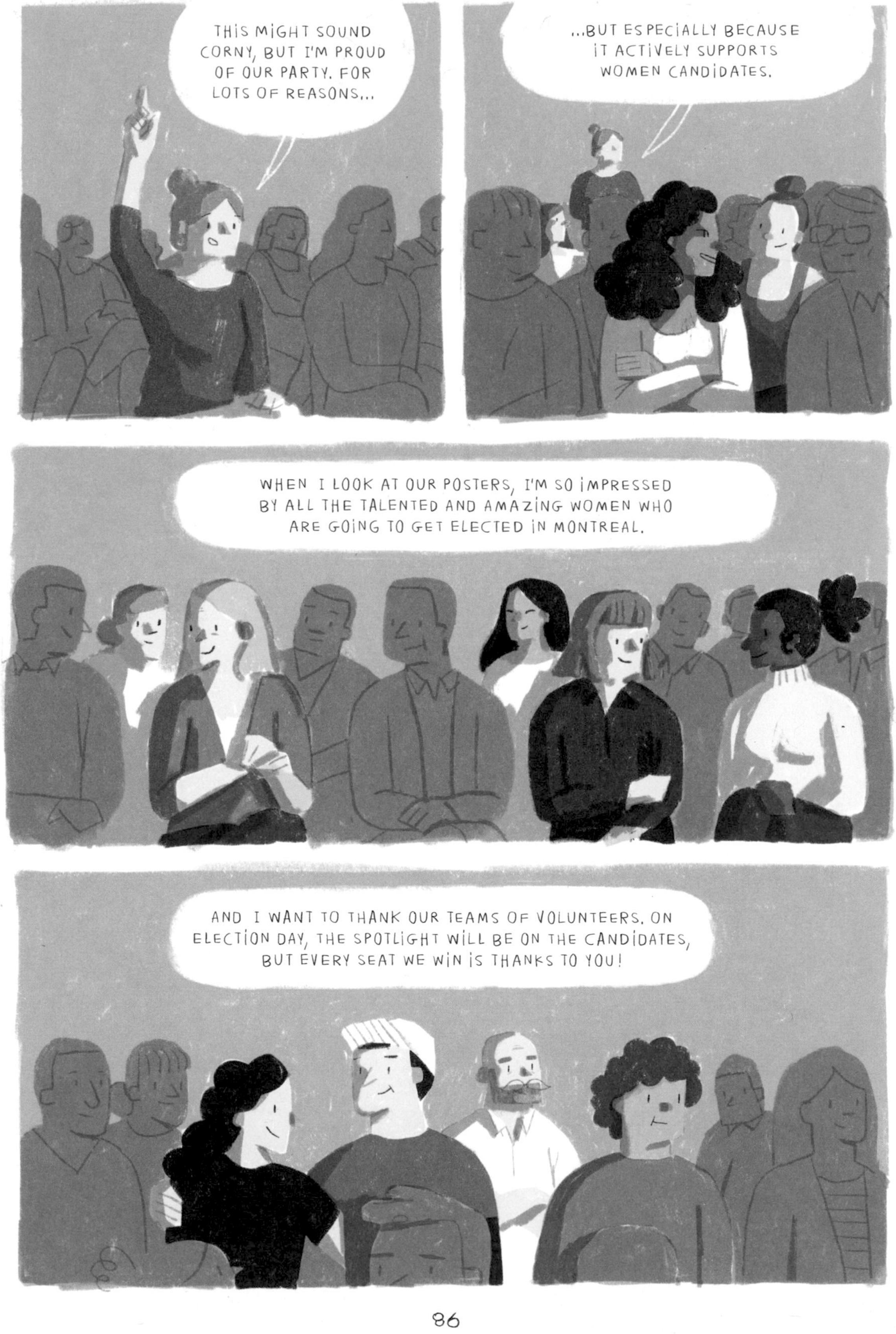
THIS MIGHT SOUND CORNY, BUT I'M PROUD OF OUR PARTY. FOR LOTS OF REASONS...
...BUT ESPECIALLY BECAUSE IT ACTIVELY SUPPORTS WOMEN CANDIDATES.
WHEN I LOOK AT OUR POSTERS, I'M SO IMPRESSED BY ALL THE TALENTED AND AMAZING WOMEN WHO ARE GOING TO GET ELECTED IN MONTREAL.
AND I WANT TO THANK OUR TEAMS OF VOLUNTEERS. ON ELECTION DAY, THE SPOTLIGHT WILL BE ON THE CANDIDATES, BUT EVERY SEAT WE WIN IS THANKS TO YOU!

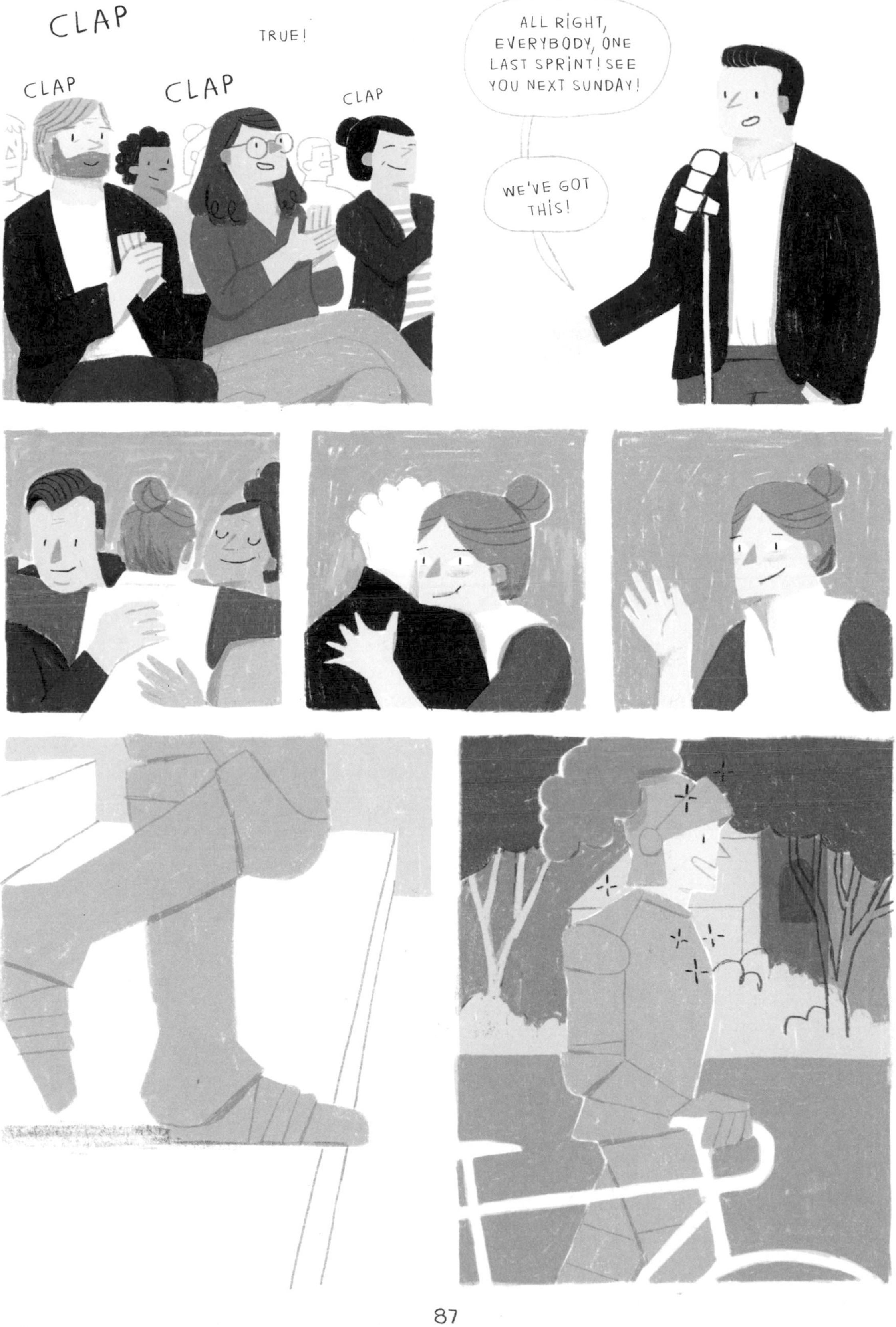
CLAP
TRUE!
CLAP
CLAP
CLAP
ALL RIGHT, EVERYBODY, ONE LAST SPRINT! SEE YOU NEXT SUNDAY!
WE'VE GOT THIS!

THE BIG DAY

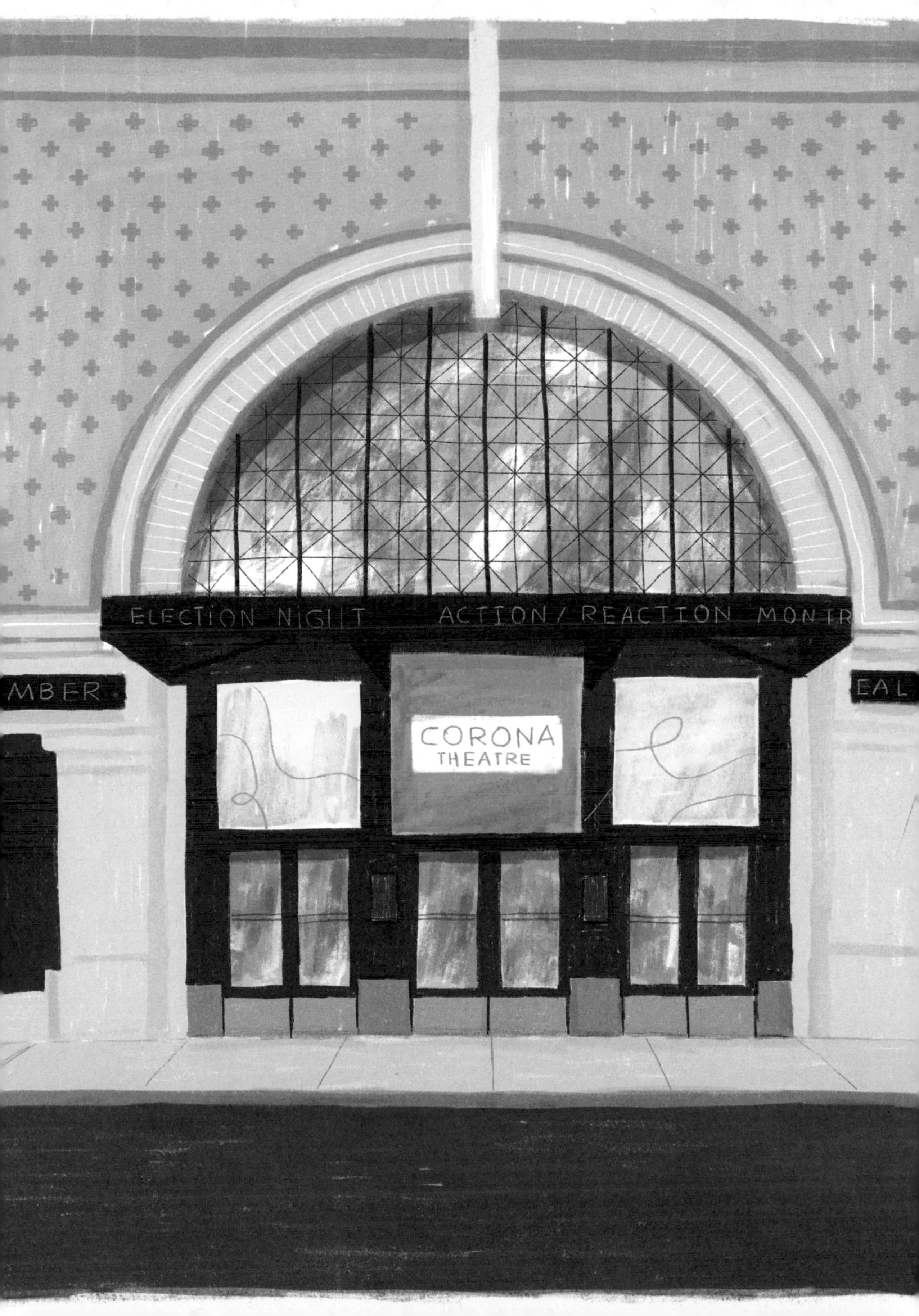
ELECTION NIGHT ACTION / REACTION MONTR
MBER
EAL
CORONA
THEATRE

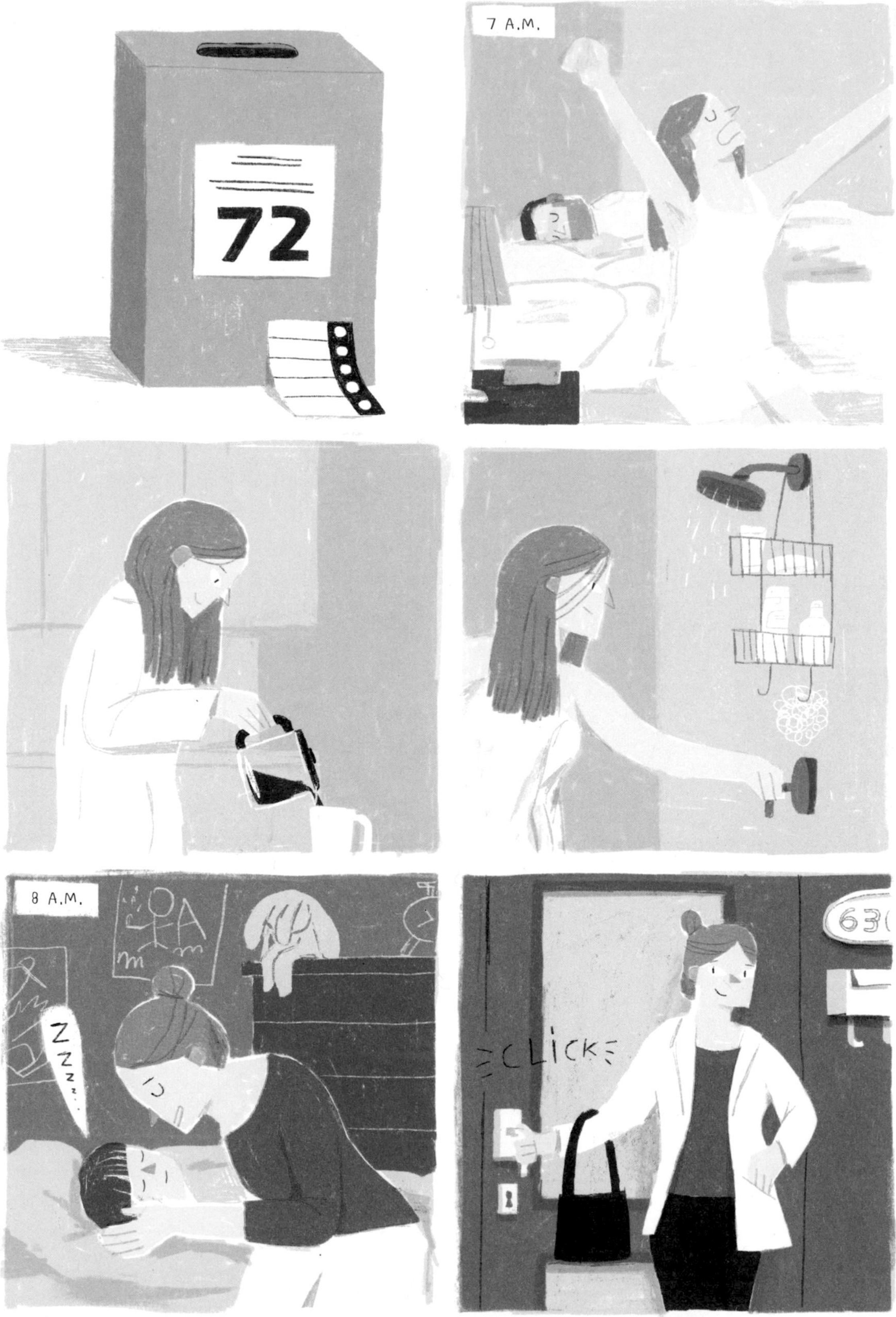
72
7 A.M.
8 A.M.
Z Z z z
CLICK
63

9 A.M.

10 A.M.

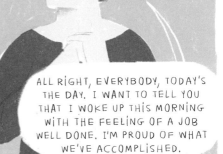

ALL RIGHT, EVERYBODY, TODAY'S THE DAY. I WANT TO TELL YOU THAT I WOKE UP THIS MORNING WITH THE FEELING OF A JOB WELL DONE. I'M PROUD OF WHAT WE'VE ACCOMPLISHED.

WE'VE GOT SIX HOURS TO GIVE IT ONE LAST PUSH AND GET THE VOTE OUT. PUT A SMILE IN YOUR VOICES, EVERYBODY!

LET'S GO! WE'RE GOING TO WIN THIS ELECTION!

11 A.M.

12 P.M.

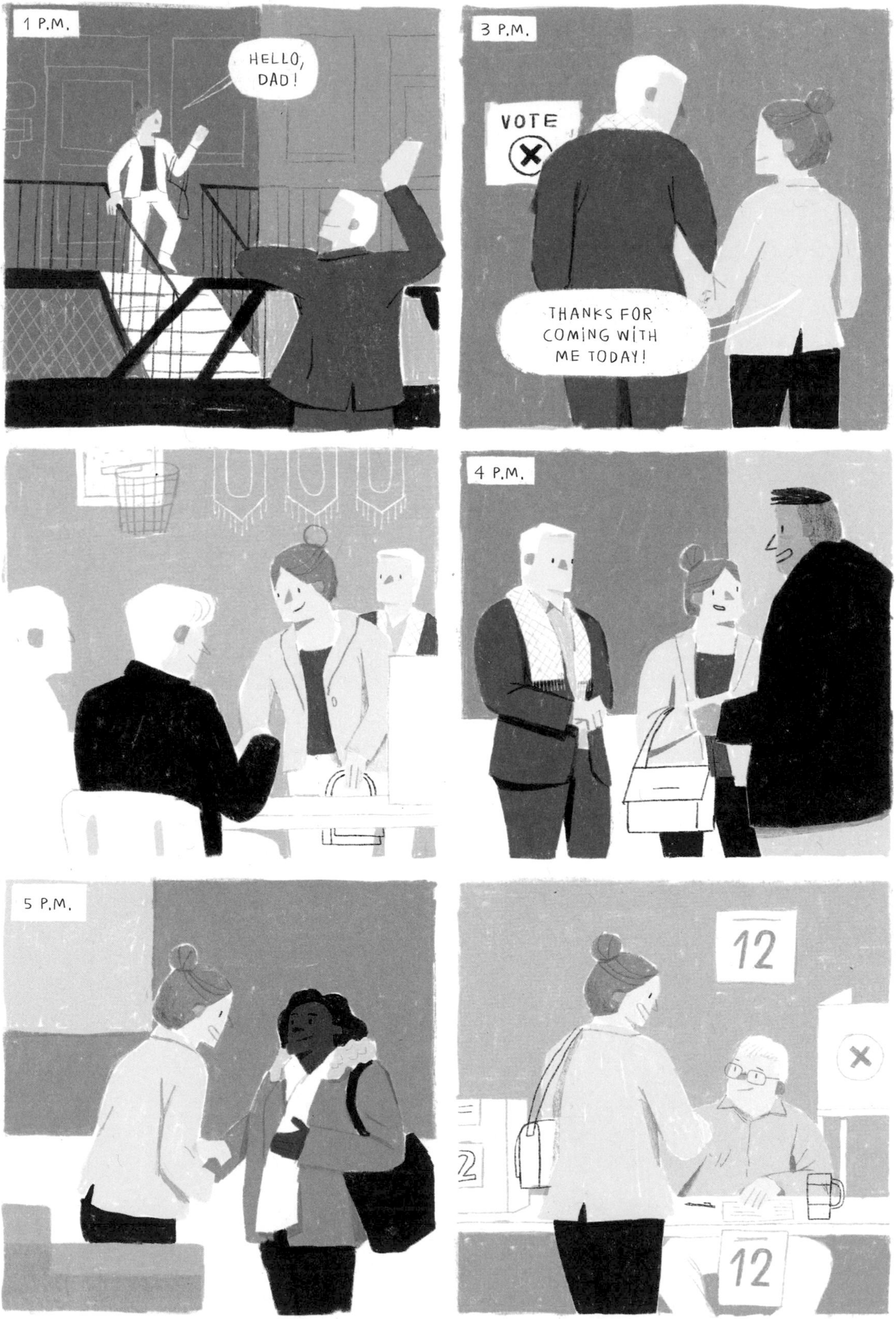
1 P.M.
HELLO, DAD!
3 P.M.
VOTE
THANKS FOR COMING WITH ME TODAY!
4 P.M.
5 P.M.
12
12

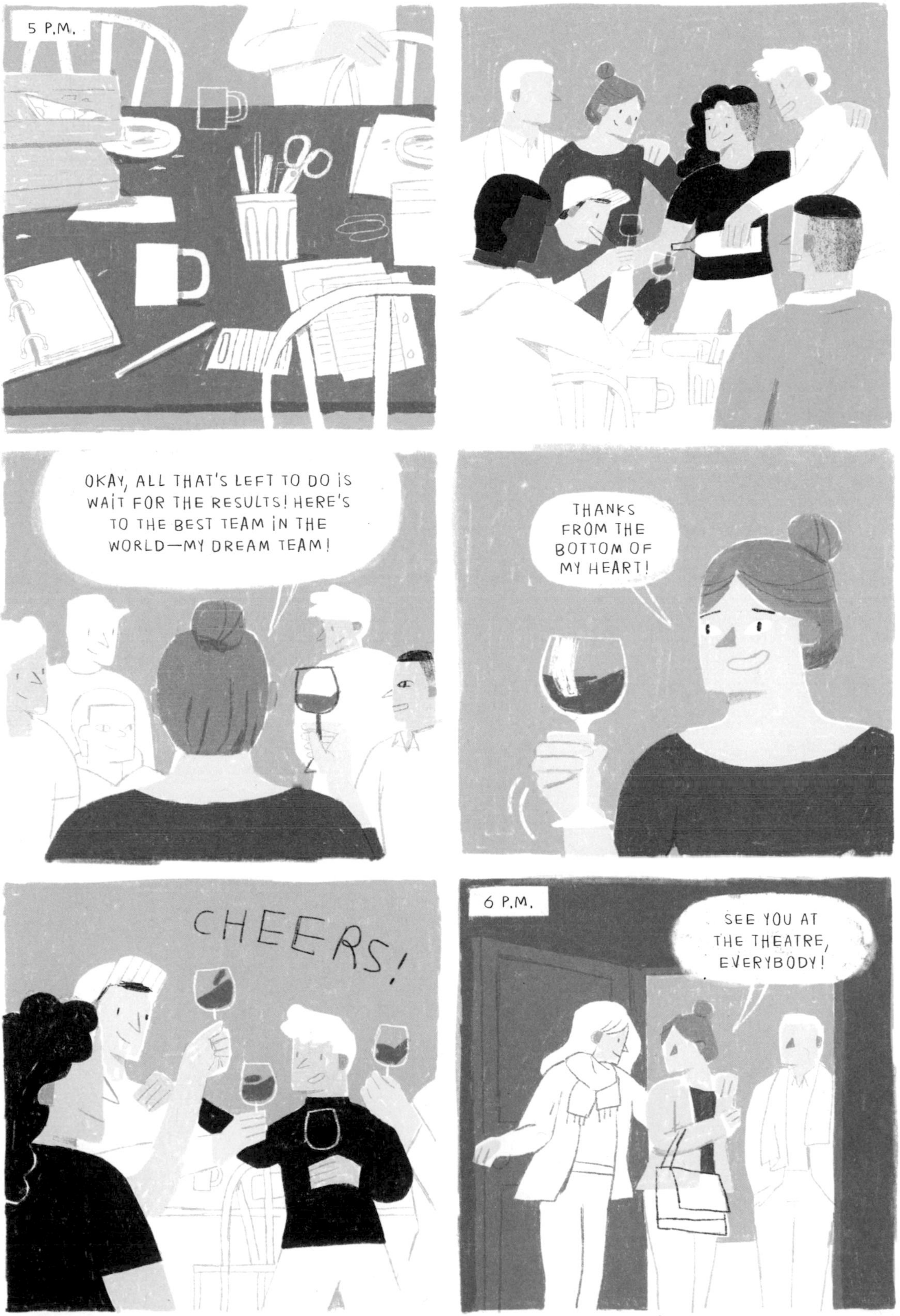
5 P.M.
OKAY, ALL THAT'S LEFT TO DO IS WAIT FOR THE RESULTS! HERE'S TO THE BEST TEAM IN THE WORLD—MY DREAM TEAM!
THANKS FROM THE BOTTOM OF MY HEART!
CHEERS!
6 P.M.
SEE YOU AT THE THEATRE, EVERYBODY!

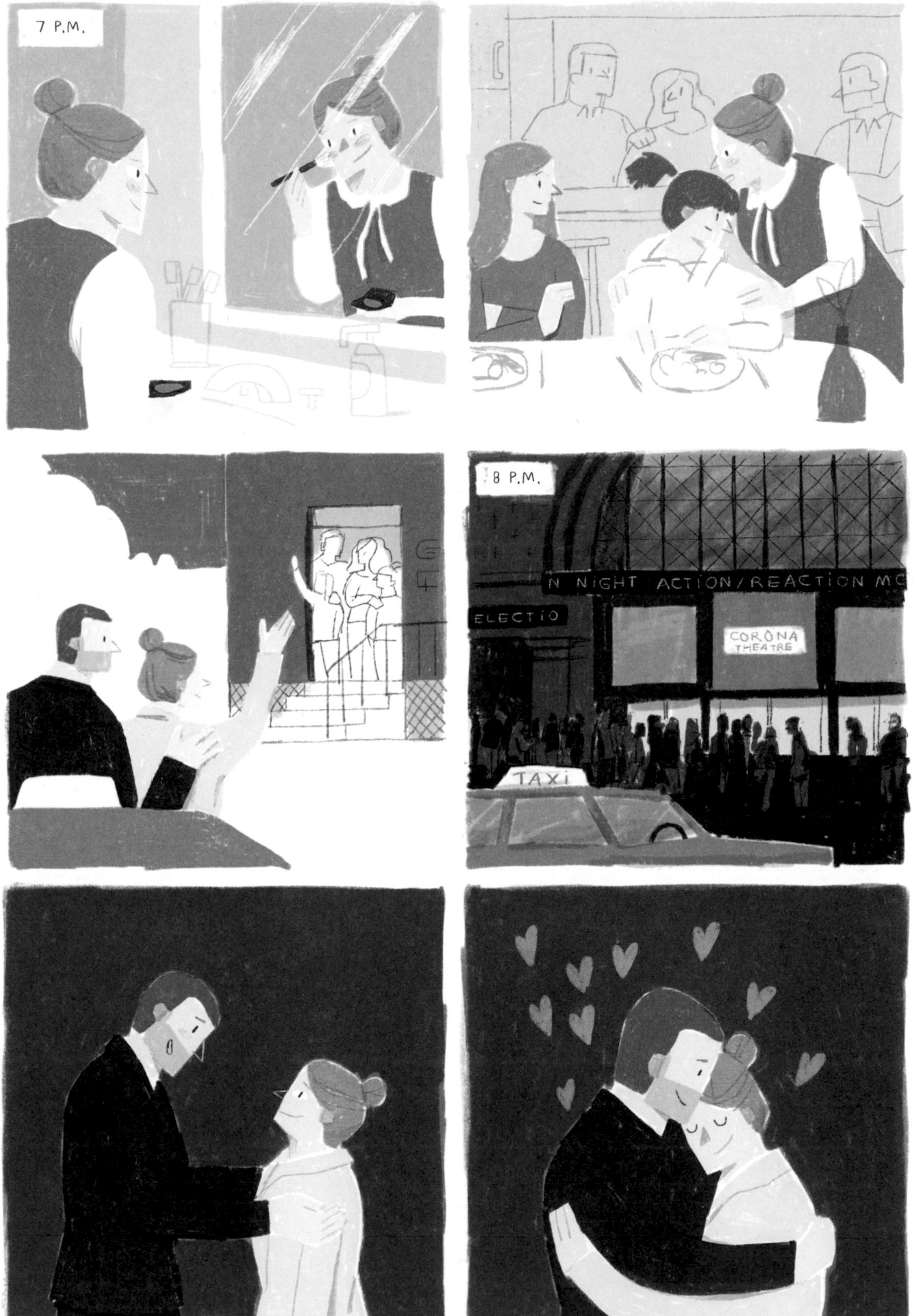
7 P.M.
8 P.M.
N NIGHT ACTION/REACTION MO
ELECTIO
CORONA
THEATRE
TAXI

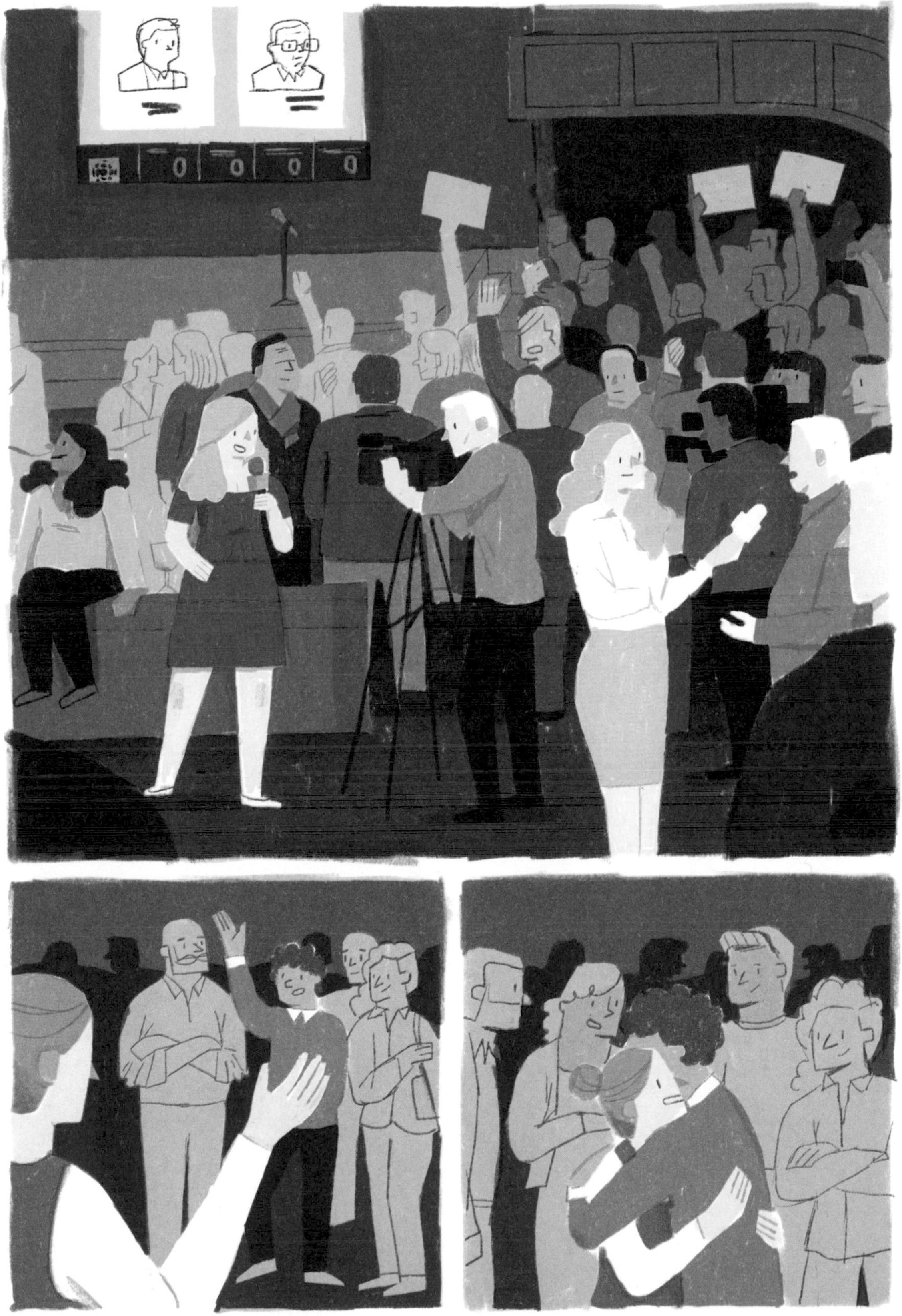

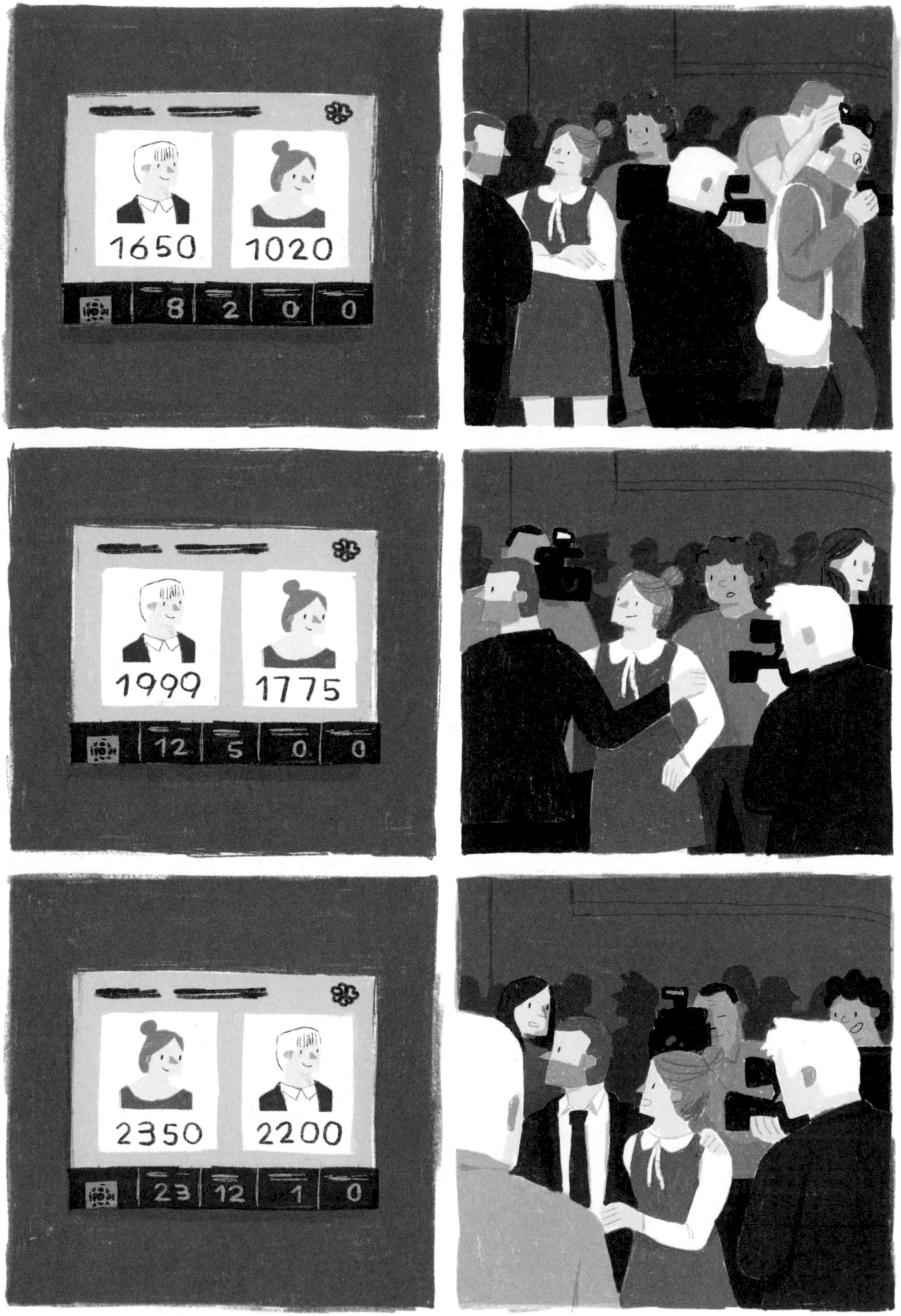
1650
1020
8 2 0 0
1999
1775
12 5 0 0
2350
2200
23 12 1 0

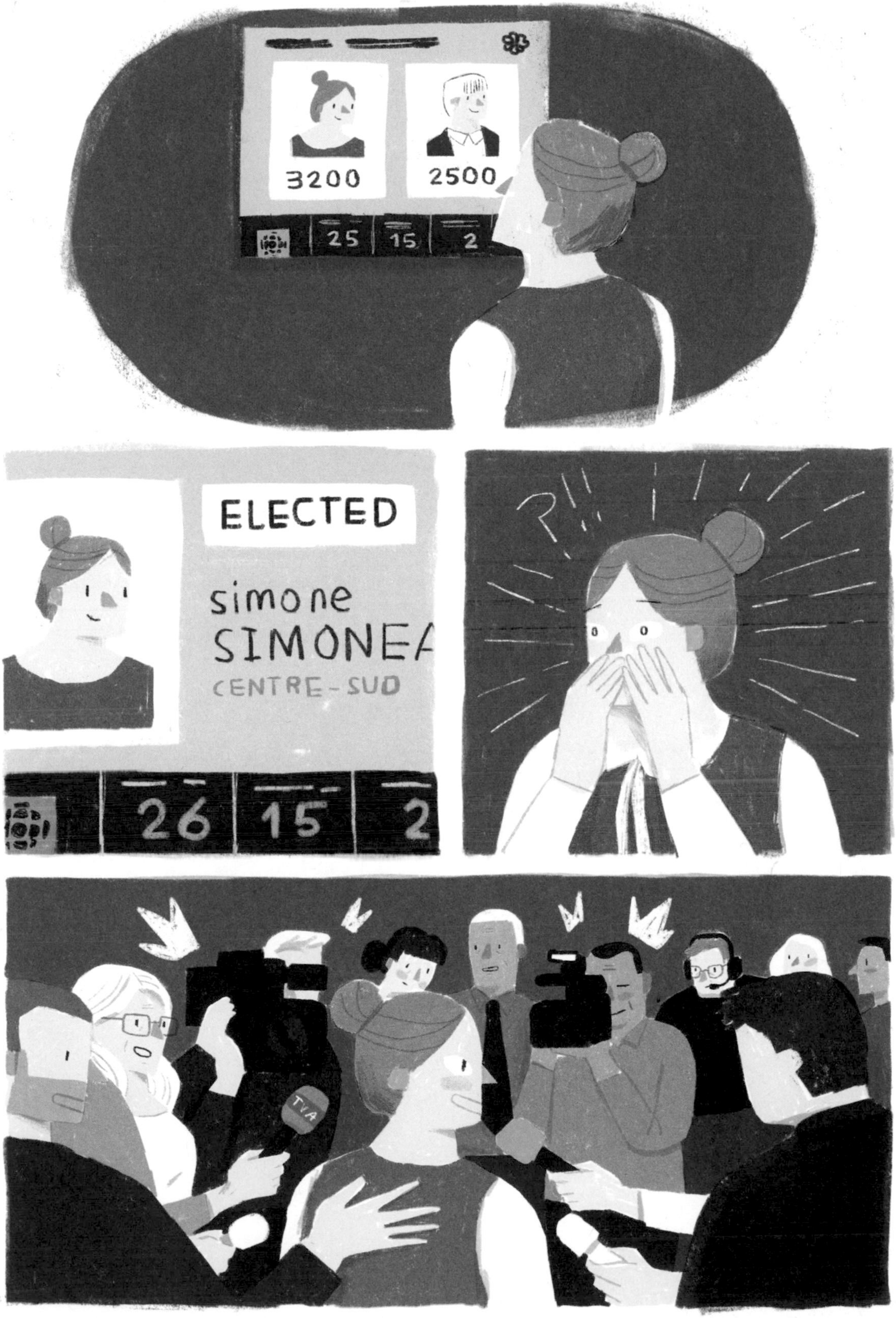
3200
2500
25
15
2
ELECTED
simone
SIMONEA
CENTRE-SUD
26
15
2
?!!
TVA

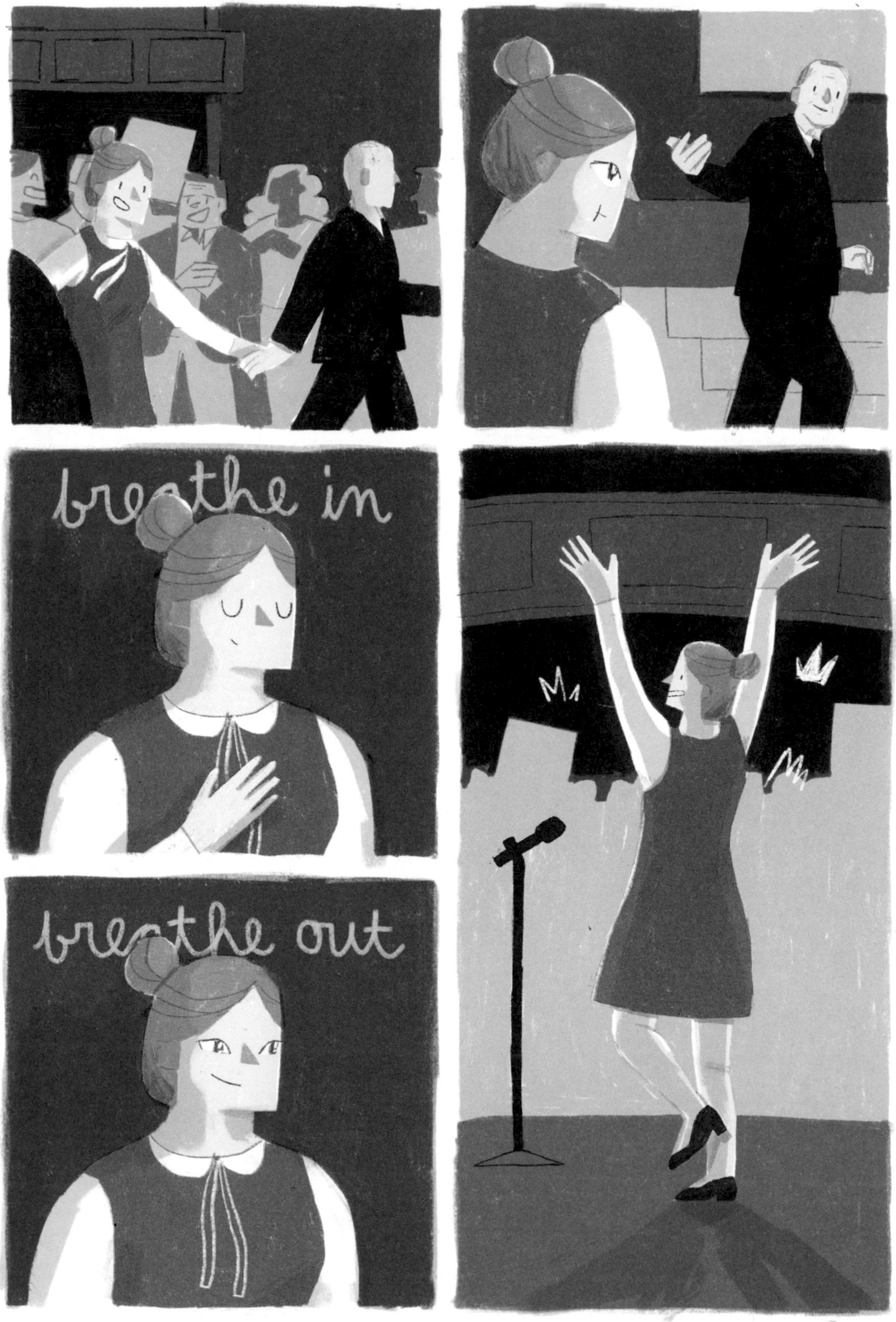
breathe in
breathe out

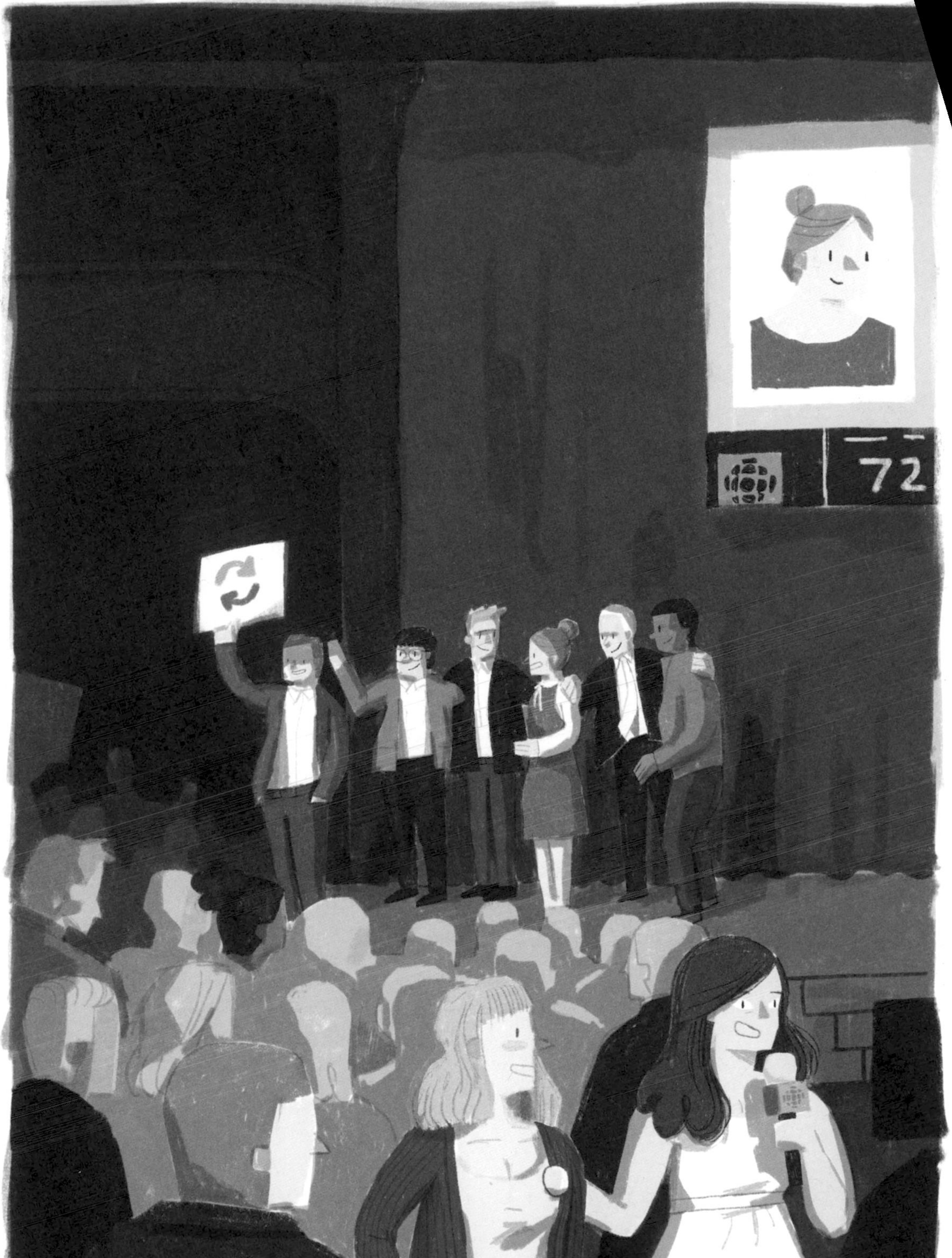
72

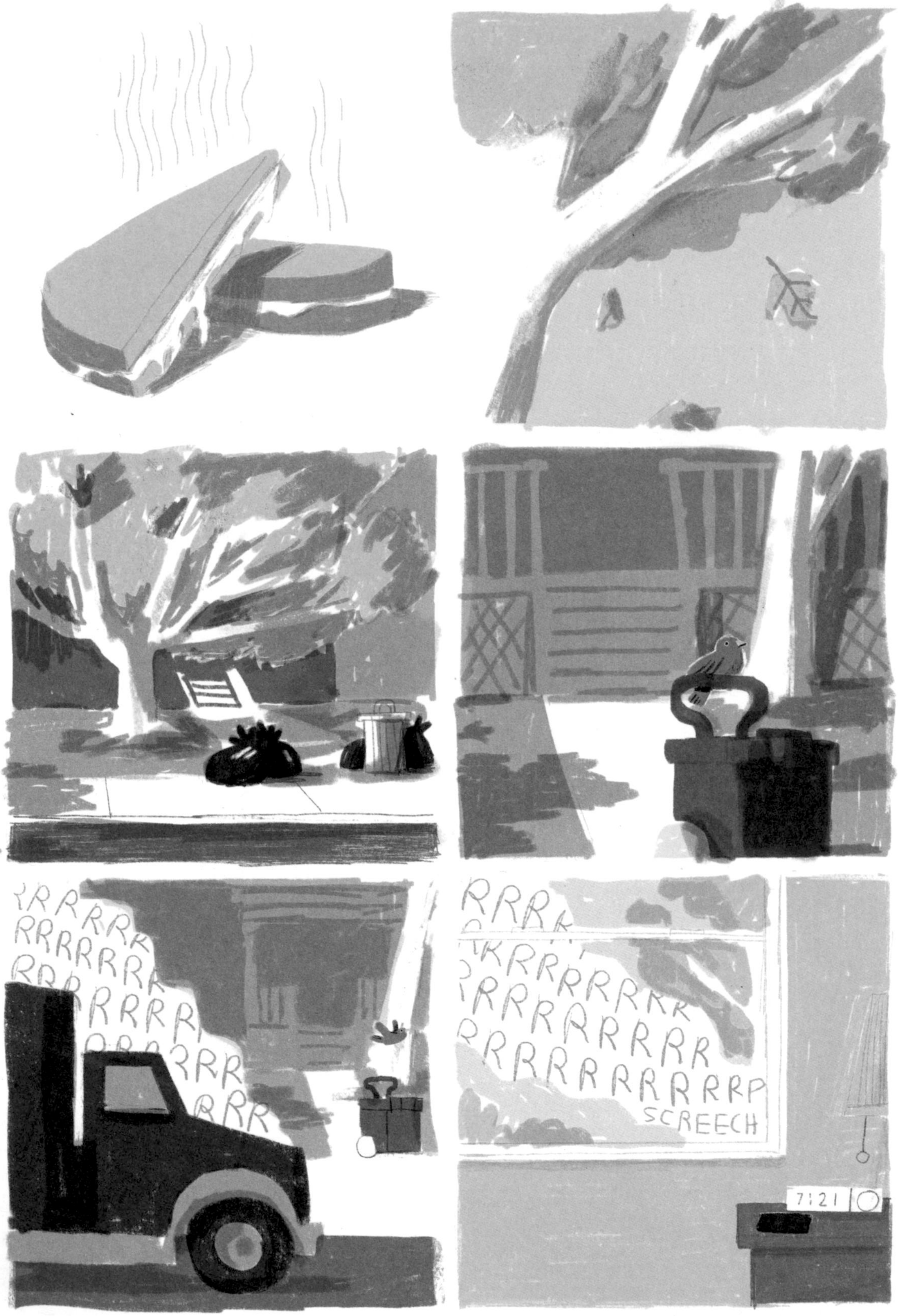
SCREECH
7:21

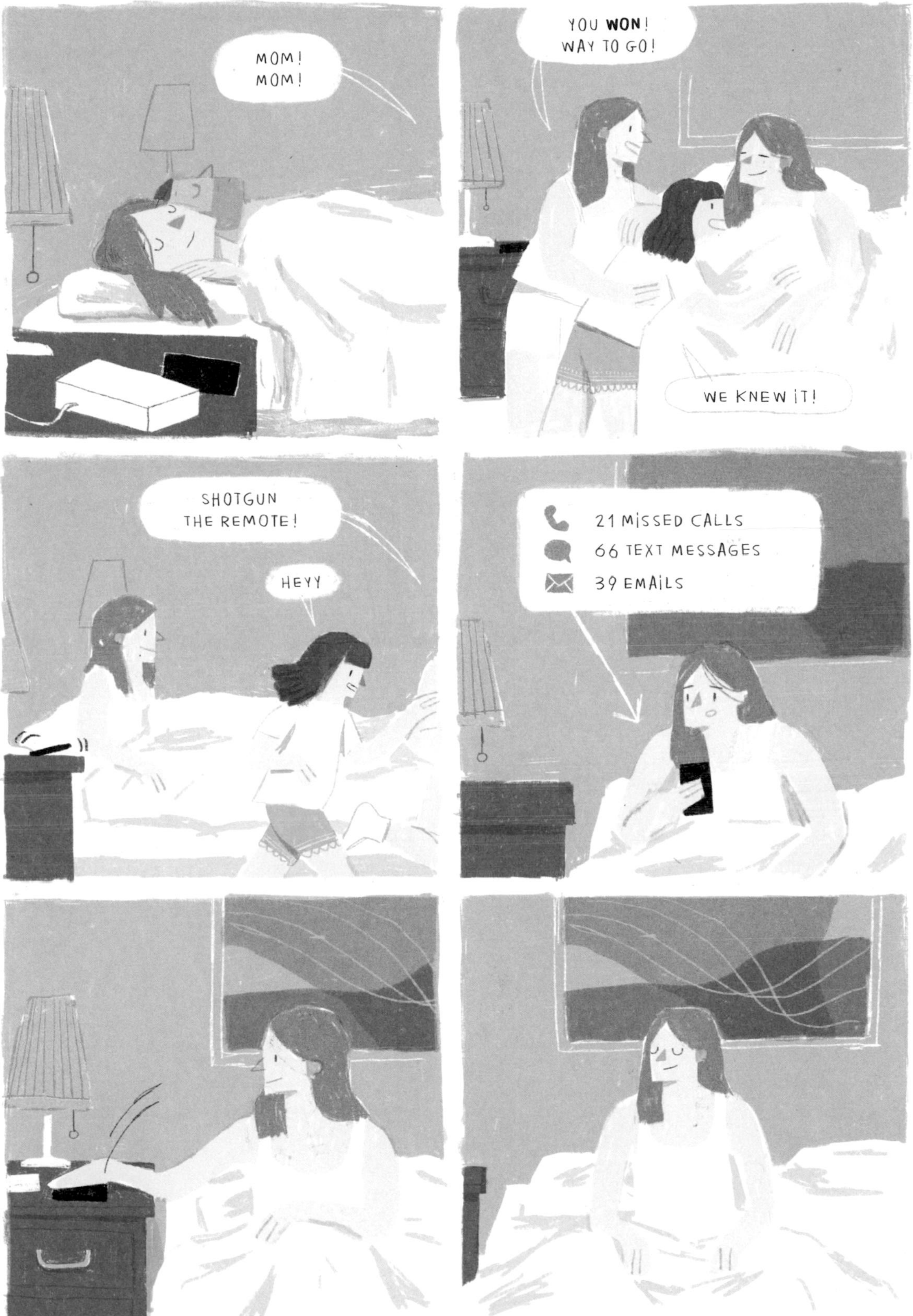
MOM!
MOM!
YOU WON!
WAY TO GO!
WE KNEW IT!
SHOTGUN
THE REMOTE!
HEYY
21 MISSED CALLS
66 TEXT MESSAGES
39 EMAILS

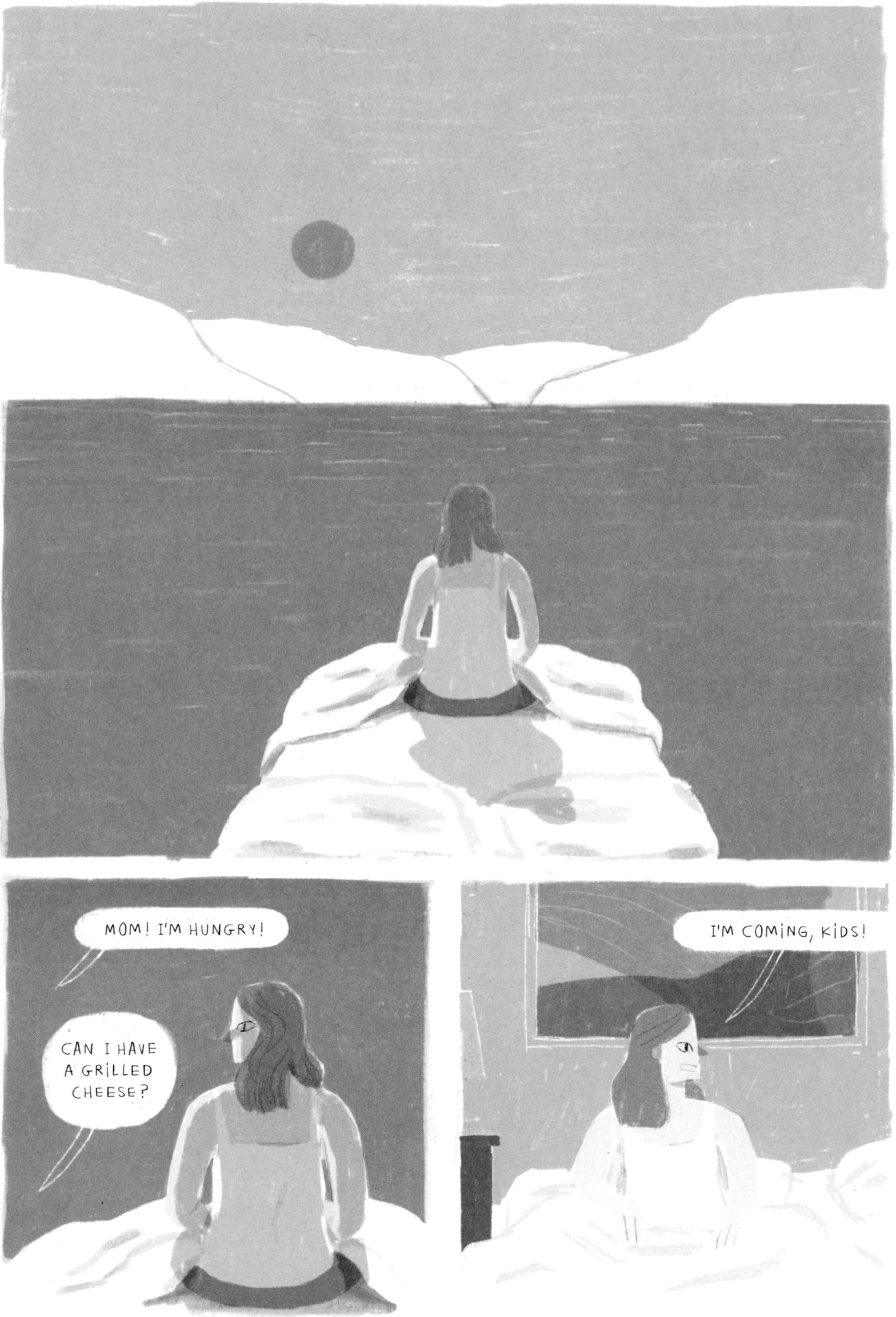
MOM! I'M HUNGRY!
CAN I HAVE A GRILLED CHEESE?
I'M COMING, KIDS!

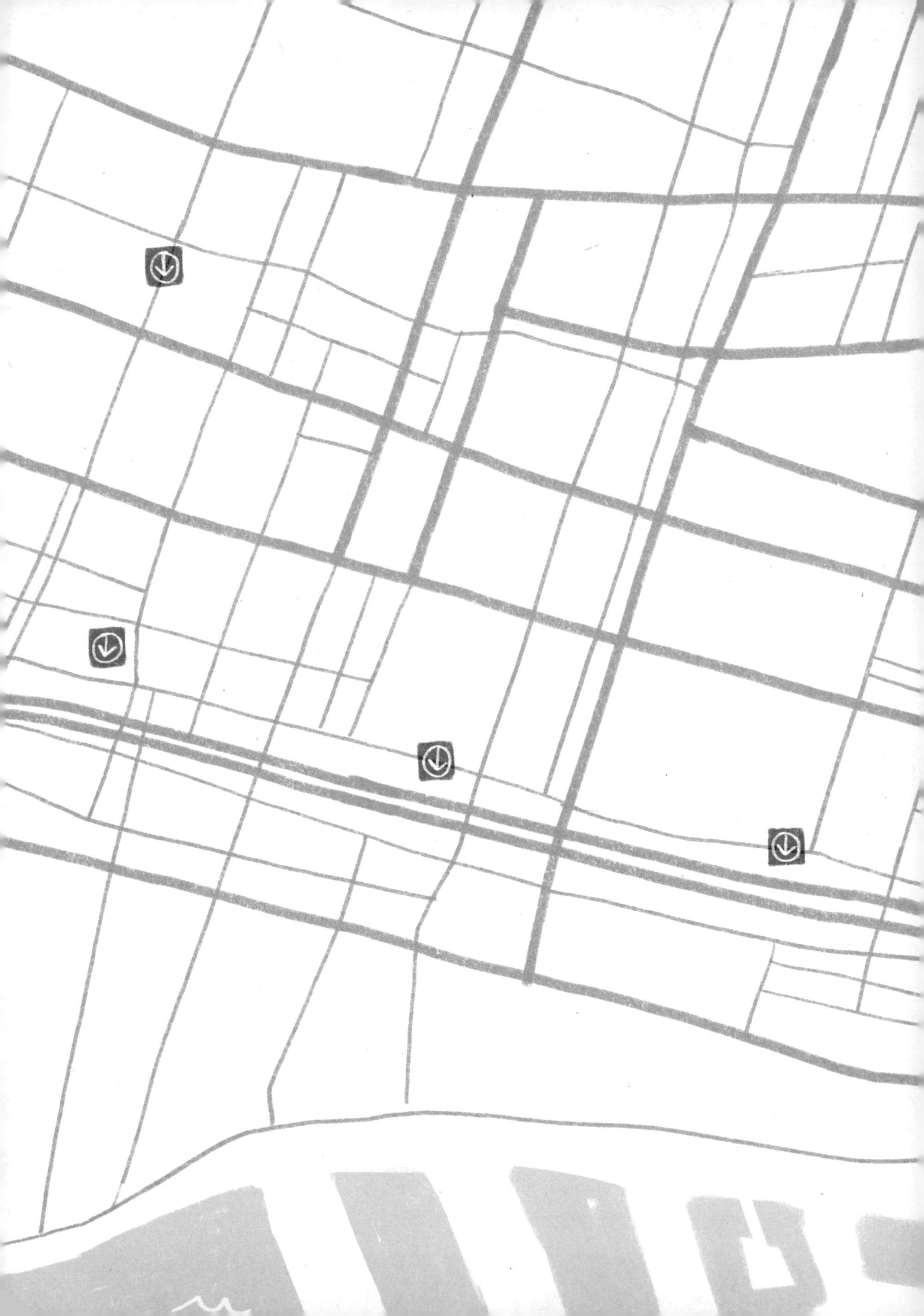